SO-BCO-645

THE DIVIDED
UNION

ustrations

THE DIVIDED UNION

A CONCISE HISTORY OF THE AMERICAN CIVIL WAR

PETER BATTY & PETER J. PARISH

The History Press

Cover illustration: *The Battle of Shiloh*, by Thure de Thulstrup (1848–1930). Library of Congress

First published 1999
This edition published 2009

The History Press Ltd
The Mill, Brimscombe Port
Stroud, Gloucestershire, GL5 2QG
www.thehistorypress.co.uk

© Peter Batty & Peter J. Parish, 1999, 2009

The right of Peter Batty & Peter J. Parish to be identified as the
Authors of this work has been asserted in accordance with the
Copyrights, Designs and Patents Act 1988.

All rights reserved. No part of this book may be reprinted
or reproduced or utilised in any form or by any electronic,
mechanical or other means, now known or hereafter invented,
including photocopying and recording, or in any information
storage or retrieval system, without the permission in writing
from the Publishers.

British Library Cataloguing in Publication Data
A catalogue record for this book is available from the British Library

ISBN 978 0 7524 5003 2

Printed and bound in Great Britain

Ill

Preface

The Civil War is both the great central dramatic event of American history and the greatest test which Americans have ever had to face. It was the biggest war anywhere in the western world between 1815 and 1914, and almost as many Americans died in the conflict as in all the other wars in which the United States has taken part. More than 600,000 men lost their lives, rather more of them from disease and the tender mercies of the medical care available at the time than actually on the field of battle. 600,000 is a huge death toll by any standard, but its full impact may be measured by pointing out that, as a proportion of the total population, the equivalent figure for American casualties in a late twentieth century war would be more than five million.

The Civil War was in many ways a transitional war which began with infantry charges and cavalry chases redolent of Napoleonic times and ended in trenches and earthworks around Richmond and Petersburg, and in Sherman's sweeping advances through Georgia and the Carolinas, designed to bring the war home to ordinary people and break their will to resist. The change in the standard infantry weapon from the old smoothbore musket to the new rifled musket which could kill at much greater range forced changes in battlefield tactics and shifted the balance of advantage on the field of battle to the defensive side. As the need to dig in became more and more important, the spade became a vital part of the infantryman's equipment. There were changes too in artillery, and dramatic changes in naval warfare, with the coming of steam-powered, ironclad ships, and even the first experimental use of submarines. This was also the first war in which railroads and the telegraph played a vital role, and superior industrial capacity could give one side a decisive advantage, once it had learned to deliver its products where they really mattered. Despite all these developments, European generals showed little interest in learning lessons from the Civil War. It was not until after the First World War that the romantic appeal of Lee and Jackson began to give way to a more realistic appreciation of the generalship of Grant and Sherman.

This was also the first war to be covered extensively by the camera, although the equipment of the time did not make it possible to photograph battlefield action. The graphic and often horrific images presented by Mathew Brady, Alexander Gardner and others made a dramatic impact on the folks at home. This was just one aspect of what became, in effect, the first media war, with journalists sending vivid, if often less than totally accurate, reports from the battlefront, and Americans, the most avid newspaper readers of their time, devouring reports, rumours, analysis and speculation in enormous quantities. The printed word was backed up by the huge volume of mail which passed back and forth between soldiers and their families and friends. One of the most significant 'firsts' of this remarkable conflict was that it was a war fought by armies of predominantly literate soldiers, especially on the Northern side, backed by a population with the highest level of literacy in the mid-nineteenth century world.

For all the limitations on the right to vote — which, for example, excluded the female half of the population — the United States was the most democratic society of the age. To non-American eyes in particular, one of the most astonishing features of the conflict was that, in the midst of civil war, elections were held on schedule, including a presidential election in 1864, when Lincoln's eventual victory was anything but a foregone conclusion. In this titanic struggle, popular commitment to the cause was vitally important, and morale on both the battlefront and the home front could be decisive. If the South was to win its independence against the opposition of a more powerful foe, its best hope — perhaps its only realistic hope — was to break, or at least to wear down, the Northern will to maintain the struggle.

Between the Revolution and the Civil War, the American Union had its bouts of fragility and insecurity, with frequent fears of division and threats of secession. The outcome of the war settled once and for all the indivisibility of the United States, and disposed of secession as a credible weapon in the hands of the discontented. In preserving the Union, the war also transformed it. If it is an over-simplification to say that the conflict converted the Union into a nation, it was certainly a giant step in that continuing process. It also brought about the abolition of slavery, which in 1861 would have seemed inconceivable as a short-term prospect to the mass of Americans, and it converted four million slaves into American citizens. But the promise of emancipation was followed by the turbulence and ultimately the disillusionment of the Reconstruction period, and the replacement of slavery by a new set of instruments and institutions dedicated to the maintenance of white supremacy. The war and its aftermath conspicuously failed to inaugurate a society based on racial justice and equality, but the constitutional amendments and the precedents set during the Reconstruction years provided a platform and an inspiration for the so-called Second Reconstruction of the civil rights era a century later. Overall, the Civil War was more successful in what it preserved — the union of the states — than in what it created or might have created, in the shape of a racially just society. The tortured relationship between the American national identity and the problem of race helped to bring about the Civil War, and has continued to plague the United States ever since.

The outcome of the Civil War had huge significance not only for America but for the wider world. One only needs to contemplate for a moment the likely consequences if the war had ended, not in the preservation and reinforcement of the Union, but in the division of the United States into two — or possibly three or four — separate countries. The 'balkanisation' of north America might have led to the chronic tensions and border conflicts which have plagued so many other regions of the world. The longer-term effects on the balance of power, first in the Atlantic and then throughout the world, offer a subject for endless speculation. Without recourse to moral judgments on what might have been desirable or undesirable, one can simply observe that a twentieth century world without an American superpower would have been a very different world indeed. In the second half of this century, the whole notion of 'the free world' or 'the West' would scarcely have been possible without the power of the American example and the fact of American power. Viewed in this context, The American Civil War was clearly one of the great world events of modern history.

The war retains its hold on both the popular imagination and the attention of professional historians. Few historical events have inspired such a vast and varied historical literature. Civil War Round Tables flourish not only in the United States but in other countries, and battle re-enactment societies devote meticulous attention to detail in re-living the military encounters of the 1860s. Major battlefields, expertly managed by the National Parks Service, are both tourist attractions and places of pilgrimage.

The aim of this book is to provide a straightforward, readable and generously illustrated narrative, which focuses above all upon the war itself, because it was the unfolding and often unpredictable drama of the battles and campaigns which shaped everything else. Threaded through the narrative of events are discussions of the experience of war for both soldiers and civilians, the social and political impact of the conflict and the great issues that it raised. And those issues have a very modern ring — nationalism, federalism, race, democracy, majority rule and minority rights, liberty, industrial development and technological advance.

This book is the product of a collaboration between a maker of television documentaries and a professional historian. They share an enthusiasm for Civil War history which, as it happens, was fostered for each of them by their first visit to the Gettysburg battlefield. In their collaboration on this book, they have accumulated massive debts to the published work of a large number of distinguished Civil War historians, and to the personal advice of many of them. Such merit as the book may have is largely due to them. Its deficiencies, and any surviving errors, can be laid at the door of the authors. We accept joint responsibility for them all.

Peter Batty
Peter J. Parish
September 1999

1 A union dividing

For the United States, the 85 years between the Declaration of Independence and the Civil War were a period of extraordinary change and growth. The four million Americans who had broken away from Britain in 1776 had become 31 million by 1861. Much of this increase was natural, but a significant part was due to immigration — four million alone in the two decades leading up to the conflict — and the newcomers brought innovative ideas and new ways of life. They had settled mainly in the Northern states, particularly in the cities of the Northeast, like New York, Boston and Philadelphia.

Although the United States was still predominantly a nation of farms, villages and small towns, the cities of the North were growing rapidly and were attracting rural Americans as well as immigrants from Europe. When Britain ruled the country, Philadelphia was its largest city, with 42,000 inhabitants. By the middle of the nineteenth century New York was easily the most populous, well past the half million mark. Chicago barely existed in 1830, yet 30 years later it had 100,000 inhabitants and was playing host to the Republican Party Convention that nominated Abraham Lincoln for president. In contrast, towns, and certainly cities, were few and far between in the South even by the 1840s and 1850s, and large areas remained wilderness. With a population of 150,000, New Orleans was the only large city while Charleston had a mere 35,000 inhabitants. A Northern visitor commented: 'From the quiet appearance of their towns, the stranger would think business was taking a siesta.'

Americans generally, North and South, believed passionately in the success of their democratic institutions and felt it their 'Manifest Destiny' to bring these institutions to the less fortunate wherever they might be, particularly if they were on their own continent. Many claimed it almost their God-given right to fill the vast, empty spaces to the west and north and even south of them — empty of course save for the indigenous peoples who were considered their cultural and political inferiors.

Territorial expansion was achieved in a number of ways. Through the so-called Louisiana Purchase of 1803, the United States acquired from France, at a bargain price, a vast tract of land between the Mississippi and the Rocky Mountains. Texas was annexed in 1845 and, a year later, the long diplomatic wrangle with Britain over the Pacific Northwest ended in a treaty that recognized America's claim to the Oregon Territory from which today's states of Washington and Idaho, as well as Oregon, have emerged. War with Mexico brought in 1848 the great prize of California, along with a huge area in the Southwest, including New Mexico, Arizona and much of what is now Utah, Nevada, Colorado and Wyoming. In order to open up the enormous regions of the Mississippi Valley and beyond to settlement, it was first necessary to drive out the

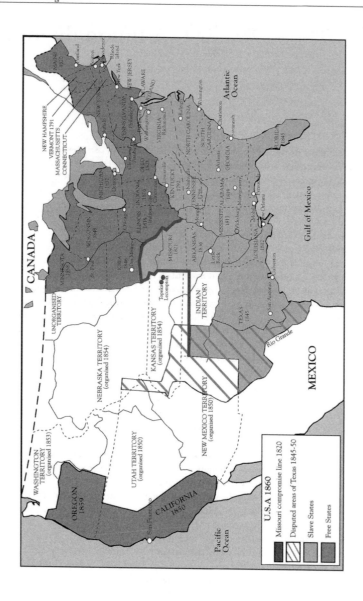

1. *Map of USA 1860*

original inhabitants, the American Indians, and this was achieved through a series of ruthless and cruel expropriations.

By the eve of the Civil War, the original 13 states of the Union had grown to 33. Most of the new ones were located west of the Allegheny–Appalachian mountain chain. Indeed by 1861 as many Americans lived west of those mountains as east of them, largely in the valleys of the Mississippi and its tributaries or along the shores of the Great Lakes, for until the railroads came, waterways held the key to the advance of settlement and the movement of goods. As a result, the Atlantic seaboard which had spawned the United States was beginning to be overtaken by its thrusting offspring to the west. This growth was drastically altering the entire balance of power within the Union as well as affecting relations between the federal government in Washington and the individual states — and it was the West which became the arena for sectional competition between North and South.

Without the inventions of the telegraph and the railway, especially the latter, the new territories and rapidly expanding population could have been more of a liability than an asset. Transportation held the key to the nation's development, and by the middle of the nineteenth century the railway builders had accelerated the process begun by their road and canal predecessors of forging a man-made network of communications to link the far-flung regions of the new land. Natural obstacles were being overcome and traditional routes superseded. In the past, geography had facilitated north-south communication but obstructed easy movement between east and west. The Mississippi, for instance, ran north to south, as did the Atlantic sea-coast. The formidable barrier of the Appalachian and Allegheny mountain chain unfortunately ran north to south, too, but goods and people now needed to flow easily between east and west. Even as late as 1840 it took two weeks or more to travel from New York to St Louis or Chicago, but, by the eve of the Civil War, with the help of the railroad, that journey was down to just two days. The impact of such changes was enormous, not only in narrow economic terms but also in their social and political effects. However much sectional differences were forcing the Union apart, the revolution in transport was binding it more closely together.

Living costs were dropping dramatically — wholesale prices, for instance, declined by 40 per cent during the four decades leading up to the Civil War. Farmers could now get their goods to the shops more quickly, while consumers could more readily afford to buy them. In addition, improved transportation was creating a national market. Production of food alone during that same period quadrupled and the percentage of it sold instead of eaten locally almost doubled. This increase further encouraged the rush to the town. In 1820 one in 14 Americans lived in cities. By 1860 it was one in five.

Similarly significant was the way in which the population of the Northern states had topped that of the Southern ones. When war eventually came, the North had a numerical advantage of well over two to one — 22 million to nine million — and of those nine million in the South, almost four million were black slaves, so the effective advantage was more like almost four to one. Paradoxically, the country that had sprung from a revolution which proclaimed that all men are created equal had, by the mid-nineteenth century, become the largest slave-owning nation in the world.

The United States had inherited the institution of slavery from Britain. The first Africans

2.   *Despite all the difficulties and hardships they endured, slaves developed close family relationships*

had been brought to Virginia in 1619, just 12 years after the establishment of the initial settlement there at Jamestown and the year before the Mayflower reached Massachusetts Bay. By the end of the seventeenth century their numbers had grown considerably and at the time of independence one in five Americans was black, most but not all of whom lived in the South. Much of the trade in slaves, which had become highly lucrative, was in the hands of Northerners, primarily merchants from New England.

After independence, slavery had been quite quickly abolished in the seven Northern states, but it was retained in Virginia, Maryland, Delaware, Georgia, and North and South

Carolina. In South Carolina, slaves actually outnumbered whites. As the Union expanded, free — that is non-slave — Northern states and slave Southern states marched in parallel across the West. The pattern was set as early as 1787 when the North-West Ordinance decreed that slavery should be banned throughout the vast territory between the Ohio River and the Great Lakes. The number of free states was swollen by the admission of Vermont in 1791, Ohio in 1803, Indiana in 1816 and Illinois in 1818. New recruits to the ranks of the slave states were Kentucky in 1792, Tennessee in 1796, Louisiana in 1812, Mississippi in 1817 and Alabama in 1819.

Thus by 1819 the number of free and slave states was evenly balanced at 11 each. Since each state, no matter what its size, had equal representation in the Senate, the more prestigious of the two legislative chambers that comprised Congress, a united South could effectively block or at least delay legislation from the lower House of Representatives, where representation was based on population. This parity in the Senate was enormously important to the South, particularly when the North's superiority in numbers had given the non-slave states a clear majority in the House of Representatives. However, the balance between slave and non-slave states looked like being upset in the crisis over Missouri's admission to the Union as a slave state in 1819.

Missouri had been carved out of the huge area acquired in the Louisiana Purchase of 1803 and it straddled what had hitherto been the ad hoc dividing line between slave and free states. Its application for statehood raised the whole question of whether slavery should be allowed to expand westward into the newer territories, as the South clearly wished, and in particular what powers, if any, Congress possessed to control that spread.

Northern opposition to Missouri's admission as a slave state was inspired less by any moral crusade against slavery than by political calculation of its effect on the voting balance between North and South. This in turn could affect the prospects of legislation on other issues important to the North, such as protective tariffs, disposal of the public lands, and federally financed internal improvements. The Missouri question generated fierce and protracted debate and, for Southerners, it seemed to pose the most direct challenge yet heard, in Congress at least, to the future of slavery.

Eventually there emerged the first of the great sectional compromises that avoided immediate collision at the expense of shelving the more fundamental political problems. Missouri was admitted as a slave state in 1821 but this was balanced by the admission of Maine, in northern New England, as a free state. In addition slavery was to be excluded from the remaining territory of the Louisiana Purchase north of the 36° 30' line of latitude. It was a settlement that seemed to favour the North since, as a glance at a map of the United States of this time will show, the great preponderance of the remaining territory was north of that line. Increasingly, it seemed that the only way in which the South could counteract that advantage would be to persuade the Union to take on new lands south of its current borders.

The Missouri Compromise lasted almost 30 years, during which time the South became increasingly set in its ways. Part of the trouble was that the fruits of the nation's spectacular growth were not being evenly shared between North and South. In sheer numbers of people, technological innovation, commercial expansion and industrial productivity, the North was forging ahead, and much of the South felt left out or at least deprived of what they considered a fair share of the increased rewards. The South was seen, and saw itself, as different from the rest of the nation, largely because it was not changing when all around it was, or not growing and developing in the same way or at the same rate as other parts of the country. Such feelings were close to the heart of Southern grievances and Southern fears.

In the decades before the Civil War, the economy and distinctive way of life of the deep South rested on the twin foundations of cotton and slavery. It had not always been so: up to the end of the eighteenth century, tobacco and rice had been the main non-food crops produced by slave labour in the South, while cotton played only a very minor role. The future prospects of slavery as an institution were far from clear; it was already on the way out in the North and even some Southerners — in Virginia and Maryland for example — were beginning to doubt its economic viability as well as its continuing ideological acceptability.

However, thanks to rising demand for cotton from the mills of Lancashire and elsewhere, and to the invention of the cotton gin in 1793, both cotton and slavery were given a new lease of life. The gin — invented by a Northerner who had been working as a tutor in the South for barely a year — was a simple device for mechanically separating the fleecy cotton-fibre from its tough seeds, a process that hitherto had been enormously time-consuming and labour intensive because the fibre stuck so tenaciously. Its great significance was that it made large-scale cotton cultivation possible, particularly of the more easily grown short-staple varieties. Whereas before it had taken a slave 10 hours to produce a pound of lint, with the gin 300–1,000 pounds could be processed in a day.

From a mere 9,000 bales a year in 1790, output soared to almost five million bales by the eve of the Civil War, helped by a near insatiable appetite for cotton from the expanding textile industries not only of New England but also of old England and Europe in general, where improvements to existing machinery were speeding up the manufacture of cotton thread and hence reducing its cost. By the middle of the nineteenth century Europe, including England, was obtaining nearly 90 per cent of its cotton from the South and cotton exports amounted to more than half of the United States' total exports between 1815 and 1860. Hence the boast among many Southerners that cotton was King and that it ruled the American economy, if not indeed the whole North Atlantic economy.

The most readily available source of cheap labour in the South to meet this boom had been the slaves. Thus cotton and slavery became interdependent and the South grew ever more reliant on both, dangerously so as the years went by. The South's stock of capital and its means of income were inextricably bound up with slavery. On a typical plantation, whether for sugar in Louisiana, tobacco in Virginia and North Carolina, rice in South Carolina, hemp and indigo in Missouri and Kentucky, or cotton in all the states of the deep South, the investment in slaves was generally far greater than that in land and tools combined. An agriculture based on slavery remained labor intensive, and the bulk of its capital was tied up in its slave labor force. Instead of investing their profits in machinery, Southern planters usually bought more slaves, not simply with the aim of producing yet more cotton or sugar, but also to achieve the enhanced social status that in Southern society only large-scale ownership of slaves could bring.

Agriculture in the South thus underwent scant technological change following

3. *Dealers had no compunction over splitting up families as this advertisement shows. Slave marriages were not recognized by the law*

the invention of the cotton gin. Indeed the proportion of the labor force engaged in agriculture actually increased between 1800 and 1860. As a result the South lacked for the most part the capital resources — as well as the will — to embark on broader and more diversified economic development on anything like the Northern pattern. It did not develop a substantial urban middle class, nor even a sizable artisan class. Similarly, its economy did not diversify.

The South too was easily the most poorly educated part of the country. Free schooling was the exception rather than the rule and schooling as such did not have a high priority before the Civil War: only half as many white children attended school as in the North. Nearly half of the South's population was illiterate, whereas the proportion in the North was perhaps no more than 10 per cent. The per capita circulation of newspapers and magazines among Southern whites was less than half that among Northerners, and the voluntary associations and self-improvement societies that proliferated in the North, as they did in Victorian England, were virtually unknown in the South. The slave states feared change and progress, preferring stability and tradition. A Southern politician proclaimed: 'We want no manufactures: we desire no trading, no mechanical or manufacturing classes. As long as we have our rice, our sugar, our tobacco and our cotton, we can command wealth to purchase all we want.'

Some Southerners enjoyed the image of themselves as Cavaliers, direct descendants not only of those seventeenth-century English gentlemen but also of the Norman conquerors of Anglo-Saxon England, while Northerners were dismissed as the puritan offspring of those defeated Anglo-Saxons, more inclined to be led than to lead, and less interested in gallantry, honor and chivalry. People in the South were much preoccupied with honor and they believed that their reputations counted for a great deal. This was not just true of the upper classes. If a yeoman farmer's daughter found herself pregnant before marriage, a shotgun wedding was no more than family honor required. Loyalty to community and social group was equally strong. In a slave society the ownership of slaves was perceived as bestowing honor on the master. What could be more ennobling to a master, they would think, than loyal servants answering his every beck and call.

Southerners saw themselves, too, as generous, hospitable, outgoing, impulsive, leisure oriented, respectful among equals, kind towards inferiors, appreciative of gracious living, given more to the heart than to the head, and enjoying the moment rather than planning for the future. Men prided themselves on their chivalry towards women, who led more restricted lives than Northern women, though both were unliberated by today's standards. Northerners were despised as graceless, grasping, grinding workaholics, unreliable in their relationships, untrustworthy in their dealings, contriving and controlled. A popular saying in the South was that 'the Northerner loved to make money, the Southerner to spend it'.

With its more clearly defined class system and its military tradition, the South could see itself as more akin to Europe than the North. Sons were often sent to military schools, even when they were not necessarily bound for military careers. The 1860 census listed five times as many military schools in the South as in the North, but only half as many professional and technical establishments, and for size of population, proportionately more white Southerners went to West Point military academy than Northerners.

4.   Most slaves were bought and sold at degrading auctions like these at least once in their lifetime

Southern men often called each other Colonel or Major and there was a general reverence for the martial arts.

Arguments would be settled by dueling or fisticuffs, depending on the social strata to which the parties belonged. Dueling was considered part of the South's aristocratic code of honor, a reliance on the spontaneous individual gesture to avenge insult rather than on communal legal action. Many prominent Southern politicians fought duels. One Southern president, Andrew Jackson, killed an opponent, while a South Carolina governor wounded more than a dozen adversaries. As the arguments in Congress between Northerners and Southerners grew ever more bitter during the 1840s and 1850s, it was not uncommon for the latter to throw down the gauntlet at the former. Northerners invariably declined — dueling had virtually died out in the North since the turn of the century — which helped convince Southerners that Northerners were basically cowards.

Southerners too learned to use guns from an early age and were more familiar with them than were Northerners. Significantly, almost twice as many Southerners took part in the Mexican War as Northerners. Moreover, the principal generals were all from the South. During the two decades leading up to the Civil War, the United States Army was commanded by a Southerner and all four secretaries of war during the 1850s were Southerners.

By the eve of the Civil War virtually every Southern state had its own military institute. Whereas volunteer militia companies were equally popular in both the North and South, those in the North tended to be social clubs, while the Southern ones took their training and drill more seriously. Charleston, South Carolina, boasted 22 such companies, although its male population of military age amounted to just 4,000.

One reason for the South's interest in military matters was the need to control its slaves. An important feature of Southern life was the slave patrol, usually a mounted detachment of three or four white men who went the rounds each night to check on slave movements, enforce a curfew if need be, and, most especially, deter clandestine gatherings. Since each unit was on duty about once every two weeks, some 50 or more white men in each locality were needed to serve the patrols. Not all, of course, would be slave-owners. Slave revolts were rare in the South but the threat of them was a constant worry and colored much Southern thinking in the pre-Civil War period.

Not least of the reasons why the South failed to generate an adequate commercial or industrial sector of its economy was fear of the social and racial consequences of such development. Blacks were employed in industry and some lived and worked in the towns, but there were deep-rooted doubts in the South about the compatibility of slavery with industrial or urban growth. As a result, the states that grew all the cotton possessed only 6 per cent of the nation's cotton-manufacturing capacity. Moreover, the South's share of the nation's manufacturing capacity as a whole declined between 1800 and 1860. In 1860 Massachusetts produced more manufactured goods than all the Southern states put together, while Pennsylvania produced twice as much as they did, and New York had nearly as much banking capital as the entire South.

The fact that slaves counted as property had a distorting effect on the measurement of wealth. Thus, the per capita wealth of Southerners on the eve of the Civil War was twice that of Northerners, whereas their per capita income was smaller by 27 per cent. With less than a third of the nation's non-slave population, the South claimed nearly two-thirds of the country's wealthiest men. European visitors remarked that, whereas in the North the farmer would boast of improvements in the form of new buildings, roads and railways that greater wealth had brought to his community, in the South the planter would show off his increased number of slaves. The boom in cotton had also doubled the price of those slaves during the 1850s alone. With the abolition of the external slave trade, the demand could be met only from natural increase or purchase from other plantations within the South.

Thus yet more and more of the section's puny capital came to be locked up in slavery, an institution that was increasingly setting the South apart. Not for nothing did Southerners label it 'the peculiar institution', meaning not that they thought it odd but simply that it was theirs; it distinguished them from other Americans and made their chosen way of life superior, or so they said, to that of the rest of the country. In the past, Southerners had been prepared to explain the existence of slavery within their midst as a 'necessary evil', arguing that its precipitate abolition might lead to social disruption and racial conflict. Now they boasted of its 'positive good' in supporting a way of life far superior to that in the North or indeed elsewhere, and in bringing the benefits of Christian civilization and a higher standard of living to the slaves themselves who had been 'rescued' from the 'barbarism' of their African homeland. Furthermore, they claimed, all great societies in history had had their basis in slavery or serfdom — Ancient Greece, Charlemagne's France, Elizabethan England. Even the Bible sanctioned bondage: the apostle Paul bade slaves obey their masters and advised a runaway to return to his owner. Some of the bitterest words were saved for the condemnation of the 'wage slaves' in the North, who were said to be worse off than their black Southern counterparts who, so the argument went, at least had guaranteed employment, free medical care and a minimum standard even in old age.

There were many, of course, who disputed these claims, including some Southerners who maintained that, moral questions apart, slavery was a direct cause of the South's relative backwardness. For example, because it was widely believed that blacks would break the lighter hoes and ploughs that were commonplace in the North by the early nineteenth century, the old-fashioned, clumsy, heavier farming implements persisted throughout the South, with a consequent loss of efficiency. The shallow-furrow shovel ploughs drawn by mules, which had long since been replaced in the North by horse-drawn, deep-furrow ones made of iron or steel, continued to be used, for the conventional wisdom among Southerners was that black slaves would be careless with horses. As a result, on the eve of the Civil War the South possessed 90 per cent of the nation's mules but only 40 per cent of its horses.

Since time was not their own and they had little leisure, slaves had scant motive to be efficient. They could work hard, especially when the overseer was watching, and they were forced to labor long hours, but they did not generally enjoy the pay incentives or opportunities for advancement which prompted the free labor in the North to produce things more quickly or more cheaply. Slave owners relied less on the carrot than the stick, though some did offer inducements to their bondsmen in the form of extra days off, small plots of land to cultivate for themselves and even cash payments. Immigrants did not go South in large numbers because they could not, or would not, compete with slave labor.

Certainly slavery was, more often than not, a profitable system, particularly for many of the major slaveowners. It was these large planters who dominated much of the politics of the South and, although only a small group, they commanded great respect from their non-slave owning neighbors. If the archetypal Southern white was a yeoman farmer owning at most two or three slaves, and quite probably none at all, there is no question that the whole tone of Southern society was set by this small minority of large slave-owning planters.

In much of the South the plantation was the center of the community and, since institutional law was less established there than in the North, it provided both judge and jury, prosecution and punisher. The South was an extremely violent society. Whereas crimes in the North were mainly against property — burglary, breaking and entering, stealing, and so on — the majority in the South were against people: assault and battery, grievous bodily harm, eye-gouging and other horrors. There was as much recorded violence in Mississippi in 1850 as in all the New England states put together, despite its population being only a fraction of theirs.

Many, of course, believed that this greater violence resulted from the very institution of slavery. Denying a man his liberty is in itself an act of supreme violence. Born into bondage and knowing little else but work from the age of 12, fed, dressed and housed at their owner's whim, and expected to show humility to any white within sight, slaves were the absolute chattels of their masters who could in effect do what they liked with them: sell, exchange, beat and even kill them without much fear of legal stricture.

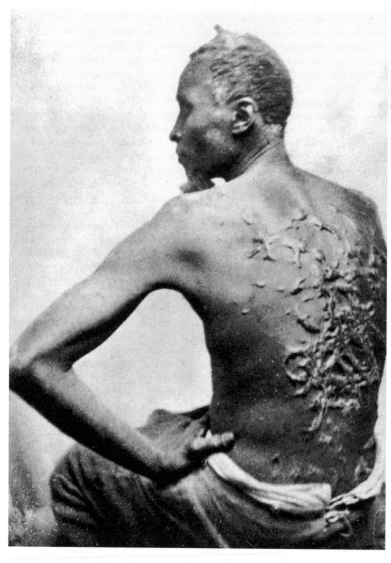

5.   *Evidence of savage treatment. The master was his own law when it came to punishing his slaves*

Slaves could not wed without their owner's permission and even then the marriage had no status in law. The resultant family could be scattered to the wind at any time by being sold off around the region. There was no harsher sight in the pre-war South than that of the break-up of a hitherto close-knit slave family. Most slaves could expect to be sold or exchanged at least once in their lifetime, with all the personal trauma and brutal upheaval that such a move implied. Moreover, women slaves were vulnerable to sexual exploitation, not just by the master and his immediate family but by almost any passing white male. Nor could slaves own property or earn money, though a few owners relented and even on occasion allowed them to buy their freedom. But until they were free, money, property and family could be taken from them at any time.

On the other hand, it was in the interest of the master to provide at least minimal care for his slave property. After all he was in business; a dead slave or one who had run away provided no labor, and a reluctant or maimed slave was a less effective worker. Good workers were often rewarded with better food and housing, and there was also a sort of pecking order whereby those employed in the house, and some other key slaves, enjoyed additional privileges.

Owners encouraged their slaves to raise families, not just because it meant more young slaves but also because they realized that men with wives and children were less inclined to rebel or run away than those with no such responsibilities. Some masters created genuine relationships of trust and affection with their bondsmen, who in many cases responded likewise.

Most planters, though, regarded their slaves as children — childlike was a common description, lacking in probity, judgment and common sense — and just as conventional nineteenth-century morality instructed parents to be strict with their children and punish them if necessary, so slave owners had little compunction in using the whip to chastise their chattels. Many communities in the South had codes of punishment for slaves, stipulating the number of lashes for each designated offence, though when it came down to it every owner made his own laws and could decide the level and nature of the punishment as well as the reason for it.

Some towns even had public whipping-places, while others employed 'slave-breakers' whose duty was to subdue troublesome bondsmen where the masters were perhaps too squeamish for the task themselves. The implements used sometimes defy description and did not stop at mere whips and sticks. Clearly, slavery was a harsh, inhumane, dehumanizing system. Evidence of its brutality was there for all to see in the advertisements for runaway slaves: the owners' descriptions of them frequently referred to numerous welts on their backs or ugly distinguishing marks elsewhere on the body, the results of repeated whippings and savage beatings over many years.

Yet amid such bleakness, the blacks showed remarkable stoicism. By and large denied education, they used their collective voice to develop a culture, and out of the depravity and repression came that most distinctive and haunting form of music, the Negro spiritual, which vividly conveyed both their intense yearning for freedom and their deep surrender to sadness. In the parts of their lives beyond the control of the master, the slave community evolved a rich and active life of its own, based above all on religion and family, which offered the best available escape from the tribulations of their lot.

25

Although slavery did not make the creation of stable family relationships easy, most blacks forged firm bonds of kinship. In the pre-Civil War period the slave population in the United States was increasing naturally by marginally less than the non-slave population while the death-rates were roughly similar. Imports of slaves were banned after 1808, and yet the slave population increased almost six-fold between 1790 and 1860. No other slave society in history had been so demographically successful.

Since blacks counted overall for well over a third of the population in the South — and in many areas the proportion was considerably higher — slavery was crucial in the eyes of most whites as a means of controlling the blacks in their midst. It also served as a yardstick of social status. Although not all Southern whites owned slaves, they all possessed white skins, and while slavery lasted even the most wretched white was assured of a place in Southern society. No matter how miserable his present circumstances or desperate his future, he had the comfort of knowing that he would always be the social superior of the blacks within his community. Slavery thus provided a level below which no white man could fall, and at the same time slave ownership furnished a way by which he might rise within his group in a manner that was not possible in the North.

This helps to explain why the non-slave owning majority of Southern whites were willing to follow the lead of the plantation aristocracy down the path to secession. On the eve of the Civil War one in four Southern white families owned slaves — and in the deep South the proportion was nearer one in three. By way of comparison, in 1950 only one in 50 American families owned stocks and shares equivalent in value to a slave a century or so earlier. If the United States now is thought to be firmly committed to the continuance of the capitalist system, it perhaps makes it easier to appreciate why Southerners then were so reluctant to give up their peculiar institution.

2 Irreconcilable differences

Cotton and slavery led the South ever further apart from the rest of the country. While parts of the North, especially in the Northeast, became increasingly urban and industrial, the South remained agricultural and rural in outlook. Its economy's lack of diversification made it greatly dependent on foreign markets and hence concerned for the maintenance of free trade, which immediately brought it into conflict with those powerful Northern interests that were equally determined to protect their burgeoning industries through tariffs.

The South was also heavily reliant on other parts of the United States, particularly the Northeast, for the supply of many of its manufacturing needs and as a market for its cotton. New York merchants handled most of the cotton trade and took hefty commissions for doing so, which in turn helped to sustain those suspicions of Yankee deviousness already current within Southern social circles, where a favorite conversational gambit was to argue that 'the North grows rich at our expense'. Its problem was that, while trying to cling to the traditions and mores of a pre-capitalist way of life, the South was also striving to sell more of its cotton and other products in world markets. It was constantly attempting to combine the pursuit of profit with adherence to cherished values.

Opponents of slavery in the South were harassed and ever tighter restrictions were imposed on the bondsmen themselves as the nineteenth century wore on. Despite the rarity of slave uprisings, Southern whites could never relax their guard. Although a plot in Charleston in 1822 had not come to anything, the Nat Turner revolt of nine years later in Virginia led to the deaths of 60 whites, the memory of which was to haunt Southerners throughout the Civil War period.

In the North the anti-slavery movement, earlier confined to small groups of Quakers and evangelicals, was becoming better organized and attracting more attention by the 1820s and 1830s, though it remained a source of embarrassment to the great majority of Northerners, who were indifferent to the plight of the slaves in the South and disinclined to intervene on their behalf. The poorer whites in the North, and many of the recent immigrants from Europe, feared that an influx of blacks from the South would jeopardize their livelihoods. Nor were richer white Northerners any more enthusiastic about having large numbers of blacks in their midst. Blacks living in the North were frequently treated as pariahs, as they suffered under a system of both official and unofficial discrimination. Until 1822 blacks could vote in New York, but the so-called constitutional reforms of that year took such political rights away from them. All forms of transport in New York City were segregated, as were public facilities. Housing, too, was segregated to a large extent, though with the terrible poverty prevalent in slum areas blacks and whites could be found living as neighbours in shared misery.

In 1831 William Lloyd Garrison founded his abolitionist newspaper *The Liberator* in Boston, and two years later in Philadelphia he helped to establish the American Anti-Slavery Society, the same year in which the British Parliament abolished slavery in the British West Indies. Until now the abolitionists, as the anti-slavery militants were now known, were relatively few in number, predominantly middle class, and strongly evangelical. Five years later membership of the movement had reached a quarter of a million and some 40 or so tracts and journals were being published every week, taking advantage of the communications boom of the time. The death in 1837 of the abolitionist Elijah Lovejoy at the hands of a mob in Alton, Illinois, gave the movement its first martyr.

Through speeches, sermons, meetings, pamphlets, newspapers and petitions, the abolitionists maintained an unrelenting pressure which aroused the fury of many people in the North and almost everyone in the South, where no effort was spared to keep out anti-slavery propaganda. Dissenters there were speedily ostracized and soon coerced into remaining silent or moving on, while criticism from outside was blocked at the point of entry. Mail was even tampered with to prevent abolitionist literature reaching the masses and hotel registers were scrutinized for the possible presence of propagandists from the North who, if found, were given short shrift.

Although, across the North, the abolitionists were abused and mocked, shouted down and beaten up, stoned, mobbed, attacked, threatened, imprisoned and run out of town, they were never silenced and they never let the issue die. A diverse group of religious activists and radical reformers committed to a variety of causes, they did not run a well-coordinated national campaign, but wherever they were heard or noticed they stirred the consciences of increasing numbers of people in both North and South. They placed the moral issue of slavery on the national agenda, and kept it in the forefront of public attention, so that when the issue finally exploded into political prominence it could not be compromised away like previous confrontations between North and South.

Politically, from the 1830s onwards, the United States was developing a genuinely national two-party system. Arguments over growth and modernization helped to define the ideology and electoral support of the two groupings. Broadly speaking, Democrats stood for states' rights, localism, limited government, religious pluralism and the agrarian way of life; Whigs, on the other hand, came to be associated with economic innovation, stronger central government, the promotion of commercial and industrial expansion, and cultural homogeneity under the auspices of the major Protestant denominations.

The Whigs were best represented in the North, particularly New England and those areas further west where New England's influence was felt, but they had support too in the South among merchants and town dwellers, as well as some of the larger planters. The Democrats were strong in the South, but also enjoyed wide support in the North, for example among poorer subsistence farmers and urban Catholic immigrants. They tended to be more apprehensive than Whigs of the social consequences of rapid change and growth, although they were often keener to enlarge the country in more traditional ways by territorial expansion and even force of arms than were their political opponents.

The two parties competed and bargained fairly successfully over issues like banks and tariffs and so-called internal improvements, but they were less inclined to compromise when confronted with the problems arising from further territorial enlargement,

6. *Even adding a massive dome to Washington's Capitol alarmed those Southerners who opposed any advance in Federal power*

particularly where slavery was involved. It was the Democrats, especially those in the South, who led the expansionist charge of the 1840s which culminated in the war with Mexico. Ironically it was David Wilmot, a Democrat, albeit a Northern one, who called on Congress during the first year of that war to ban slavery in any lands that might be acquired as a result of it, the very issue that fifteen years later would lead to the Civil War.

Unlike national banks or protective tariffs, slavery was not a matter that could be readily accommodated within the existing two-party system; it created moral and ideological divisions which went far too deep. Furthermore, when slavery became yoked to westward expansion, the fierce competition that it stimulated aroused raging ambition as well as profound anxiety in the North and South alike. The scene was thus set for a country-wide calamity.

The anti-slavery movement made its first impact on congressional politics towards the end of the 1830s when a group of abolitionists, mainly from the Midwest, organized such a flood of petitions to the House of Representatives that it threatened to disrupt normal business. When the authorities tried to limit the ruse, doughty defenders of the constitution, including a distinguished former president, John Quincy Adams, intervened on their behalf, which enhanced the abolitionists' credibility and helped to create for the first time an anti-slavery lobby within Congress. They even formed their own political party in 1839, the Liberty Party, and put up a candidate for the presidency in the election the following year. Although he got only a handful of votes, the publicity value was enormous.

But, as is the way of these things, the movement became too successful for some of its members and it split between those who were committed unequivocally to immediate emancipation of the slaves and those who saw this as a longer term aim. The first objective of this latter group was to contain slavery within its existing limits and to prevent its spread into the newer territories of the West. This more pragmatic approach found a readier audience in the North, where many people viewed any large-scale expansion of slavery into the western territories as a threat to their own free labor interests. The Liberty Party gave way to the Free Soil Party in 1848 and then the political anti-slavery movement widened still further into the more broadly based Republican Party, founded in 1854.

Slavery was not the only cause of North-South confrontation during the 1830s and 1840s. Ever since the passage in 1828 of the high protective tariff, dubbed by Southerners 'The Tariff of Abominations', the Southern states had been protesting not just at its unfairness but also its illegality. They managed to get it reduced in 1832, though that was not enough for many South Carolinians who argued that an individual state, as a party to the original compact that created the Union, had the right to declare null and void within its borders a federal law that it considered unconstitutional or unjust. On this basis a special state convention in South Carolina nullified the tariff acts of 1828 and 1832, banned the collection of duties within its borders and declared that any use of force by the federal government would justify secession from the Union. The Northern majority in Congress voted the President additional powers to enforce collection of the revenues, but others successfully sought conciliatory ways to avoid a direct clash of authority on this issue and the immediate crisis was averted, although South Carolinians did not discard their beliefs in state sovereignty and the right to nullify federal laws.

Later that same decade, Texas provided another crisis. In the euphoria following its independence from Spain earlier in the century, Mexico had encouraged Americans to settle in this largely empty Mexican province, but by the 1830s their growing numbers and, more especially, their increasing arrogance had made the Mexican authorities regret their previous decision. Also, the new immigrants favored slavery, which had recently been abolished in Mexico itself. In 1836 the settlers declared their own independence and, after their famous setback at the Alamo, they turned the tables at the battle of San Jacinto. The Mexican government lacked the power to prevent an independent republic of Texas being established and within the year Texas had applied for membership of the Union.

Since Texas lay south of the Missouri Compromise line and next door to an existing slave state, Louisiana, Southern interests saw it as potential slave territory. Moreover, because it was so vast, they thought it could be divided into several states, all open to slavery, whose votes in the Senate might sustain the South's majority there for decades to come. Northerners realized this too and managed to delay annexation for another eight years and to have Texas, when it eventually joined the Union in 1845, do so as a single state, albeit as a slave one.

Within a year the United States and Mexico were at war, provoked in part by the annexation as well as by the unashamedly ardent expansionist aims of the new pro-Southern administration in Washington, many members of which had their sights on acquiring the whole of Mexico. Victory for the Union brought the great prize of California, where, as it happened, gold was about to be discovered, together with enormous tracts of former

7.   *Texas looked like being the South's saviour. Because it was so big it could have been divided into several states, all slave, that might have sustained the South's Senate majority for a long time*

Mexican provinces — more than 600 million acres in total — including all or part of what is now New Mexico, Arizona, Utah, Nevada, Colorado, Wyoming and Oklahoma. The bulk of this huge new domain lay south of the Missouri Compromise line and hence offered the prospect of further expansion of slavery, though little of it seemed immediately suitable for plantation agriculture.

Northerners had been uneasy about the war from the start and many now considered it a Southern conspiracy to enlarge their interests. There was talk of an unholy alliance between 'the Lords of the Loom and the Lords of the Lash', an emotive way of referring to the cotton manufacturers of Massachusetts and the slave-owning planters of such states as Mississippi and Louisiana, who were said to have used their combined influence to lobby the ruling political parties in Washington to provoke a conflict with Mexico.

Abolitionists, too, were whipping up anti-Southern sentiment and warning of a 'slave-power' plot to take over the whole country. Even before the Mexicans had been defeated, a Northern Congressman, David Wilmot, managed to get a Proviso passed by the House of Representatives, though never approved by the Senate, to the effect that slavery should never exist in any part of the territory to be acquired from Mexico. The South was able

8.   *The discovery of gold in California in 1848 led to an early decision on its statehood*

to block the acceptance of this Proviso by the Senate, but not its repeated approval by the House of Representatives. Thus slavery was once again in the political forefront.

As long as it maintained its parity in the Senate the South could thwart the passage of legislation considered harmful to its interests and accordingly it worried over the continuing balance between slave and free states within the Union. Arkansas's admission in 1836 as a slave state had been matched by Michigan's a year later as a free state. Similarly, the admissions of Florida and Texas in 1845 as slave states had been offset by those of Iowa and Wisconsin as free states in 1846 and 1848 respectively. By the time gold was discovered in California in 1848 the tally of free and slave states was 15 each.

That discovery brought droves of new settlers to California — 80,000 in a matter of months. Faced with the potential for mischief and disorder from such a rapidly growing, unstable and diverse population, Washington sought to establish without delay an organized civil authority there. A convention held in California during September 1849 drew up a constitution that prohibited slavery, and early the following year a delegation arrived in the federal capital to seek admission to the Union as a free state.

Southern politicians were clearly alarmed and harped on the contribution that Southern lives had made to the conquest of California. In addition grievances had been mounting for some time in the South over the growing number of slaves who were escaping to the North by the 'Underground Railroad', through which runaways were passed from safe house to safe house, sometimes hidden in laden wagons or stowed away on river steamers, on other occasions led on foot at night through swamps and woods, as they fled northwards. The tag had come from an Ohioan clergyman, who had played no mean part in the 'Railroad' himself; in his words, 'They who took passage on it disappeared from public view as if they had really gone to ground.' The people who provided the hideouts and transport were of course breaking the law. The escape network was never as successful or as well organized as Southerners thought, but the few thousand fugitives who made their way to freedom in this fashion each year had a symbolic significance out of all proportion to their actual numbers.

After months of heated and acrimonious debate in 1850, a compromise was arranged whereby California was admitted as a free state and the South was compensated in other ways: the territories of New Mexico and Arizona were organized without any provision for or against slavery and, more controversially, a much more severe Fugitive Slave Act was passed. This was to produce many bitter and embarrassing confrontations for both sides during the years to come. That runaway slaves be returned to their masters was enshrined in that holy of holies, the American Constitution, and until the advent of militant abolitionists during the 1830s the concept had not been questioned. Thereafter the anti-slavery press thrived on lurid stories of heroic fugitives outwitting bloodhounds and human slave-catchers alike as they ran, crawled, hobbled and swam to freedom in the North. Abolitionists soon realized that an escaped slave or two brought in both audiences and revenue at meetings.

Enforcement of the earlier fugitive slave law had become lax, but with the passage of the 1850 Act the situation had to change. The new law was heavily weighted in favour of those claiming ownership of a runaway slave and against the fugitives. For example, fugitives claiming to be freemen were denied trial by jury. Slave cases came under federal jurisdiction, and federal commissioners were given wide authority to pursue fugitives and enforce the law. The consequences were, however, far from what the Southern politicians had hoped. The crude and often callous attempts of federal agents to enforce the new law brought home the slavery issue to many Northern communities in a way that petitions and pamphlets had never done, angering moderate opinion and helping to swell the ranks of the abolitionists. Incident followed incident as men were snatched from their families to be returned to masters in the South whom they might last have seen years before. Because there was a bounty on such returns the law was open to abuse and many blacks were wrongfully re-enslaved. Thousands did not wait but made their way further north into Canada, convinced they could never be safe again in the United States.

It was not long before the more radical among the abolitionists found ways to combat the law by forming vigilante groups, and the anti-slavery press was filled with reports of fugitives being spectacularly spirited away from under the noses of the official slave-catchers. Personal revulsion against the Act prompted Harriet Beecher Stowe to write *Uncle Tom's Cabin*, which was first serialized under a different title in an obscure anti-slavery newsletter during 1851 before being published as a book the following year. It became the most powerful piece of propaganda that the anti-slavery movement ever had and, although many readers today may find Mrs. Stowe's characters stereotyped and her simple tale somewhat naïve and mawkish, the account of white men's inhumanity to their black brethren struck a guilty chord in the North and broadened the abolitionist appeal. The book was an instant best-seller in the United States, and was astonishingly successful in Europe, too; more than a million copies were sold in England alone during its first year of publication, something unheard of for the time. It was also made into an extremely popular play and was a favorite subject for lantern-slide lecturers the world over. Everywhere Harriet Beecher Stowe went, she was feted, and in London Queen Victoria insisted on meeting her.

All of this was grist to the abolitionist mill and helped to polarize the nation still further over the slavery issue. Several Northern states went so far as to enact 'personal liberty laws' designed to thwart the operation of the Fugitive Slave Act. Nevertheless, racial discrimination remained strong in the North. A number of the free states, such as Indiana, Iowa and Illinois (and also Oregon, which was admitted as a state in 1859), had laws denying entry to blacks and barring those already there from voting, serving on juries or becoming members of the state militias. Massachusetts was something of an oasis for free blacks where men at least had almost full civil and political equality. After 1843 a free black male could even marry a white woman, though he still could not join the militia, and in 1855 segregation in schools and on public transport was made illegal in the state. Elsewhere in the North old attitudes died hard and no political party could expect to win on a platform proclaiming racial equality. Northerners might despise slavery, but by and large they were far from enthusiastic at having blacks in their midst, let alone treating them as peers.

For a while during the 1850s, many Northerners were similarly unenthusiastic about having immigrants in their midst, particularly if they were Catholic. Indeed at the local level this was a much more explosive political issue than slavery. Immigration had risen quite sharply from the mid-1840s onwards, when failed revolutions in continental Europe, potato famines in Ireland and bad harvests elsewhere had all served to make millions move westwards across the Atlantic in search of a better life. Some three million entered the United States between 1846 and 1855, increasing the population by nearly a seventh. Most settled in the North, though some went to the western territories; few sought a haven in the South. Many of them were unskilled and not of Anglo-Saxon origin, and more than half were Catholic, either from Ireland or southern Germany and Austria.

Because they tended to concentrate in the cities along the Atlantic seaboard, where the accepted religion had long been Protestant, Catholic immigrants soon ran into conflict, especially if they drank heavily, since the majority of churches then were engaged in temperance drives. Anti-Catholic feeling had always been strong in what was an intensely and essentially Protestant culture, and there had been religious riots before, although nothing to match what now ensued. Southern politicians were not slow to seek advantage from the discord and election days were the occasion for some of the worst sectarian violence. In such incidents during 1854 eight people in Baltimore and ten in St. Louis died. Twenty were killed at Louisville a year later in another dispute between rival Protestant and Catholic groups.

Anti-immigrant secret societies began to proliferate throughout the North and ironically Massachusetts became the focus of their efforts. Politicians there were quick to climb on to this particular bandwagon and in 1854 control of the state legislature passed into the hands of the 'Native American' party, generally referred to as the 'Know

Nothings' because they began with many of the trappings of a secret society. Three other New England states went the same way the following year. The tide then swept southwards to take in Maryland, Kentucky and even Texas. After that the Know-Nothing craze faded almost as fast as it had arisen, but it was an important symptom of various undercurrents of political and social discontent. Immigrants were convenient scapegoats for a deeply troubled society.

For a brief time it was uncertain whether arguments over immigration or slavery would bring about a radical realignment of the existing two-party system. Certainly anti-immigrant feeling helped to undermine it, especially among the Whigs, and thus clear the way for the emergence of a major new party. That new party grew out of renewed sectional conflict over the further extension of slavery, this time focusing on Kansas and Nebraska territories, the only remaining parts of the Louisiana Purchase which had not yet achieved statehood.

In 1854 a bill was introduced to organize these territories as a preliminary to statehood. Its author was Stephen Douglas, perhaps the most dynamic figure among the Democrats in the North and also Abraham Lincoln's great political rival in their shared home state of Illinois. Douglas was an out-and-out expansionist and was keen to promote a transcontinental railroad along a route which would benefit his own state. Somewhat naively, he hoped to duck the slavery issue at the national level by leaving it to the people in the territories themselves to decide whether or not the peculiar institution should be allowed there.

Whatever the apparent attractions of this appeal to grass-roots democracy, the proposal was political dynamite. Kansas and Nebraska were both north of the Missouri Compromise line and on that score should clearly have been non-slave states. Alarm in the North at the prospect of slavery entering hitherto forbidden territory drove disillusioned Whigs and disaffected Democrats into alliances to resist the bill. Although they were unsuccessful, they stayed together to fight the mid-term elections later that same year.

Out of these alliances at local and state level there rapidly emerged the new Republican Party, which was strong enough to mount a serious challenge in the elections of 1856. It was not merely a new party but a new kind of party, in that its appeal was confined to one section of the country, the North. However, although it opposed the further extension of slavery, it did not yet seek its immediate abolition in those states where it already existed.

In contrast to the exclusively Northern Republican Party, the Democrats could still claim to be a national party, although the South's influence within it was now stronger than ever as the tensions of the 1850s pushed more and more Southern voters into the Democratic camp. The moderate elements in the leadership were now challenged, not by a rival national party but by extremists in the South, the 'fire-eaters', who demanded, or at least threatened, secession from the Union. There were Southerners at this time who even talked of reopening the external slave trade, and others who cast envious eyes on various parts of the Caribbean as extensions of the Southern slave empire. Several abortive unofficial expeditions were launched against Cuba and Nicaragua, while the pro-Southern administration in Washington made a serious bid to purchase Cuba from Spain.

In such a feverish political climate, the task of holding the Democratic Party together nationally became more and more difficult. Events in Kansas were eventually to shatter those attempts. If hostility to the Kansas-Nebraska Act was the seed-bed of the Republican Party, the continuing troubles there proved a most effective stimulant to its growth and also to the cause of the abolitionists. By focusing on the question of slavery in the territories, the Republicans were able to assemble a political and economic, as well as ideological, case with a mass appeal that the moral crusade of the abolitionists could never match.

Republicans like Lincoln claimed that prevention of its further extension would lead to slavery's eventual extinction. Meanwhile, such a policy would preserve the territories for free white labor and secure the West for the kind of American society in which they passionately believed. This 'free soil' position was so broad in its appeal that it could draw in both those who disliked slavery and those who wanted to keep the West a white man's country.

Leaving the decision on slavery to the people on the spot produced fierce antagonism, as well as a hectic race against time, between free and slave-owning interests. Nebraska was too far north to give the pro-slavery cause much hope but Kansas, with the slave state of Missouri on its eastern border, was a different proposition. Pro-slavery settlers and interlopers from Missouri had an early advantage, but soon met stiff opposition from migrants from the North, often sponsored by emigrant aid societies, a thinly disguised description of abolitionist-backed organizations based in New England.

Southern interests soon decided that these moves were simply ruses whereby Northern businessmen were trying to take over the territory. Consequently Kansas sank into a state of virtual civil war, with newspapers across the land turning every minor skirmish into a major battle. 'Bleeding Kansas' became a favorite headline as rival gangs took turns at burning down each other's headquarters, raiding each other's settlements and battling openly in the streets of the territory's few towns. The first elections were won by the pro-slavery forces, with the help of sympathetic Missourians who slipped across the border on polling day to vote — some 1,700 of them, later rising to nearly 5,000, armed to the teeth, willing and expecting to create trouble, and soon dubbed 'Border Ruffians' in the Northern press. The anti-slavery groups replied by calling a convention in late 1855 to draw up a constitution and apply for admission as a free state. But the decisions of this gathering, boycotted by the pro-slavery side, although ratified by a majority in the territory, were dismissed as illegal by the administration in Washington, then in the hands of a pro-Southern president.

Violence and bloodshed in Kansas — over 200 people were killed there in sectional clashes during 1856 alone — were matched by violence and bloodshed in Washington when in May of the same year a Northern senator, Charles Sumner, a champion of the anti-slavery cause, was so badly beaten in the Senate chamber with a heavy cane wielded by a Southern congressman that he did not return there for three years. The action horrified Northerners, many of whom saw it as a blatant example of the barbarism bred by a slave society, while in the South the congressman became a hero and fragments of his stick prized possessions among 'fire-eaters'.

Southerners had another cause for jubilation when in 1857 the Dred Scott case came before the Supreme Court. Scott was a slave who had been taken by his master, an

9.   *White Southerners were used, when young, to being looked after by slaves in the house*

army surgeon, from Missouri to Illinois, a free state, and then on to Wisconsin, a free territory. On the grounds of his residence in these non-slave areas, he had later claimed his freedom. The Supreme Court, a majority of whom were Southerners, pronounced against him, ruling also that blacks could never become citizens on a par with whites and that Congress had no power to bar slavery from a territory, which implied that the exclusion clause of the Missouri Compromise was unconstitutional. This, of course, antagonized the North and there was talk of a slave-power conspiracy to take over first the West and then the whole country.

Once again passions were aroused and the problem became further polarized. The South's confidence was boosted by the fact that it had largely escaped the hiccup in the economy that had occurred elsewhere in the nation during 1857. While panic hit Wall Street and Northern businessmen demanded higher tariffs to protect their burgeoning industries, the South, enjoying excellent cotton crops and experiencing no dip in its export earnings, saw all this as confirming the superiority of its chosen way of life, resting on the peculiar institution.

In Kansas, meanwhile, a new constitutional convention, this time boycotted by the anti-slavery elements, met in 1857 and inevitably produced a pro-slavery document. However, when the next elections for the territorial legislature were held, the anti-slavery groups participated and their candidates won a large majority. This encouraged them to put the pro-slavery constitution to a popular vote, when it was roundly rejected. Nevertheless the pro-Southern administration in Washington recommended its adoption by Congress. The Senate promptly did so, but the House of Representatives insisted that it be put a second time to a referendum, when it was again rejected, this time by a six to one majority, which secured the future of Kansas as a free state when it finally entered the Union in 1861. Both the states admitted to the Union since California in 1850 — Minnesota in 1858 and Oregon in 1859 — were also non-slave, which tilted the balance in the Senate against the South, though, ironically, California's representatives more often than not voted the South's way.

The drama was far from over with the four years of wrangling over Kansas and Nebraska. During October 1859 there occurred perhaps the most emotionally charged episode of the whole decade: John Brown, an anti-slavery hardliner who had already made a reputation for himself in Kansas, where he had not stopped short of murdering his opponents in cold blood, led an attack on the undefended federal arsenal at Harper's Ferry, Virginia, where the Shenandoah River joins the Potomac, some 50 miles northwest of Washington. Believing in a God of wrath and righteousness — his favorite biblical saying was, 'Without the shedding of blood there is no remission of sins' — and fanatical to the point of insanity, John Brown aimed to arouse the slave population of the South and, using the captured weapons, to strike a fatal blow at the hated peculiar institution on its home soil. His band of 18 men included five blacks and three of his own sons.

Militarily the raid was a fiasco and as a call to arms to the slaves it fell on deaf ears. Brown's little group was soon surrounded by a larger force commanded by a certain Colonel Robert E. Lee, and most of them were killed or captured. Brown was tried for murder and treason against the state of Virginia, found guilty and, with six of his followers, executed within the month.

Conceived in fantasy, performed with incredible folly and culminating in horror and disaster, this incident shocked even those Americans already hardened by the lurid events of the 1850s. It touched the South on its rawest nerve, the fear of an armed revolt. For a while rumors of other insurrections swept the slave states. John Brown was seen as the personification of the now overwhelming Northern urge to destroy the South. He had given the anti-slavery threat a human dimension. When it was learned that he had had financial backing and moral support from influential and hitherto respectable people in the North, many Southerners were alarmed that such mindless violence could be countenanced.

Panic gripped the slave states, while in the feverish mood that flourished in the North John Brown was crowned a martyr. The day he was hanged bells tolled in many New England churches and groups prayed openly for his soul. He had handed his executioner a note, which read, 'I John Brown am now quite certain that the crimes of this guilty land will never be purged away but with blood'. Within a few years Yankee soldiers would be marching into battle to the strains of a newly composed song: 'John Brown's body lies a'mouldering in the grave, but his soul goes marching on . . .'

3 Forward to Sumter

The fateful 12 months that led up to the Civil War began and ended with events in Charleston, South Carolina, a city of some 35,000 people where the two rivers, the Ashley and the Cooper came together, in the words of the local boast, to form the Atlantic Ocean. Charlestonians were given to extravagant behavior as well as to exaggerated comments. They considered themselves the epitome of Southernness and their city the focus of Southern traditions and Southern ideals. On 23 April 1860 it was the chosen venue for the Democratic Party Convention to select its candidate in the presidential election of November that year.

During the months following John Brown's execution the atmosphere in the South had been highly charged. Many communities organized boycotts of Northern goods. Militia units stepped up their training. Vigilante groups prowled the rural areas for runaway slaves and would-be guerrillas. There was open talk of secession and even before the Convention began the Alabama legislature had instructed its governor to convene a state-wide meeting to consider leaving the Union should a Republican succeed in being elected at the polls in November.

With strong support from Northern delegates, Stephen Douglas fought hard for the Democratic nomination in the unfriendly atmosphere of Charleston. But he could not find the required two-thirds majority, even after delegates from several Southern states walked out in protest at the failure to include in the party platform a demand for a federal slave code in those western territories still to be organized into states. After 57 inconclusive ballots, the convention was adjourned to meet in Baltimore six weeks later.

Before that happened the Republicans had gathered at Chicago in jubilant mood on May 16 to choose their candidate. The venue was as brash and brazen as themselves — a few years before Chicago had hardly existed but now it was the fastest growing community in the land. Whoever was their choice stood a good chance of winning in most of the Northern states but was unlikely to secure many votes in the South. The key states were Pennsylvania, Illinois and Indiana, which had all gone to the Democrats four years earlier. There was no shortage of aspiring candidates, but none of the favorites was able to secure a majority in either of the first two ballots, which led the party managers to look round for a compromise candidate.

Abraham Lincoln had arrived at the convention with the support of only his fellow Illinois delegates, although his reputation had been growing beyond his own state ever since his unsuccessful campaign for the Senate two years before, when he had come to national notice in a series of featured debates with his better-known opponent, Stephen Douglas. A lawyer of considerable ability, he had spoken extensively throughout the

Midwest, and more recently in the Northeast. In the search for a compromise candidate, he had the advantage of not having been around long enough to have made many enemies in influential places. In addition, his homespun 'Honest Abe' image and his humble origins — his parents were semi-literate pioneers — were as much an asset then as they would be for any aspiring politician from the prairie states today.

In other ways, too, Lincoln fitted the Republicans' need. He was a former Whig in a party which was full of former Whigs; he combined pragmatism and realism with a deep devotion to the Union; above all, he was a moderate but one whose revulsion against the moral evil of slavery made him acceptable to the more radical wing of the party. Although he did not receive the requisite number of votes on the third ballot, enough delegates switched to him immediately afterwards to ensure his nomination.

As expected, the Republican Party's platform was strongly anti-slavery but not abolitionist. It came out unequivocally for a ban on any further extension of slavery into the territories, but it drew the line at interference with slavery in the states where it already existed. This was not enough to reassure Southern voters, who dismissed the party as nigger-loving and nicknamed its members 'Black Republicans'. Such Southerners failed to grasp not only the attraction of the Republican ideology, based on free labor and free soil, to the Northern electorate, but also the new party's appeal to the many Northerners who wanted to translate their economic and numerical strength into effective political power in Washington. They were tired of persistent Southern influence and even control over the Federal government. Republicans had made a case since the birth of their party in 1854 that Northern liberties and Northern rights were being stripped and subjugated by Southern tyranny, in particular through the South's domination of the ruling Democratic Party, to the extent that they, too, felt themselves enslaved. As one Northern congressman put it in 1858: 'We are becoming slaves to the slave juggernaut.' Both sides saw themselves as fighting to preserve their essential freedoms. What they were arguing over were two different definitions of the American dream. Southerners feared being condemned to a perpetual minority, their influence forever in decline, and hence began to consider whether their interests might be better served outside the Union than within it. Fiercely proud of the society that they had created, they were determined to resist outside interference in their affairs.

The Republicans courted the Northern voters not just with ideas but with pledges to enact a protective tariff, a homestead law, liberal immigration rules, improvements to rivers and harbors, and federal aid to build a transcontinental railroad. It was a package that had something for everyone in the North and West. When the Democrats met again in June, instead of uniting behind a single, strong nominee in the face of the now known, formidable Republican challenge, they proceeded to fall out with each other and ended up with two candidates, John C. Breckinridge, the choice of Southern Democrats, and Stephen Douglas, the champion of Northern and Western Democrats. They inevitably split the vote and let in their opponents. There was even a fourth presidential candidate, John Bell, from the Constitutional Union Party, a hastily organized movement consisting mainly of former Whigs which took its stand simply in defence of the Union and the Constitution.

Lincoln emerged as the clear winner in the November election, with a majority in the crucial electoral college vote over all three of his rivals. He owed his victory to the winner-takes-all principle by which the candidate with the largest popular vote in a state receives all that state's electoral college votes — and Lincoln had the votes where they really counted, in the Northern states with large populations. Almost all his votes came from there, which was just as well since even the state where he was born, Kentucky, gave him only a handful. In 10 of the slave states, he did not even appear on the ballot. His share of the popular vote nationally was less than 40 per cent – very similar to that polled by such twentieth-century presidential losers as Barry Goldwater in 1964 and George McGovern in 1972.

The worst fears of many Southerners seemed to be confirmed when a prominent Northern politician declared: 'The country has once and for all thrown off the domination of the slaveholders.' Lincoln's election seemed truly to be the red rag to the Southern bull that moderates had feared. The Republicans would still not be in control of both houses of Congress and the new President would also have to contend with a Supreme Court dominated by pro-Southern judges, but such considerations did not prompt second thoughts from the fire-eaters.

As usual South Carolina led the way. Within hours of the news of Lincoln's victory, the state legislature there had called for the election of delegates to attend a special convention to consider secession. On December 20, 1860, that body agreed unanimously to take South Carolina out of the Union. A local planter's wife wrote in her diary that day: 'We are divorced, North and South, because we have hated each other so.' The Charleston convention was followed during the next six weeks by similar gatherings in Mississippi, Florida, Alabama, Georgia, Louisiana and Texas, which all came to identical conclusions, though not always by large majorities. Only in Texas was the issue put to a vote of the whole electorate.

On February 4, 1861 representatives from the seven seceding states met at Montgomery, Alabama. Within five days they had agreed on a provisional constitution for the Confederate States of America and had elected Jefferson Davis, a senator from Mississippi, as their provisional president. Davis was, in fact, not present at the convention and had not sought the job, although he had expected to play some military role in the rebellion, since he had been to West Point, had served in the United States Army during the Mexican War and was a former secretary of war. He was a moderate, but passionately concerned for Southern values; the other candidates had cancelled each other out, and he was a compromise choice. When the news of his election was brought to him at his Mississippi plantation home, he let it be known straight away that he was prepared to do what he considered his duty and he left within the day for Montgomery.

Elsewhere in the South there was less enthusiasm for secession. In the states of the upper South, where cotton was not king and where slavery had a less secure hold, there was much greater reluctance to break up the Union. Conventions had met in Virginia, Missouri and Arkansas and had all rejected secession, in some cases by substantial majorities. As late as April 4, 1861, Virginia, the South's traditional leader, had voted two to one against leaving the Union. The remaining slave states, North Carolina, Delaware, Maryland, Kentucky and Tennessee, had all stayed their hand, not bothering to call conventions.

Although not expecting resistance from the North, all the seceding states quietly reinforced their existing militias and set about recruiting volunteers for new groups,

10.   *When Jefferson Davis*
      resigned his Senate seat in
      January 1861 he spoke
      more in sorrow than in
      anger: 'Whatever of
      offence there has been to
      me, I leave here. I carry
      no hostile remembrance'

which in some cases were named 'Minute Men' after the units that had fought the British in the War of Independence. Where feasible, they took over federal arsenals and forts located within their borders and used the weapons and ammunition to equip their own forces. One of the first decisions of the provisional Confederate administration was to sanction the formation of a Confederate army some 100,000 strong — the Federal army at that time numbered only 16,000, most of whom were in the western territories defending the settlers against the American Indians.

The seceding states stoutly asserted that their action was legal and was simply aimed at protecting their basic rights against what they saw as the encroachment of federal power in Northern hands. In setting up the Confederacy and drafting its constitution, they did not place much emphasis on slavery. However, their Vice-President, Alexander Stephens of Georgia, who ironically had originally opposed secession, was franker than most when, just a few weeks after its creation, he said that the Confederacy's

> cornerstone rests upon the great truth that the negro is not equal to the white man; that slavery — subordination to the superior race — is his natural and normal condition. This, our new government, is the first in the history of the world based upon this great physical, philosophical, and moral truth.

Northern abolitionists were not slow to seize on this and to describe secession as 'a rebellion in the interests of darkness, of despotism and oppression'.

Abolitionists apart, Northerners by and large were slow to respond to the acts of secession — and when they did their response was often confused. There were many

11.   The war begins. Fort Sumter under bombardment, April 12–13, 1861

who simply thought that Southerners were bad losers, unprepared to accept the will of the majority as expressed through the ballot box. There was also plenty of anger and resentment, though no consensus on what to do next in this unprecedented situation. A willingness to 'let the erring sisters go in peace' was voiced in some quarters, even, for a while, by the normally vehement editor of the influential *New York Tribune*, Horace Greeley, and there was widespread anxiety to avoid any precipitate action which might drive more states to secede. But the advocates of caution were matched by those who demanded vigorous measures against the Southern 'traitors'. In the lame-duck session of the old Congress, as well as in a hastily convened 'peace conference' in Washington, compromise proposals were keenly but fruitlessly debated.

Although elected in November, Lincoln was not due to be inaugurated as president until the following March, and under the strange political timetable which then operated, the newly elected Congress would not normally have met until December 1861. At this critical time for the Union the reins of government were still in the hands of the previous Democratic, and generally pro-Southern, administration which, not surprisingly, showed no inclination to act decisively against the seceded states. At least one Cabinet member, the Secretary of War, was openly conniving with secessionists in the release of Federal arms into Southern hands.

Two years earlier, in his 'House Divided' speech, Lincoln had forecast that 'a crisis must be reached and passed' on the slavery issue. Now, as he waited to assume office, he went

12.   *The war begins. Fort Sumter under bombardment, April 12–13, 1861*

out of his way to reassure the South that he had no intention of interfering with its peculiar institution inside the existing slave states, and even that the notorious Fugitive Slave Act would continue to be enforced. He offered to consider an 'unamendable' amendment to the Constitution which would exempt slavery from any future Federal interference but he was not prepared to countenance any proposed compromise that would permit slavery's further extension.

As Lincoln left Illinois in mid-February for his inauguration in Washington on March 4, on what should have been the most triumphal journey of his life, Jefferson Davis was being sworn in as provisional president of the Confederacy in Montgomery, Alabama, and a Confederate Congress was in the process of formation. The slave states of Maryland and Virginia, which surrounded the Federal capital, had not yet seceded but their loyalty to the Union was uncertain, and because of the rumors of a possible Southern coup in Washington, Lincoln travelled the latter part of the way in disguise and under an assumed name.

Despite threats to his life, Lincoln had lingered en route, as was traditional, to make speeches and to receive petitions, but his audiences were apprehensive and he appeared far from confident. Most of them were seeing him for the first time. Just 52 years old, tall, angular and with a somewhat lean and hungry look, Lincoln disappointed many of his onlookers. He had struck some as woefully inadequate for the task ahead; nothing he said seemed to reassure them and indeed his natural oratory appeared to forsake him.

The secession of the seven states of the deep South had presented the federal government with all manner of administrative problems, from the delivery of mail to the enforcement of law and order, but these did not in themselves threaten an immediate collision between North and South. The presence of forts manned by federal garrisons within some of the seceding states was a different matter. Many of them were quickly abandoned or became subject to local agreements. Two, however, were not so easily disposed of: Fort Pickens at Pensacola, Florida, and Fort Sumter in the middle of Charleston harbor. An unarmed merchant ship, *The Star of the West*, sent to Sumter in early January with provisions for the garrison and 200 troops to relieve them, had been fired on by South Carolina shore batteries and had returned home without discharging either cargo.

For the next two months the Washington administration did nothing and tacitly accepted informal truces at both forts. But the day after his inauguration Lincoln was told by the commander at Fort Sumter, Major Robert Anderson, that the garrison had supplies for only a further six weeks. After much discussion with his colleagues, Lincoln decided to send relief expeditions to both Sumter and Pickens. He had already tried to relieve Pickens but due to a mix-up of orders his wishes had not been carried out.

Both forts had now taken on a symbolic value out of all proportion to their military importance: the Confederacy feared that its case for recognition as a sovereign nation would be compromised as long as another power maintained an armed presence within two of its main harbors, while the federal authority felt that it could not afford the loss of face if the forts were surrendered to states in rebellion. It was strangely appropriate that, in the case of Sumter, the severest test ever to face the Union should arise over the attempted relief of a federal garrison marooned on a fort protecting the birthplace of secession.

Lincoln went ahead in early April with his decision to despatch a relief convoy to the beleaguered Fort Sumter, with orders that the troops should be deployed only if the South Carolinians resisted the landing of provisions. He gave advance notice of his plan to both the fort commander and the secessionist governor of South Carolina. He thus placed on Confederate shoulders the onus of firing a first shot. If Lincoln was indeed setting some kind of trap, the Confederate leadership, including Jefferson Davis, walked unhesitatingly into it, though they probably felt that there was little alternative to confrontation by this stage. Excitement was already running high, and there was a widely shared belief that a shooting-match would unite the Confederacy and bring the remaining slave states into the fold.

Since he knew that the relief convoy was expected to arrive off Charleston by April 11 or 12, Davis ordered the local Confederate commander to seek Sumter's surrender. On April 10 Anderson rejected the demand, though he admitted that without relief his food supplies would be exhausted within a few days and, when pressed, hinted that this might happen by April 15. With the relief expedition expected before then and fearing some Union trick or bluff, the Confederates decided that they could not wait and at 4.30 a.m. on April 12 their troops began firing on Fort Sumter, watched by an enthusiastic crowd along the Charleston waterfront. Some of the ships of the relief force arrived in time to witness the bombardment, though there was no attempt to intervene.

13.   *The Northern commander at Fort Sumter, Major Robert Anderson*

The firing lasted 34 hours before Anderson decided that he and his 100 or so men had had enough; the Confederate guns had shot off more than 4,000 rounds in the general direction of the luckless fort, while the Federals had replied with just under 1,000 rounds. Major Anderson in fact never used any of his heavy cannon, thinking that they would be a bigger hazard to his own forces than to the enemy's. The damage to the fort was extensive, though miraculously no one had been killed. The only casualties happened later when a soldier died while firing a salute during the surrender ceremony and another was fatally wounded in an ensuing explosion. They were to be the first of many dead as America's bloodiest struggle developed.

Once the Confederates had actually fired on the flag, Northerners rallied firmly to the Union's defense. Baffled and bemused before, they now knew where they stood and seemed almost relieved. In the South the Sumter success raised secessionist fervor to a new pitch and appeared to confirm the conventional wisdom that one Southerner could whip 10 Yankees. But it had killed the dream that independence could be won without a fight. Four more states came into the Confederate camp — Virginia, North Carolina, Tennessee and Arkansas — on the grounds that force was now intended against their fellow Southerners. Lines were being drawn and positions taken. The war was about to begin in earnest.

4 Early euphoria

Within a day of Sumter's surrender, Lincoln called 75,000 militia into service for three months to suppress the rebellion in the South. This immediate response to the most serious crisis that the Union had ever faced was ridiculed by one critic with the comment, 'You might as well attempt to put out the flames of a burning house with a squirt-gun.' However, a wave of patriotic enthusiasm swept the North to match the high spirits which had been so evident in the South for several months. Recruiting rallies took place in every local community and the music of marching bands and the tramp of drilling feet filled the air. Thousand upon thousand of young, and not so young, men flocked to the colors, egged on by family, friends and neighbors. 'So impatient did I become for starting,' said one volunteer, 'that I felt like ten thousand pins were pricking me in every part of my body.' No one, it seemed, wanted to miss the opportunity of a lifetime to participate in a great adventure.

Such enthusiasm was unrestrained by any realistic sense of what lay ahead. Rather than four years of carnage and horror, the general expectation was that it would all soon be over, settled by one exciting encounter, with sufficient gallantry and romance to satisfy would-be heroes but not enough bloodshed to turn drama into tragedy. *The New York Times* predicted that the rebellion would be put down within 30 days; the *Chicago Tribune* thought it might take three months. Lincoln's old adversary, Stephen Douglas, proclaimed: 'There can be no neutrals in this war — only patriots or traitors.' An obscure ex-army officer named Ulysses S. Grant wrote to his father: 'Whatever may have been my political opinions before, I have but one sentiment now. That is, we have a Government, and laws, and a flag, and they must all be sustained.' The first flush of martial enthusiasm united North and South in their different ways to a degree that would seldom be achieved again later in the war. A British journalist traveling in the South saw nothing but 'flushed faces, wild eyes, screaming mouths hurrahing for "Jeff Davis and the Southern Confederacy"'. The famous British war correspondent, William Howard Russell of *The Times*, reported from New Orleans: 'As one looks at the resolute, quick, angry faces about him, and hears but the single theme, he must feel the South will never yield to the North, unless as a nation which is beaten beneath the feet of a victorious enemy.'

Virginia had opted for the Confederacy on April 17, though its act of secession was not ratified until a state-wide referendum was held on May 23, and Arkansas, North Carolina and Tennessee had followed suit within a matter of weeks. Without these four states the Confederacy's war effort would have been crippled from the start, since they constituted half of its manufacturing capacity, grew half its food, supplied half its mules and horses, and provided more than two-fifths of its armed forces. They also altered the whole

14. *The Northern state militias answered the call to arms, some looking as if they were dressed more for opera than for war*

strategic outlook by bringing the front line much closer to the free states of the North; Virginia lay just across the Potomac from the Federal capital itself.

If the Confederacy had enjoyed similar success in bringing the top tier of slave states — the 'border states' — within the fold, it might have decisively changed the balance of advantage between the two sides. Washington, D.C. would have been enveloped in hostile territory and, further west, the Ohio River would have provided a formidable natural line of defence. Lincoln was under no illusion about the importance of these states to the Union's survival. They were in many ways its hinge, sharing economic links with the North but having in common with the South its social system and peculiar institution. Their people looked equally disfavorably on the abolitionists to the north and the fire-eaters to the south. It would take a judicious mixture of subtlety and strength to secure them for either the Union or the Confederacy. Perhaps Lincoln's greatest achievement in the difficult first year of the war lay in the measure of Union control that he was able to secure over these states.

The pattern varied from one border state to another. Delaware was by this time only nominally a slave state, and its small size and geographical situation left little doubt that it would remain firmly in Union hands. Its neighbor Maryland was altogether a different matter. It enveloped Washington on its northern side, and secessionist feeling was strong in parts of the state, not least in its major city of Baltimore. If it had gone the same way as Virginia, the position of the Federal government in Washington would have been untenable.

15.   *As 14*

As it was, when some newly recruited Massachusetts regiments were moving south within a week of Sumter in order to man the defenses of the national capital, they were attacked by a pro-Confederate mob while changing trains in Baltimore. In the fracas that followed, four soldiers and twelve civilians lost their lives. Enraged Southern sympathizers burned bridges and blocked roads to prevent further reinforcements reaching Washington. For a while, overland communication between the Federal capital and the North was cut, and the only troops who got through were carried by boat down Chesapeake Bay to Annapolis, from which point they could march to Washington.

Although rumors of a coup against the President or of an imminent Confederate attack were rife for several days, they had no substance in fact, not least because the Southern forces were as little prepared for action as their opponents. By the end of April Lincoln had at least 10,000 troops in and around the capital and the immediate crisis was over. For lack of more suitable accommodation, many of the soldiers were billeted in the unfinished Capitol building before being put to work fortifying the city.

During the next few weeks, Lincoln took steps to secure Maryland. The writ of habeas corpus was temporarily suspended throughout the state so that suspected trouble-makers could be detained without trial. Eventually its state legislature was prevailed upon to vote against secession, though its citizens remained deeply divided on the issue. Some 30,000 white Marylanders and, later, 9,000 blacks, were thought to have fought in the Union army, while about 20,000 became Confederates.

Kentucky was also crucially important to both camps because of its size and situation, and its pivotal position was symbolized by the fact that it was the birthplace of both Abraham Lincoln and Jefferson Davis. Lincoln joked that while he hoped God was on his side, he knew he must have Kentucky. The state's governor made a hopeless attempt to keep it neutral, and certainly a false or rash move by either side could have driven it into the arms of the other. The Confederacy squandered its initial advantages and eventually Union forces took over the state without much hindrance. Altogether during the war, some 50,000 white and 24,000 black Kentuckians fought for the Union, as against 35,000 who joined the Confederacy.

Kentucky typified the singular tragedy of the border states in the Civil War, for there the notion of the war as a conflict between brother and brother, neighbor and neighbor, became a literal reality. Relatives of Mrs. Lincoln, for example, fought in the Rebel army. Occasionally, members of the same community, or even the same family, confronted each other on the field of battle. One of the most poignant moments of the war occurred at Missionary Ridge near Chattanooga in 1863 when the 4th Kentucky Union Regiment came face to face with the 4th Kentucky Confederate Regiment. In this regard, the border states were very much the exception to the rule; for people in most parts of the North and in the deep South, the war was a conflict between distinct cultures and distant societies, strange and even alien to one another.

Missouri, the most westerly of the border states, was a tangled web of local rivalries and conflicting loyalties and was to suffer more than any other state from internal feuding and the ruthless bush whacking of irregulars. Initially the pro-Southern groups held the upper hand and the early military engagements in the state went the Confederacy's way. However, during the course of the war, some 80,000 white Missourians and 8,000 blacks served in the Union army, as against 30,000 who joined the Rebel ranks and another 3,000 or more who fought as guerrillas on the Southern side.

Next to the border states and the traditional leader of the upper South, Virginia was not totally united in its decision after Sumter to back secession. The western counties beyond the Alleghenies, where the farmers were almost to a man non-slave holders, had voted overwhelmingly against it. Lincoln sought to make the most of this pocket of Unionism and by somewhat irregular — and, some would argue, scarcely constitutional — means succeeded in carving out the separate state of West Virginia, which was admitted to the Union in 1863. However, although the whole Appalachian Mountain area running down from West Virginia through eastern Kentucky and western North Carolina into east Tennessee, where slavery had never had much of a foothold, was a bastion of pro-Federal feeling deep inside the Confederacy, the region's rugged and inaccessible terrain made it difficult for the North to take advantage of it militarily.

The dilemma with which secession and war confronted many people in the border states and the upper South is well illustrated by the case of Robert E. Lee. A professional soldier in the Union army with a reputation which led Lincoln initially to offer him command of the Northern forces, Lee was also a Virginian and a slave holder, though an apologist rather than an enthusiast for the peculiar institution and at best a lukewarm supporter of secession. Nevertheless, he threw in his lot with the South on the grounds that he could not raise his hand against the state of his birth. In many respects he always remained a Virginian first and a Confederate second.

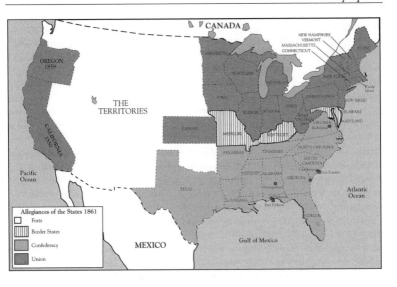

16. Map of Allegiances of the States 1861

Few countries were ever less prepared for war than the United States in 1861. The regular army was minuscule and scattered, mostly in small units, west of the Mississippi. Nearly a third of its officers resigned to join the Confederacy. The War Department in Washington was staffed by a few clerks and run by veterans of previous campaigns. The Commander-in-Chief, Winfield Scott, known as 'Old Fuss and Feathers', had fought in the War of 1812, was 74 years old and suffered from dropsy and vertigo. There were scarcely any maps of the South, and the professional training provided at West Point had always devoted more time to mathematics, engineering and the construction of fortifications than to strategy or staff work.

The navy was in equally bad shape. Less than half its ships were in commission and those that were had been designed for deep-water activities rather than service on rivers or inshore among the bays and inlets and shallow channels of the Southern coast. Most were obsolescent sailing vessels, since the highly conservative United States Navy had been slow to learn the significance of steam power. Officers were often as antiquated as their ships and knew little of the Rebel coast or its ports. Like the regular army, they had never expected to be waging a war in their own backyard.

Lincoln quickly realized that the war was likely to be a lengthy affair. He had first called out the state militias, dismissed by many as 'marching-and-chowder' societies and widely regarded as social clubs rather than potential fighting units. Clearly they could not be relied on to form the basis of an effective force in a protracted conflict. In early May he appealed for 42,000 volunteers on three-year engagements; he also increased the regular army by 23,000 men and the navy by 18,000. When Congress met in July, he asked for 400,000 more volunteers — a sure sign of growing realism about the likely scale of the conflict — and, not to be outdone, Congress raised the number to 500,000.

During these early months more men responded to the call than the army could organize, train and equip. Recruitment was the responsibility of states and localities, and governors and mayors vied with each other to meet the demand for troops. At the grass roots level, the initiative in raising a regiment was usually taken by local worthies whose ambition to become colonel ran far ahead of their military prowess or experience. Most companies elected their own officers and NCOs. Since units were based on counties and districts, where peer pressure was at its most intense, camaraderie was usually strong. Equipping and supplying the regiments, including clothing, was also in the hands of localities and states. Poor organization, shoddy materials and sometimes rank profiteering all helped to make a difficult situation worse. The result was a weird array of weapons and a motley of uniforms, ranging from the standard dark blue jacket and light blue trousers of the regular army to the gaudy 'Zouave'-style dress based on that worn by French colonial units in the Sahara. Some Union regiments were clothed in grey and some Confederates in blue, which led to some tragic mix-ups in the early battles. It was not until the second year of the war that Union soldiers were virtually all wearing blue; Confederate grey was never so consistent.

Initially, the South mobilized rather more quickly than the North. Its militias had been on alert since the first states had seceded. In May Jefferson Davis, like Lincoln, had quadrupled his call for troops to 400,000. With a pool of white manpower barely a third that of the Union's, the South had nearly two-thirds as many men under arms as the North by the first summer of the war. The recruiting pattern was similar, though the supply of weapons and arms at the beginning came mainly from captured Federal arsenals located within the Confederacy. Volunteers were encouraged to bring their own guns and horses. Each regiment decked itself out in uniforms of its own choice, hence the tragic confusion of the initial skirmishes. The Southern states may have had a military tradition but they certainly did not have a maritime one. Consequently the Confederacy could not boast a navy at the outset, apart from a few customs-cutters filched from Federal service at the time of secession. The main shipbuilding facilities were all in the North and most of the existing merchant vessels were Yankee-owned. Very few sailors defected to the South. Accordingly the Confederacy had to start from scratch, laboriously and expensively building up a fleet of mainly small ships, and seeking to acquire menacing commerce raiders built in European shipyards. The Confederates lacked the resources to get rid of the blockade initiated by Lincoln during the first week of the war, which, although never wholly effective, swallowed up much Southern energy in efforts to evade it. The Confederacy was never self-sufficient and hence relied on outside suppliers for weapons and other necessities, although it was often luxury goods that were brought in by the blockade-runners because of the premium prices they could command.

Why the people of the North went to war is one of the most difficult questions raised by the whole conflict. Many observers at the time, and numerous historians since, have

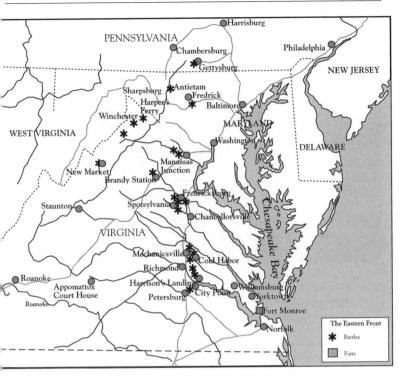

17. *Map of Eastern Front*

expressed astonishment at the vigor of the Union's reaction to the fall of Sumter. Why should ordinary Northerners support a war to coerce back into the Union rebel states that had been a thorn in their flesh for many years? Why should they take up arms against the 'Slave South' when they had had little or no direct experience of slavery themselves, and when they had for so long been conspicuously reluctant to translate their disapproval of the South's peculiar institution into action against it?

No doubt the fact that the Confederacy fired the first shot, and fired at the flag, had much to do with the immediate reaction. This affront stirred a deep pride in the Union and a patriotic fervor to which Lincoln skilfully appealed but which the South had grossly underestimated. Many Northerners, too, were devoted to their own way of life and their own notions of freedom. They resented the threat to it posed, as they saw it, by the 'slave power' and now by the new Confederacy, and the attack on Sumter confirmed their worst fears. However, no one had any real idea of the scale and character of the struggle upon which the Union was embarking. The initial burst of enthusiasm was not for the kind of endurance test that the Civil War became.

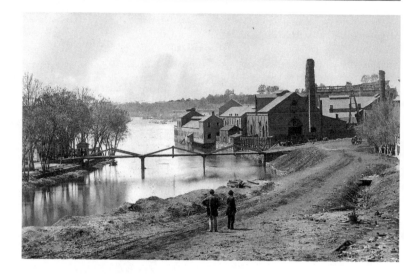

18.   *Richmond's Tredegar Iron Works were, for much of the war, the South's main weapons'*
      supplier, apart from imports

The South's war aims were more readily understandable. They had no designs on anyone else's territory. They simply wished to be left alone. They did not need to win, merely not to lose. For them the war was a defensive struggle. It was the North that would have to make the running: to invade and conquer the Confederacy or at least to break its will to resist.

British military experts, recalling their own army's predicament during the War of Independence, argued that a country as large as the Confederacy could not be conquered. To date no nation of that size had been successfully subdued. Napoleon, whose example was frequently invoked, had failed in Russia. *The Times* in London declared; 'It's one thing to drive the rebels from the south bank of the Potomac, or even to occupy Richmond, but another to reduce and hold in permanent subjection a tract of country nearly as large as Russia in Europe.' The South was fighting for its life, the North was not. Northern morale might well have proved the more vulnerable to frustration or war-weariness.

In waging a defensive war, the South would have the advantages — and also face the costs — of fighting on its own territory. Geography was in its favor, at least in Virginia. Between Washington and Richmond no fewer than six rivers ran from west to east, each affording a barrier to a would-be attacker. In the West, however, the situation was different. The waterways flowed north to south, offering invasion routes into the heartland of the Confederacy — and there would be the rub. The South's wretched roads were an obstacle to an invader, while the limitations of the rail network within the Confederacy limited the mobility of the defending forces.

Lacking any substantial manufacturing capacity, the South had to develop an arms industry almost from nothing. Its degree of success in doing so is one of the more astonishing stories of the war. For instance, of the 31,000 miles of railroad in the United States in 1860, only 9,000 were in the Confederate states. Variations in the gauge of the track made transfers from one stretch to another extremely costly and tedious. Many of the Northern lines, on the other hand, were of a uniform gauge. Moreover, of the 470 locomotives produced during 1860 only 19 were made in the South. Plants for fabricating agricultural implements were turned almost overnight into armories producing cannons and rifles. The Tredegar Iron Works at Richmond was the jewel in the South's modest industrial crown. Without it the Confederacy would have been in dire straits, although small-sized gunpowder mills and other workshops were quickly established elsewhere in the South.

Southerners used ingenuity and improvisation to overcome deficiencies in resources. Confederate churches were persuaded to give up their bells to be melted down for cannon, Southern women took to saving the contents of their chamber pots to be rendered into nitrate for gunpowder, and liquor stills were converted to produce percussion caps for rifles. Even so in the early days the Confederacy relied heavily on imports from Europe, as well as on booty from the defeated Union armies and occasional clandestine purchases of weapons and ammunition from Yankee traders prepared to sell anything to anyone for profit.

Knowing that the South could never be self-sufficient in the tools of war, Winfield Scott and others favored a strategy of slow strangulation. A blockade of the Rebel coast, coupled with an advance down the Mississippi, would cut the Confederacy off from external sources of supply and hence steadily squeeze the life out of it. Appropriately dubbed 'the Anaconda plan', it eventually helped bring about the Union's success, though such a gradualist approach could not satisfy Northern public opinion which, once aroused, insisted upon immediate and aggressive action.

Egged on by newspaper editors like Horace Greeley, Northerners demanded revenge for Sumter and the quick and decisive victory which, they believed, would surely be theirs. Following Virginia's secession referendum on May 23, the Confederacy had had the nerve to move its capital from Montgomery in the deep South to Virginia's state capital of Richmond, a mere 120 miles from Washington. Thereafter the cry of 'On to Richmond' from some of his less temperate supporters became difficult for Lincoln to resist, particularly as many of the 90-day volunteers summoned to the colors in mid-April were in danger of returning home that summer without having seen any action.

At this time, 35,000 Union troops were concentrated across the Potomac in front of the Federal capital. Another 18,000 were to be found to the northwest, guarding the exit from the Shenandoah Valley around Harper's Ferry, which had already changed hands twice, while 15,000 or so more were located to the southeast along the coast, mainly at Fort Monroe on the James Peninsula. The Confederates had 22,000 men based at Manassas railway junction, barely 25 miles from Washington, commanded by the victor of Sumter, General Pierre Beauregard, with another 12,000 lurking in the Shenandoah Valley keeping an eye on the Harper's Ferry forces.

This deficiency in numbers worried some people in the Southern camp but they

19.   *General Pierre Beauregard was a hero throughout the South because of his capture of Fort Sumter*

saw compensating advantages in the prospect of fighting on their own soil, with better intelligence and shorter supply lines, plus the advantage of an important east-west rail link which would allow them to switch their forces more easily than their opponent. In addition, there was still the widely-shared assumption that a handful of Confederates was more than a match for an army of Yankees.

The newly appointed Union commander, Irvin McDowell, was not keen to challenge that assumption just yet. He knew only too well how untrained and ill-disciplined his men still were and he pleaded for further time in which to put the more obvious weaknesses to right. But Lincoln was unwilling to wait. 'You are green, it is true,' he told him, 'but they are green also; you are all green alike.' And so on July 16, 1861 the Northern troops vacated their camps across the Potomac from the Federal capital and marched southwards. The intention was to outflank from the west the Confederates based at Manassas.

Nothing went to plan from the outset. The Federals took an unconscionably long time — almost two and a half days — to move into their positions, with the result that all hope of surprise was lost. The intense July heat did not help, although that did not excuse the mislaying of rations and ammunition en route by many of the men, nor the frequency with which stragglers dropped out of line to consume blackberries or to forage for

20.   *Many of the Northern units acquitted themselves well at Manassas, such as the 71st New York Regiment depicted here. But it turned out not to be the walkover that their leaders had led them to believe*

chickens. Hitherto no American general had had to cope with such numbers on the road. This Union army was the largest the North American continent had ever seen, more than twice the size of the Franco-American force which George Washington had commanded at Yorktown during the War of Independence.

Because they were venturing into unknown enemy country for the first time and lacked even the most modest of maps, McDowell's advancing army spent an inordinate amount of effort on reconnaissance. In addition, the Harper's Ferry forces failed to pin down the Confederate contingents in the Shenandoah Valley, either through a mix-up in orders from Washington or, more likely, sloth on the part of the local commander. Thus, unbeknown to the Union side, the South was able at a critical phase to switch its troops via the railroad.

However, by Sunday July 21 the North felt that it was ready to strike its opening blow. That morning the cream of Washington society, men, women and children, politicians, clergymen, even a member of Lincoln's Cabinet, rode out as if for a picnic. All were eager to see the Rebels get thrashed, convinced that this would be not just the first major skirmish of the war, but probably the one and only battle. Many fondly believed that it would all be over by nightfall and the boys would be back home for the harvest. Before the sun set that day, many such illusions were shattered and many reputations made and lost.

At a crucial moment in the battle, when all seemed lost for the Confederates and the South Carolinians looked like fleeing the field, their commander tried to rally them by indicating the staunchness of the Virginians under their leader Thomas J. Jackson. 'There stands Jackson like a stone wall' was the shout and thus was the legend of 'Stonewall Jackson' born.

All went well at first for the Federals, who managed to cross the Bull Run stream in some force. Outnumbered, the Southerners fell back and back. Confusion reigned, not helped by the multiplicity of uniforms which made it difficult at times to distinguish friend from foe. Some Union troops shot at their own forces who happened to be dressed in grey. Others held back their fire as a contingent dressed in blue advanced towards them. They turned out to be a Virginian regiment, which shot at close range and with devastating effect.

As the Northern attack wilted and McDowell failed to call up his reserves waiting idly in the rear, the initiative passed to the Confederates, particularly as they had been reinforced by the troops transferred by rail from the Shenandoah region. Now these fresh troops became critical as both sides tired. Many men were collapsing from thirst and heat exhaustion. Some were even dying of sunstroke. Others stopped fighting to tend wounded comrades. A few simply ran away, appalled by what they had seen and heard. For the first time the Northerners were experiencing the Rebel yell, a high-pitched, wailing scream delivered on the run. Intended perhaps to relieve tension and to instil a sense of solidarity and strength within the advancing ranks, and thought to originate from either fox-hunting or cattle-calling, it often struck terror into the opposition. A Federal soldier said:

> There is nothing like it this side of the infernal region. The peculiar sensation that it sends down your backbone under these circumstances can never be told. You have to feel it, and if you say you did not feel it, and heard the yell, you have never been there.

By late afternoon many Northern soldiers were so jittery and disoriented that they were no longer bothering to check whether their rifles had been discharged before ramming down another shot and, in some cases, not even waiting to remove the ramrod from the barrel before firing and so sending it whistling across to the enemy like an arrow. Having gone without food or drink since the night before, they had had enough and began to retreat.

Within the hour the retreat had turned into a rout, as the roads back to Washington became clogged with fleeing civilians as well as panic-stricken troops, many of them discarding their weapons and packs as they ran. It became known later as 'the great skedaddle'. For a while the Federal capital seemed wide open to the Rebel hordes, but the Confederates were not sufficiently organized to follow up their remarkable victory. For a time it was difficult to know which side was the more confused by the events of the day. Many Southerners, though, would forever rue what seemed a great opportunity missed.

If the Federal government had been forced to abandon the national capital it might well have been 'all over by nightfall', though not in the way the beau monde of Washington had envisaged that same morning. It is debatable whether the morale, not only of the

21. *The North's retreat from Bull Run, as they preferred to call Manassas, was not a pretty sight. Many of the soldiers flung off their uniforms and mingled with the civilians as best they could*

troops but of the North as a whole, could have survived such a blow. As it was, morale plummeted in and around the Federal capital as the full realization of defeat sank in. It seemed that one Southerner could indeed whip 10 Yankees.

The Confederate failure even to threaten Washington in the aftermath of Manassas was the first of the great might-have-beens of the war. However, Lincoln and his government did not flee, and there was no coup and no major political crisis. For their part, the Rebels perhaps accepted too readily that they were in no fit state to attack the Federal capital. One of the most persistent themes of the Civil War battles was to be this inability of the winning side to follow up its victory.

Walt Whitman, the journalist turned poet, described for the *Brooklyn Standard* the scene as the dejected troops re-crossed the Potomac:

> . . . baffled, humiliated, panic-struck. Where are the vaunts, and the proud boasts with which you went forth? Where are your banners, and your bands of music, and your ropes to bring back your prisoners? . . . The sun rises, but shines not. The men appear, at first sparsely and shame-faced enough, then thicker, in the streets of Washington — appear in Pennsylvania Avenue, and on the steps and basement entrances. They come along in disorderly mobs, some

22.   *The Stone House on the Warrenton Turnpike near Manassas was on the route of both the Federal advance and retreat, as well as the scene of some bitter fighting*

in squads, stragglers, companies . . . During the forenoon Washington gets all over motley with these defeated soldiers — queer-looking objects, strange eyes and faces, drench'd (the steady rain drizzles on all day) and fearfully worn, hungry, haggard, blister'd in the feet. Good people (but not over-many of them either) hurry up something for their grub. They put wash-kettles on the fire, for soup, for coffee. They set tables on the sidewalks . . . Amid the deep excitement, crowds and motion, and desperate eagerness, it seems strange to see many, very many, of the soldiers sleeping — in the midst of all, sleeping sound. They drop down anywhere, on the steps of houses, up close by the basements or fences, on the sidewalk, aside on some vacant lot, and deeply sleep. A poor seventeen or eighteen year old boy lies there, on the stoop of a grand house; he sleeps so calmly, so profoundly. Some clutch their muskets firmly even in sleep. Some in squads; comrades, brothers, close together — and on them, as they lay, sulkily drips the rain.

Back at the Confederate base, the joy at the victory and the bickering over the possible missed opportunity went on in equal measure, though with the drenching rain that fell all around the battlefield, creating rivers of mud where previously there had been merely meandering dirt roads, any thoughts of further advance were dismissed for the moment. It was a time for both sides to lick their wounds after the bloody day. Nearly 40,000 men had been involved, and of them some 600 or more on each side had either been killed or would die later from their injuries. Another 3,000 had been seriously wounded and about 1,200 Northerners taken prisoner.

The battle of Manassas, or of Bull Run as the North preferred to call it (the Union tended to name battles after the nearest geographical feature, while the Confederacy favored towns or settlements), was the most costly to date in American history, though the losses were to be dwarfed by those in later Civil War engagements. No one could imagine what was in store for the divided nation. When Lincoln had been told of the defeat, his terse comment was, 'It's damned bad.'

The Southerners had, in fact, been within a whisker of defeat themselves but they had had the advantage, especially when the troops on both sides were so green, of remaining by and large on the defensive for most of the day. The sheer inexperience of most of the soldiers, including not least the officers, had led to the battle's confusion, and it was clearly going to be some time before either army would be turned into an efficient fighting machine.

The illusion that the war would be a brief, romantic affair of honor was now shattered once and for all. Manassas gave the South an enormous psychological boost and the North a short, sharp shock. If it left a lingering feeling of inferiority that colored much of the North's military thinking during the next year or two, it also bred a new realism. The North now knew that it had a real fight on its hands.

5 Southern setbacks

Manassas proved to be something of a false start to the war. Both sides drew from it the lesson that a little less haste and a lot more preparation were needed. If the South could scarcely believe its good fortune, its leaders were also conscious of the chaos and confusion which the battle had caused in its own ranks. Not everyone agreed with this defensive posture. General Beauregard for one, the victor of Sumter and, by his account, the victor of Manassas too, urged an attack on Washington without delay. But caution prevailed in Richmond — as it prevailed for more obvious reasons in Washington.

The post-Manassas panic in the North quickly gave way to a new, more sober determination. The luckless McDowell was cast in the role of scapegoat; his replacement, George B. McClellan, who had enjoyed one or two small successes in western Virginia, was an ambitious young officer, combining a self-confidence bordering on vainglory with a prudence which sometimes induced paralysis. He was, however, well suited to the immediate task of turning thousands of raw recruits into an organized and disciplined army.

McClellan took immense pains in fortifying the Federal capital to make it safe from any surprise Rebel attack. He also diligently restored morale within the newly named Army of the Potomac and saw to it that everyone was at least well drilled — to the point that McClellan's drilling obsession became something of a joke among Washington society. By mid-autumn he had 150,000 men on his roll, reasonably well disciplined and equipped, but while the cooler weather might have encouraged others to venture forth against the foe, he preferred to spend the daylight hours parading his troops in and around the capital, to the enormous delight of many small boys, though to the intense irritation of Lincoln and his Cabinet.

However, in late October 1861 a minor sortie was made across the Potomac above Washington at a place called Ball's Bluff. It ended in another humiliating fiasco and suggested that McClellan's marching army was not yet quite ready for real action. Those killed included an old friend of the President himself, Colonel Edward Baker, a former Republican senator from Oregon. Asked when his army might be ready, McClellan replied only when he had another 125,000 men under his command.

Such estimates of the situation showed the extent of his reliance on the intelligence provided by Allan Pinkerton, an ambitious Scot who had founded one of the first American private detective agencies and specialized in giving his clients the information they wanted to hear. Certainly he seemed anxious to flatter the General, or rather to pander to his caution, by exaggerating the numbers that opposed him, often by a factor of two or three. This was the period when the popular song in Washington and northern

23. *McClellan became the Northern commander after the Manassas debacle but the euphoria over his appointment was brief*

Virginia was 'All Quiet Along The Potomac', the words of which had been written by a Northern woman and the music by a Southern man. If the lyric originally expressed relief, its message soon acquired a note of irony.

Victory, or at least avoidance of defeat, was only one part of the strategy by which the Confederacy hoped to achieve independence. If the Northern armies could be kept at bay, the Confederates expected to obtain European recognition, particularly that of Britain and France. Recognition in itself, it was thought, might bring independence; at the very least it would embroil Britain and France with the Union government in Washington. One of the keys to the outcome of the Civil War was that the South set great store by international intervention, while the North was determined to keep the conflict a strictly domestic dispute.

The South's faith in the power of King Cotton to achieve its aim had become almost unquestioned. The argument on which it was based was simple: the bustling textile mills of Britain and France depended on the South for four-fifths of their raw cotton, and the economic prosperity and social equilibrium of parts of those countries required that the supply be uninterrupted. It was believed that self-interest would compel the European powers to give diplomatic recognition to the Confederacy in order to ensure their supply of cotton.

24.   *With Washington ringed by a series of forts, a surprise attack was now ruled out*

Punch, the London satirical weekly, pointed to a modicum of truth in this when it mischievously rhymed:

> Though with the North we sympathize
> It must not be forgotten
> That with the South we've stronger ties
> Which are composed of cotton.

What the Confederates appeared to have forgotten, or chose to ignore, was that crops in recent years had been so good that stocks had been mounting in Europe. Also, the rising prices of the previous decade had encouraged other countries, such as India and Egypt, to grow cotton.

Some Confederate leaders initially favored using cotton to buy weapons and supplies to sustain the struggle against the North and there was talk of rushing millions of bales to Europe by fleets of steamships. However, the South lacked not only the vessels but also the dynamism and administrative skill to put such a scheme into practice. Cotton had hitherto been exported in Yankee or European ships. Nor was there much evidence of immediate need, though that argument was countered by the suggestion that the bales could be stockpiled in Britain and France to await demand or to serve as security for loans — a possibility that was gradually reduced by the Union's blockade of Rebel ports.

The alternative policy, much easier to implement, was simply to deny Europe its supply of Southern cotton in the expectation that such an embargo would force the British and

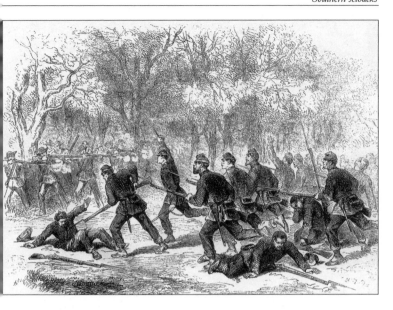

25.   *The setback at Ball's Bluff in October 1961 prompted most observers to conclude that the Union army was still not capable of a major offensive*

French governments to intervene, at least to the extent of giving diplomatic recognition. So complete was the hold of King Cotton on his subjects that the ban was almost 100 per cent effective during the first year of the war — thanks to voluntary initiative rather than official action. Planters were encouraged to turn over their acres to food production, and by 1863–4 the cotton crop was only at one-eighth of its pre-war level.

However, as events proved, King Cotton's rule did not extend across the Atlantic. Indeed, the whole embargo policy rested on ignorance and misunderstanding of the realities of international politics. It was Britain that mattered most, and a British government, led by Lord Palmerston, was sure to base its policy not on sympathy or sentiment but on calculation of British interests, political, strategic and economic. Nor would it react kindly to the element of threat or blackmail such an embargo carried. Palmerston may well have found the prospect of the break-up of a potentially dangerous rival in the north Atlantic not unwelcome, but he could see no basic British interest which would be served by involvement in the American conflict; he was, moreover, concerned for British Canada's vulnerability to Union attack, since few regular troops were stationed there, certainly not enough to withstand a sustained assault. Even in purely economic terms, whatever the distress in the Lancashire cotton towns, most other industrial and commercial interests in Britain profited handsomely from serving the needs of the belligerents.

26. *Allan Pinkerton, seen here smoking a pipe at army headquarters, ran McClellan's intelligence gathering, but tended to inflate the size of the opposing force, thinking that was what his commander wanted to believe*

The textile mills of the Northern states were of course also denied the South's cotton, but one of the sharpest ironies of the Civil War is that they were able to continue production partly through purchases of raw cotton from British traders, who in many cases were simply reselling at a considerable profit Southern cotton bought some years previously. In addition Confederate middlemen were themselves not reluctant to trade with the enemy if the opportunity arose.

Wishing to deny the South supplies of weapons from outside, the Union put its trust in the naval blockade announced by Lincoln within a week of Sumter, although at the time he had only three seaworthy warships to mount a watch over nearly 4,000 miles of coastline. The Confederacy countered by inviting ships of any nationality to apply for licenses as privateers, which enabled their owners to sell as contraband any cargoes captured from Union merchant vessels on the high seas. Jefferson Davis also indicated that he was prepared to pay a bounty of a fifth of the value of any Federal ship which the privateers sank. Lincoln riposted by warning that the crews of any such privateers falling into Union hands ran the risk of being hanged for piracy, though none ever were.

Because Britain was then the largest maritime nation in the world, both sides worried about her attitude towards their respective decisions. Along with France she had disavowed privateering as a form of warfare since 1856. On the other hand, under international law, blockades could be declared only against other sovereign nations and Lincoln's proclamation of a blockade appeared to be giving the South the recognition that it craved.

27. *Southerners were convinced that a shortage of cotton would encourage Britain and France to intervene on their side, and hence took every opportunity to burn stocks. Instead their former customers looked elsewhere for their supplies*

However, just a month after Sumter, Britain issued a formal Declaration of Neutrality, which satisfied neither North nor South, each of whom feared that the other might be unduly favored. Any British moves that even hinted at recognition of the Confederacy were bitterly resented and vigorously opposed in Washington.

A major crisis came in November when a Union frigate stopped and boarded a British mail packet, the *Trent*, bound from Havana, Cuba, to the Danish West Indian island of St Thomas. Among its passengers were two Southern politicians, both former United States senators, en route to Europe to win favor for the Rebel cause. They were forcibly taken to a Boston prison, to the delight of public opinion in the North, and the warship's captain, Charles Wilkes, was feted as a hero. The House of Representatives even voted him a special medal.

When the British Parliament heard the news, its reaction was very different. Prime Minister Palmerston warned his Cabinet: 'You may stand for this but damned if I will.' His attitude found a ready response in the London press and in the country generally. It seemed as if war between Britain and the United States could scarcely be averted. The Royal Navy strengthened its fleet in the Atlantic. Preparations were made to send a military force to Canada, if necessary to invade the North or at least repel a suspected attack from the Union. Many in London were convinced that Washington had its eyes on Canada as a replacement for the possible loss of the Southern states.

Jingoism reared its head in both capitals, though saner counsels began to emerge. It was tactfully suggested to Lincoln that perhaps the incident had not been officially planned and that the frigate's captain had been acting on his own initiative, which had indeed been the case. The administration was anxious to find a way out of the embarrassing and potentially dangerous crisis that would not appear to be a humiliating climb-down. Lincoln released the two Southerners but at the same time applauded the warship's captain for his patriotism. The Rebel envoys proceeded to Europe, where they achieved

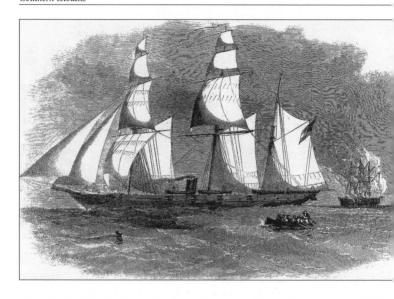

28. *Built in Birkenhead, the* Alabama *was the most successful as well as the most famed of the South's fast, well-armed commerce raiders that preyed on the North's merchant fleet and helped to circumvent the North's blockade of Southern ports*

little or nothing, especially in London where it mattered most. The North in its turn tried to tighten the blockade of Southern ports.

However, blockade runners employed a fleet of small, speedy vessels which, usually under cover of a darkness, could penetrate the Union's puny screen of warships located at the entrance to the South's main rivers, and could take out cotton and bring back much needed weapons, ammunition, medicine and clothing. Some of these blockade-runners preferred to trade in luxuries such as fine wines, brandies, silks, perfumes and cigars that commanded premium prices in Southern salons. Some, including some British captains, became millionaires within the year, but it was a high risk business. Since secrecy as well as speed was a prime requirement, and many of the ships were steam driven, smokeless fuel was a necessity and much of it came from Welsh anthracite mines. British-controlled ports such as Nassau in the Bahamas, just 150 miles off the Florida coast, or St. George in Bermuda, some 350 miles from the Carolinas, were vital centers of the blockade-running business, which stimulated much new activity in these quiet waters.

The other arm of Confederate maritime strategy was the construction, mainly in British shipyards, of fast, well-armed commerce raiders which could prey on Northern shipping across the oceans of the world. These vessels, of which the most famous was the *Alabama*, were destined to cause serious diplomatic incidents between the United States and Britain and they succeeded in driving much of the Northern merchant fleet from the high seas.

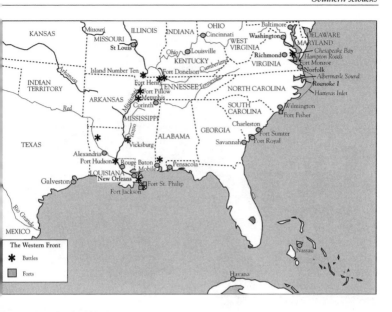

29.   *Map of Naval Actions*

The North in its turn was finding the blockade a costly and weary business. Because the gunboats mounting guard over Southern ports had to return every so often to home bases for supplies and fresh crews, much valuable time and effort was lost. Accordingly it was decided to seek safe havens along the Confederate coastline itself. During August 1861 a Union amphibious force was successfully put ashore at Hatteras Inlet in North Carolina, followed two weeks later by another at Ship Island, Mississippi. Then in early November, Port Royal Sound, South Carolina, within easy reach of both Charleston and Savannah, came under Northern control, followed a few months afterwards by another wide strip of North Carolina coast, including Roanoke Island. These footholds on the perimeter of the Confederacy helped to make the blockade more effective, though nine out of 10 ships were still getting through to Southern ports by the end of 1861.

1862 witnessed the advent of the ironclad ship. Both North and South had been struggling to come to terms with the transformation in naval warfare which was taking place at this time. Sail was replaced by steam, wooden ships by armour-plated vessels and traditional smooth-bore cannon by rifled guns, housed in revolving turrets which could fire explosive shells. There were, of course, teething troubles with most of these innovations. Paddle-wheeled steamers were ponderous and vulnerable, though the introduction of the screw-propeller changed things dramatically.

It was the need to protect engines and boilers from the new, more powerful guns that hastened the introduction of iron cladding — and with it a new kind of naval warfare.

30. Crew members of the Monitor *cooking on deck. Conditions below were uncomfortable: hot, humid and very cramped*

Since the Crimean War, the French had set the pace in naval development, with the British some way behind and the Americans not yet in the race at all. Now the conflict between North and South became a test-bed for the revolution in naval warfare and, as such, was observed with interest by all the maritime powers.

Ironically, the North had been slower off the mark than the South, though its greater industrial capability soon allowed it to catch up and to build its first *Monitor* in half the time that it had taken the Confederacy to modify a captured wooden vessel named the *Merrimac*. The eagerly awaited first clash between the ironclads occurred in early March 1862 at Hampton Roads, a wide, shallow channel some 8 miles long where three Virginia rivers came together to flow into Chesapeake Bay. A small Federal fleet of wooden warships was located there to blockade the entrance to the James River which fed Richmond.

The *Merrimac* was the first to put in an appearance on March 8 shortly after its commissioning upstream, when it wrought havoc among the Northern gunboats and supply ships, whose shells simply bounced off its armor-plating like 'peas from a popgun' in the words of a local newspaper reporter. By the end of the day two of the

31.   *Despite the advent of the ironclads, it was wooden ships such as these that played the biggest role in naval operations*

biggest Federal vessels had been destroyed and others crippled. News of the debacle caused alarm and despondency in Washington, where it was assumed that the rest of the Union squadron was doomed. But by coincidence the *Monitor* was already on its way southwards from New York, where it had been built, primarily to protect the approaches to the Potomac on which Washington stood. It reached Hampton Roads the very next day.

While the ironclad *Merrimac* with its casemate of 10 protruding guns looked odd to conventional eyes, the *Monitor*, considerably smaller, with its hull barely visible above the water and sporting a single turret containing just two guns, would appear bizarre in any age. 'A tin can on a shingle' was how one observer derided it. For four hours these two ironclad sea monsters threw everything at each other to little avail in one of the most unusual maritime combats ever witnessed. At the end of it both ships withdrew to lick their wounds, but surprisingly not to fight another day. Within a couple of months the *Merrimac* was scuttled by its captain to prevent capture when the Confederates evacuated Norfolk, while the *Monitor* foundered later the same year in a gale off the North Carolina coast with the loss of many of its crew. The age of the ironclad had undoubtedly dawned, but there were still many practical problems to be overcome. The North, and to a lesser extent the South too, laid plans for the construction of many more ironclads, but most of the naval war was in fact still fought by wooden vessels.

32. Map of Western Front

It was not just the Atlantic coastline that saw such action. Equally important encounters were to take place on the rivers of the West, particularly the Mississippi and its great tributaries. The North's 'Anaconda' strategy called for not only a blockade of the Southern ports but also a move down the Mississippi to cut the Confederacy off from its lifeline to the west and to Mexico, and then to divide it still further into unviable sections.

In the early weeks of 1862, the North badly needed some action and a boost to its morale. The Army of the Potomac was idle, and McClellan lay ill with typhoid fever. The administration was worried about popular reaction to its backing down over the *Trent* affair. Its financial difficulties forced it to resort to the issue of large amounts of new paper currency, the 'greenbacks'. Wall Street was in a state of panic and the New York press full of stories of scandals arising out of war contracts. Confidence in the ability of the Lincoln administration to win the war, and of the Republican Party to win the next elections, declined into one of its periodic troughs.

Then, in February, some welcome relief came with news of Union successes in the West. The unlikely hero of these victories was Ulysses S. Grant, who had left the regular army seven years earlier, had failed at everything which he had tried since, and whose reputation as a drunkard had proved impossible to shake off. However, any ex-regular officer was welcome when war came and Grant, finding himself in command of some 15,000 men on the Kentucky-Tennessee border, seized his opportunity with relish.

The Tennessee and Cumberland rivers, tributaries of the Ohio, offered avenues into the interior of the Confederacy — to drive a wedge between the Rebel forces in Virginia and those on the Mississippi. The initial targets were two river forts, Henry and Donelson, some 12 miles apart on the Tennessee and Cumberland respectively, just below the Kentucky-Tennessee state line. With the help of a small fleet of three wooden and four armored gunboats, Grant set out to clear these first obstacles.

Fort Henry was bombarded into surrender in a few hours on February 6, the Confederates at that time not having a river fleet of their own. However, the majority of the garrison was able to escape to Fort Donelson before Grant's troops arrived on the scene. Not to be outdone, he swiftly moved them on to Donelson, together with 12,000 reinforcements, while the gunboats made the longer journey down one river and up the next. It was not until February 13 that he was ready to begin his siege.

Donelson was a different proposition from Fort Henry. It was better sited on higher ground and its dozen or so heavy guns, protected by deep earthworks, were able to wreak havoc for a while on the Union fleet. Three of the Northern gunboats were put out of action and their commander mortally wounded. But Grant's men had surrounded the fort and it was clearly just a matter of time before the Confederates would be compelled to surrender. On the 15th the garrison tried to break out and had almost succeeded when the attempt was abandoned. However, more than 3,000 men managed to slip away during the following night, despite the intense cold. The next day the remaining 13,000 or so offered to lay down their arms.

When their commander asked for terms, he was bluntly told by Grant that nothing 'except unconditional and immediate surrender can be accepted'. The surprised Confederate general concurred, and the victor instantly acquired the nickname of 'Unconditional Surrender' Grant. Publicity men could scarcely fail to exploit the happy

33. *Nashville, with its railyards and factories, was something the South could not afford to lose at this stage of the war*

chance that his initials were also those of the United States, Uncle Sam and unconditional surrender. Lincoln promoted him to major-general, and the North made the most of its best news for months.

The South, on the other hand, was depressed by its first significant setbacks, particularly since the loss of Henry and Donelson exposed Nashville to danger. The city was evacuated on February 23, the first Rebel state capital to fall. More importantly, Nashville was a major communications and manufacturing center with gunpowder mills, foundries and clothing factories which had been feeding the Confederate war effort. Meanwhile, Union gunboats ranged down the Tennessee River, even into northern Mississippi and Alabama. The main Confederate army retreated south to Corinth, in northern Mississippi, a vital rail junction where the line connecting Memphis to Chattanooga and the East met the line which ran south to Mobile on the Gulf Coast.

During March Grant moved his troops down the Tennessee River to Pittsburg Landing, only 22 miles from Corinth. Here he was joined by three new divisions, one of them led by William Tecumseh Sherman, an eccentric, brilliant and intensely nervous 42-year-old, who, before the war, had run the military academy at Baton Rouge which was later to become Louisiana State University. Grant's forces now numbered nearly 40,000 and were soon to be increased to more than 75,000. The Confederate commander knew this and, in order to regain the initiative, was determined to strike before the reinforcements arrived.

The Union men at Pittsburg Landing were so confident that they had not prepared any defenses, believing the Rebels were too demoralized to attack and expecting in any case to move against them before very long. But while they were drilling rather than digging trenches, the Confederates advanced unnoticed from Corinth to within a couple of miles of the Northern lines. The attack had been planned for April 4, but the march had taken three days, much longer than anticipated, since most of the troops were raw recruits and the weather was atrocious. Union skirmishers had noticed the activity but their reports were ignored, such was the misplaced arrogance of the Northerners. Grant himself had telegraphed his immediate superior to the effect that there was 'scarcely the faintest idea of an attack being made upon us'. When told of a Rebel build-up in the woods opposite his positions, Sherman had derided the worried colleague: 'Take your damned regiment back to Ohio . . . there is no enemy nearer than Corinth.'

The Confederates were themselves having second thoughts about whether or not to proceed, fearing that the Yankees must have something up their sleeves. But on the morning of Sunday, April 6, by which time their presence was known to almost all and sundry, they fell upon Sherman's force near a small, little-used, Methodist meeting-house on a low hill called Shiloh, which in Hebrew means 'place of peace'.

Because Union patrols had run into some of the Rebel pickets during the night, the front-line troops were able to fall back in time to tell the others, so that not everyone was caught by surprise. However, the first few hours of what Sherman came to call 'the devil's own day' were extremely confusing for both sides, since most of the fighting took place in woods. So frenzied was the initial battle that many troops fired on their own men, thus adding to the appalling losses.

By mid-morning, although many of the Federals had fled far to the rear in panic and disorder, most had simply fallen back to an old wagon road which had sunk from frequent use and hence provided some cover. Because it also sported a stout split-rail fence, common in the South, fringing a sizable open field which the assaulting Confederates would have to cross fully exposed, it seemed a more than suitable refuge. Within minutes though it became a hell on earth, a veritable 'hornet's nest' in the words of one Rebel, and the name has stuck.

Wave after wave of Confederate attacks were halted and the bodies soon piled up against the wooden barrier. Thwarted and enraged, like 'maddened demons' according to a Federal soldier, the Southerners brought up more than 60 guns and hurled round after round into the cramped area. One occupant compared the cannonade to 'a mighty hurricane sweeping everything before it'. Much of the brush caught fire, which added to the horror, as many of the wounded lying in the field were burned to death.

The Rebels lost their own commander in the struggle and it took until late afternoon for them to force the 2,000 or so surviving Yankees along the Sunken Road to surrender. By then Grant, who had been 7 miles down river when the onslaught began, was rushing

34.   Grant had not been born with the middle initial S but his adoption of it allowed him to utilize later the magic two letters in front of his name

reinforcements into position and preparing a defensive line around Pittsburg Landing. In addition he had brought up his own artillery and they were pounding the exhausted Rebels, most of whom had not eaten for 12 hours and were more intent on foraging for food within the evacuated Federal encampment than continuing the fight. As a result the battle fizzled out. The Confederates had gained 2 miles but had not broken the Union will.

During the night Northern gunboats came up the river to add to the horror and hell as they lobbed shell after shell against the luckless Southerners. Some 10,000 wounded and 2,000 corpses lay on the battlefield. Neither side knew how to cope with the catastrophe and many men died needlessly, their suffering for all to see and their cries unheeded. Wild pigs came out of the woods to feed on the bodies, living and dead. Nature joined in, too, with a full display of lightning and heavy rain, lashed by a cold, hard wind. Few soldiers in either army slept much that night. The bone-saws of the handful of surgeons who were available were worked overtime in tents and makeshift huts around the field. Their rasping was an added nightmare and the ever-rising pile of arms and legs a terrible spectacle. A Confederate survivor commented: 'This night of horrors will haunt me to my grave'.

But before morning 25,000 fresh troops had arrived for Grant and when the Rebels renewed their attack at first light they met a stubborn resistance all along the line. Step by step they were forced back to their starting position of the day before. By mid-afternoon they had ceased their assault and begun to withdraw through the mud and rain to Corinth.

35.   *Sherman, the most controversial of all Grant's generals and still hated in the South to this day*

Grant chose not to chase them, which surprised many since the Confederate retreat was far from orderly. But as at Manassas nine months before, the winners were as confused and disorganized as the losers.

Neither side at this stage had the ruthlessness of purpose or the depth of resources to strike the final blow regardless of the consequences. Neither army was strong enough to annihilate the other. Besides, few of the Federals had eaten or drunk much during the long fighting day and were simply not capable of dedicated pursuit. One wrote home to his family:

> We chased them one-quarter mile, when we halted . . . and threw ourselves on the ground and rested. Oh, mother, how tired I was, now the excitement of the action was over . . . The dead and wounded lay in piles. I gave water to some poor wounded men, then sought food in an abandoned camp near us.

Nearly 4,000 men were killed at Shiloh and of the 16,000 or so wounded, another 2,000 would die. It was said that in places the bodies had fallen so close together that it was possible to walk some distance over them without touching the ground. This was America's worst bloodbath to date. No previous battle had produced casualties on anything like this scale. A watershed had been reached in people's attitudes. It was now being realized that the struggle would be prolonged and the cost in blood and tears appalling. One Southern novelist likened it to stumbling into a buzz-saw. Another said:

'The South never smiled again after Shiloh'. Herman Melville in his poem Shiloh wrote, '. . . what like a bullet can undeceive!' A negotiated peace now seemed more distant than ever. 'Oh my God, my God, what are we in for?' was a common reaction on both sides. One survivor wrote: 'God grant that I may never be the partaker in such scenes again.' But the war was to get worse, far worse, before it would be over.

6 Bloody stalemate

In the spring of 1862 the Rebels seemed to be on their knees, particularly in the West. The day after Shiloh, Union land and river forces captured Island Number Ten, so called because it was the tenth island downstream from the Mississippi's confluence with the Ohio. They had besieged this key Confederate stronghold, close to the Kentucky-Tennessee border and hitherto considered impregnable, for almost a month before its 7,000 men, including three generals, surrendered. Its loss threatened Memphis, 100 miles to the south and a major east-west rail link between the trans-Mississippi west and Chattanooga, and on to Atlanta, Charleston and Richmond. Jefferson Davis among others regarded this line as the backbone of the Confederacy.

Later in that same month of April came the South's heaviest blow and perhaps the North's most remarkable success to date. At the very mouth of the Mississippi, New Orleans, the Rebels' largest city and leading port, fell into Union hands as a result of a bold stroke by one of the great characters of the conflict, Flag Officer David G. Farragut, an architect of the eventual Northern victory.

Realizing how thinly stretched Confederate naval and military forces were in the area, Farragut first set out to batter into submission the two massive forts guarding the approaches to New Orleans. When that failed, he decided to run his ships, mostly wooden ones, past their 100 belching guns. An eyewitness compared the resultant battle to 'all the earthquakes in the world and all the thunder and lightning storms together, in a space of two miles, all going off at once'. Even so, Farragut managed to get through with the loss of only one gunboat and serious damage to another three, forcing the bewildered city to surrender without a shot being fired.

Not resting content with this, Farragut took seven of his ships further upstream, first to Baton Rouge, the state capital of Louisiana, which also quickly surrendered — the second Confederate state capital to do so — and then on to Natchez, the star of Mississippi, which fell before the month was out. He was halted at Vicksburg, 400 miles upstream from New Orleans, but meanwhile on June 6 other Federal gunboats, approaching from the north, had captured Memphis, which by then had become isolated by the Rebels' evacuation of Corinth at the end of May.

That evacuation had been a direct result of their failure at Shiloh, a battle from which not even the victor, Grant, had gained honour or advancement; he had been demoted to a desk job back at base. The fact that he had been unprepared against a possible attack had come in for criticism, both in the Northern press and within Congress itself. There was talk again of his heavy drinking under stress. Lincoln was pressed to sack him from the army altogether, but had argued that he could not afford to get rid of generals who were

36.   *David Glasgow Farragut,
hero of the Union's daring
naval victory at New
Orleans*

keen to fight. Depressed, Grant considered returning to civilian life but was dissuaded by Sherman, who wrote later: 'I argued with him that, if he went away, events would go right along, and he would be left out. Whereas, if he remained, some happy accident might restore him to favor.' Grant took the advice of his friend and the happy accident eventually came about.

In the East, meanwhile, things were going much worse for the Union. McClellan had been prodded by Lincoln into moving the Army of the Potomac against the Confederates in front of Richmond. But rather than doing so head-on, as at Manassas the previous summer, McClellan had preferred to try to outflank them by laboriously transporting his troops down the Potomac and through Chesapeake Bay to the tip of the Virginia Peninsula between the York and James rivers. Here the Federals had retained a foothold at Fort Monroe, opposite the naval base of Norfolk and close to Hampton Roads, the scene of the great battle between the *Monitor* and the *Merrimac* earlier that month. The Confederate capital was but 70 miles distant. Nearly 400 vessels, from river steamers to barges and tugs, shuttling to and fro during a three-week period towards the end of March, were needed to shift the 100,000 or so men with all their impedimenta, including weapons, ammunition, horses, wagons, ambulances and pontoon bridges, the 200 miles from the Washington area to Fort Monroe.

Lincoln had been far from enthusiastic about this indirect approach, though he was reluctant to discourage his army chief from any sort of action. To McClellan's chagrin he

37. *Stonewall Jackson had been a philosophy professor before becoming a general. He was eccentric in other ways too! He always insisted on sitting or standing bolt upright. In this way, he claimed, the digestive organs could function more efficiently*

had insisted on 35,000 soldiers being left behind to defend the Federal capital. Another 25,000 were based in the Shenandoah Valley, where the presence of Stonewall Jackson ensured that they could not be moved to aid either Lincoln or McClellan. Out-numbered four or five to one, Jackson launched a series of lightning attacks on the Union forces there, which prevented the release of any Northern troops to participate in the pincer movement against Richmond that Lincoln had in mind.

Jackson's campaigns in the valley made him a hero to the whole South and a legend in his own time. As examples of inferior forces tying up much larger groups through imaginative leadership and persistent, daring soldiering, they can hardly be bettered and are indeed still studied at most military academies today. Yet Jackson was far from the image one has of the natural general. He was fanatically religious and a total abstainer, with such faddishness about food that he sucked lemons by the score, and wholly denying himself pepper for fear it might make his left leg itch.

Opposing McClellan's force of nearly 100,000 men in the peninsula that April were just 17,000 Rebels. McClellan, however, appeared to be in no hurry and settled down to

38.   The Confederate batteries at Drewry's Bluff halted even ironclads like the Monitor

besiege one Confederate strongpoint after another, much to Lincoln's annoyance. The trouble was that the army's intelligence constantly, and sometimes ludicrously, exaggerated the size of the opposition. In addition, there was McClellan's naturally cautious nature. He had a touch of 'the slows' in Lincoln's words; some of the Southerners were less kind and nicknamed him 'the Virginia Creeper'. Nor did the weather favor the Northerners as torrential rain turned the few roads into rivers of mud. There also proved to be many more creeks, streams, marshes and inlets between Fort Monroe and Richmond than had been expected, which again delayed progress.

Five Union gunboats, including the ironclad *Monitor*, tried to storm the Confederate capital on May 15 by way of the James River but they were halted at Drewry's Bluff, just 7 miles short of it, where they suffered heavy damage from the well-sited guns of the fort there. However, by May 20 McClellan had pushed to within 5 miles of Richmond, where fear now gripped the Rebel leadership. Jefferson Davis sent his wife and children away. His archives and his government's gold were packed aboard a train that was steamed up ready to leave at a moment's notice. The Virginia state legislature voted to raze the city to the ground rather than see it fall into Yankee hands. Union patrols set their watches by the chimes of the capital's churches.

Richmond was defended by 60,000 Confederates and threatened by more than 100,000 Federals, though McClellan was convinced that he was outnumbered by almost two to one and pleaded with Lincoln for reinforcements. However, the only forces that might have answered his call were bottled up in the Shenandoah Valley by Jackson's hit-and-run raids, which not only discouraged any Union redeployment but thoroughly demoralized the Northerners. Like many in Washington, Lincoln was not yet convinced of his own army's capabilities, nor of its commander's dynamism. McClellan did not receive his reinforcements. Moreover, early in June the Rebel high command caught its opponents unawares by switching Jackson's men to help protect Richmond.

Shortly before this, on May 31, McClellan's advance on the Confederate capital was thwarted at Seven Pines, or Fair Oaks as it is sometimes called, at a cost of 11,000 casualties to both sides, one of whom was the Rebel commander, General Joseph Johnston. This battle was the first in which tethered balloons were used, under fire, for observation. A Northern scientist-cum-showman by the name of Thaddeus Lowe was responsible. They seldom went higher than about 300 feet and were linked to the ground by telegraph. Flights at dawn were preferred, when not only were air currents usually favorable, but the intelligence gleaned from the location of campfires and the early movements of patrols could be most valuable.

General Johnston was replaced by Robert E. Lee, fresh from a desk job in Jefferson Davis's office. Few at the time thought the appointment of much significance. McClellan in particular was very disparaging and reported to Washington that he was 'likely to be timid and irresolute in action'. However, before long Lee was planning a counter-offensive against McClellan, who seemed mesmerized by his recent setback and surrendered the initiative, convinced as usual that he was outnumbered.

Lee launched his counter-attack, his first major engagement as a field commander, on June 26 at Mechanicsville, to the north of Richmond, where his cavalry screen, led by Jeb Stuart, had reported that McClellan's line was weakest. And so it turned out. For the next seven days some of the fiercest fighting of the war raged along the Chickahominy River to the east of Richmond and southwards towards the James. Battles at places like Gaines Mill, Savage Station, Oak Grove, Frayser's Farm, Malvern Hill, all now comfortable suburbs of metropolitan Richmond, have passed into legend. The carnage was terrible and had a great impact on the Federal commander, who was not insensitive to such suffering, something that appealed to his men and was certainly commendable in itself, though unfortunately not perhaps what the times called for in a general with a real will to win this kind of war.

Confederate losses alone were almost 20,000 and Federal 11,000, with a further 6,000 Northerners taken prisoner. McClellan was forced to withdraw his army on July 2, first to Harrison's Landing on the James River and then, a month later, to his original base near Washington. As at Shiloh earlier that spring, the Seven Days Battles changed the

39.   *Thaddeus Lowe ascending in his balloon Intrepid to reconnoitre the battlefield at Fair Oaks, Virginia*

conception of combat for the soldiers on both sides, and added one more nail to the coffin of romantic notions of warfare.

Compromise and reconciliation seemed out of the question. The struggle had become a grim, remorseless, bitter, and gory affair. As its scale and violence escalated, the end receded ever further from view. With yet more men and more material resources being sucked into it, the conflict appeared to be running out of control. No one seemed to sense this more than McClellan. In a letter to Lincoln he made a despairing plea for a war which would be conducted 'upon the highest principles known to Christian civilization,' one which would not be waged against the population at large but against armed forces and political organizations. Alas, it had already gone beyond that stage.

The battles in Virginia had given the North a new bogyman and the South a new hero in Robert E. Lee, who for his part was deeply disappointed that he had not managed to trap and destroy McClellan's army once and for all. However, he had set in train a dramatic turnaround in the fortunes of war. Richmond in June had been panic-stricken; two months later it would be Washington's turn. Meanwhile recriminations abounded in Washington and beyond. McClellan accused Lincoln of denying him the men he needed; many Republicans blamed McClellan's timidity on his Democratic sympathies. Ordinary Northerners were despondent and bewildered and the President's popularity slumped.

Recruiting became increasingly difficult as it became increasingly necessary. Losses had to be replaced, but, even more importantly, it was clearly going to take many more men to win the war than had previously been predicted. Lincoln had called on the state governors to supply him with an additional 300,000 three-year volunteers and within the month he was appealing for a further 300,000 nine-month militiamen. When they were slow in coming forward, there was talk of conscription. The Confederacy had already introduced the draft in April. By way of compromise the Northern state governors were given quotas of troops to be raised, and it was suggested that, if they were not met, then some form of enforced recruiting might be needed. Most governors managed to meet their quotas, either by fudging the figures or resorting to a kind of conscription at the state level. This latter provoked disturbances in some areas. Various incentives were used to encourage recruitment and more and more volunteers were paid bounties.

Meanwhile Lee and Jackson, not content simply to await events, were harrying the Federal forces both in the Shenandoah Valley and in the area between the two capitals. A second confrontation at Manassas in late August produced an even more humiliating result for the Union than the first. Three times as many men were involved on this occasion, but the casualties were six times higher. Such was the war's escalation. The North suffered almost twice as many casualties as the South and was plunged further into gloom. Bitter feuding inside the Federal high command went hand in hand with political turmoil in Washington. Public opinion generally was alarmed by its military leadership.

Rumors abounded that Britain was about to recognize the Confederacy. The House of Commons had recently debated such a motion, although the government had prevented it from coming to a vote. However, the Foreign Secretary, Lord Russell, had asserted that 'the great majority are in favor of the South', while the Chancellor of the Exchequer, William Gladstone, had maintained that, 'it is indeed much to be desired that this bloody and purposeless conflict should cease'. Later, in a famous, or in Northern eyes infamous, speech at Newcastle Gladstone went much further: 'Jefferson Davis and the other leaders of the South have made an army; they are making, it appears, a navy; and they have made what is more than either, they have made a nation.'

These were worrying sentiments for the Union. Indeed the secretary of their legation in London had written: 'The current here is rising every hour and running harder against us than at any time since the *Trent* affair.' In mid-September when news of the second Manassas battle had reached London, Russell and Prime Minister Palmerston discussed whether the time had come for a joint offer of mediation in the conflict from Britain and France, with the implication that, if the North refused, the Confederacy should be recognized. Russell was all for immediate action; Palmerston suggested awaiting the outcome of the next battle. Clearly, it was not just American eyes that would be focused on Lee's future moves.

40.   *Robert E. Lee: Southern hero, Northern bete noire. Lincoln had offered him command of the Union forces at the war's outset. Most judge him the Civil War's greatest general*

Keenly aware of the critical situation, Lincoln realised that unless he pulled some chestnut out of the fire soon, the flames might engulf him. The chestnut that he had in mind was the emancipation of the slaves in the Confederacy; after all, the South had seceded to preserve slavery, even though the North had not gone to war to abolish it. Slave labor was making a major contribution to the Confederate war effort by helping to produce food and other war material, including weapons and also, more importantly, by releasing a greater proportion of the white male population to serve as soldiers. Blacks worked as cooks, grooms, valets, teamsters, general laborers and even musicians in the Southern armies. At least half the nurses in Rebel military hospitals were slaves. When the Northern black abolitionist leader, Frederick Douglass, argued, 'Arrest that hoe in the hands of the negro, and you smite the rebellion in the very seat of its life', he was beginning to find a ready ear.

Federal armies moving into the South faced the mounting problem of what to do with those slaves who were captured or who, increasingly, came through the lines in search of freedom. At first they were ordered back to their Rebel masters. But Ben Butler, the Northern general who commanded the Union outpost at Fort Monroe on the Virginia Peninsula in May 1861, had a different solution. When three slaves crossed into his lines, he decided to retain them as 'contraband of war'. The name stuck and thereafter blacks who followed suit were called 'contrabands'. By the early summer there were more than a thousand on his books and he was employing them around the fort. Such unilateral action embarrassed Lincoln, who was anxious to keep these matters firmly under his control. When he revoked proclamations by two other military commanders that freed the slaves in their areas, he incurred the wrath of abolitionists and radical Republicans alike. As the Union armies occupied more and more Southern territory, the trickle of blacks into their lines became a flood, particularly in places like Louisiana and along the South Carolina coast, where a great many slaves lived. Congress increased the pressure on the President. An Act of March 1862 made it illegal for fugitive slaves to be returned to their former masters. The following month slavery was abolished in the District of Columbia. In June it was prohibited from any of the territories.

By July Lincoln was discussing emancipation with his Cabinet colleagues but was dissuaded from any formal announcement lest it be construed, in the wake of Union defeats, as 'the last measure of an exhausted Government'. The Secretary of State Seward advised that it would be better postponed until it could be associated with success on the battlefield. Besides, Lincoln had long worried about the possible effect of emancipation on the border states where of course slavery was still tolerated. He had tried to persuade border state congressmen to accept a plan for gradual emancipation, with compensation to owners, but had been rebuffed. Always sensitive to popular racial attitudes and concerns, he was worried about what Northern public opinion would accept, while many moderate Republicans were concerned about the impact that an emancipation announcement might have on Republican prospects in the mid-term elections due that autumn.

War-weariness was mounting on the home front, especially in the Midwest, which had been badly hit by the loss of Southern markets and where inevitably the peace wing of the Democratic Party was making inroads. Policies which appeared to favor blacks were not likely to win many votes. Indeed racial prejudice was never far below the surface of Northern opinion. Already there had been race riots in a number of cities, such as Toledo and Cincinnati, often provoked by Irish and German immigrants fearful for their jobs. Newspaper editors warned of millions of 'semi-savages' intermingling with 'the sons and daughters' of white families. Others talked of free labor being 'degraded' by the competition of these blacks, many of whom 'will have to be supported as paupers and criminals at the public expense'. Even the Archbishop of New York had proclaimed that Catholics 'are willing to fight to the death for the support of the constitution, the government, and the laws of the country. But if . . . they are to fight for the abolition of slavery, then, indeed, they will turn away in disgust from the discharge of what would otherwise be a patriotic duty.' In this same year of 1862, Lincoln's own state of Illinois voted to ban the further settlement of blacks within its borders.

Northern soldiers reflected these attitudes, too, and not all of them welcomed the contrabands. When a delegation of leading free blacks visited the White House in August to plead the emancipation cause, Lincoln urged that they seriously consider emigration instead. Congress voted $600,000 to encourage voluntary colonization of freed slaves and much of it went in settling 450 black Americans on an island near Haiti, which turned out to be prone to smallpox. When many of them died, Washington evacuated the survivors.

That same month of August, Lincoln replied to a request from Horace Greeley at the *New York Tribune* that he turn the war into a crusade for freedom with the words:

> My paramount object in this struggle is to save the Union, and is not either to save or destroy slavery. If I could save the Union without freeing any slave I would do it, and if I could save it by freeing all the slaves I would do it; and if I could save it by freeing some and leaving others alone I would also do that.

Such language may be seen as a demonstration of Lincoln's pragmatism, or equally his skill in laying a smokescreen to cover his actions. He never departed from his insistence that this was first and foremost a war to save the Union, and his approach to the slavery issue was deliberately, and sometimes deceptively, low key and undramatic.

When, after Manassas, Lee turned his eyes towards Maryland, the leadership on both sides was keenly aware of just how much was riding on the outcome. The Confederates saw a great opportunity to assail the Union cause at what were potentially its two most vulnerable points — wavering morale at home and the prospect of intervention from abroad. Divided opinions in the North over slavery and race, the dubious chances of the Republicans in the forthcoming elections and, above all, the real possibility of British and French mediation and recognition, brought Confederate hopes to their high tide in the late summer of 1862.

Lee was keen to follow up his victory while the Federal forces were still reeling from the blow. A defeat for the Union on Lincoln's own doorstep might persuade the Yankees to sue for peace. Besides, Lee was anxious for the fighting to be moved from his beloved Virginia, especially at harvest-time. His hungry troops also had their eyes on the rich crops of Maryland.

41.   *One in four of the slaves in the South freed themselves by moving behind Union lines. Their*
reception was not always as warm or as tactful as it might have been

Thus on September 4, while regimental bands played 'Maryland, My Maryland', some 50,000 Rebels crossed the Potomac about 30 miles up river from the Federal capital and concentrated three days later at Frederick, where sympathetic Marylanders were expected to flock to Lee's lines. Few came, which was a great disappointment for him, although western Maryland had never been a stronghold of slavery. More seriously, Lee was having problems in holding his army together on account of the large number of stragglers. His soldiers had been marching and fighting for weeks on end. Ill-shod, their sore feet were finding the hard macadamized Maryland roads too much for them. Many also had stomach complaints from eating unripened fruit and corn. Nearly a quarter of Lee's strength dropped out to find their own weary way home. He himself had damaged both hands in an accident with his horse and was obliged to ride in an ambulance.

However, the news of Lee's invasion had thrown Washington into a panic. The first report reached the national capital in dramatic fashion: a Maryland farmer had ridden down Pennsylvania Avenue shouting it. Gunboats were ordered up river to defend the District and rumor had it that the Cabinet planned a midnight flight by warship to Philadelphia or New York. Even government clerks were being armed.

Lee hoped that he might get as far as the Pennsylvania state capital, Harrisburg, to cut its important railroad links with Baltimore, Philadelphia and the Midwest. But because

42. *Lincoln went down to Antietam after the battle to see the devastation for himself and also to pressure McClellan into pursuing Lee. The trouble was that the Northern generals had scant confidence in their own ability and were frightened of the Southerner*

of the need to protect his rear by disposing of the Federal garrison at Harper's Ferry, he dispersed his army over a wide area in a risky maneuver which relied on a cautious Union response. He could not have known that his security was about to be breached by a cruel piece of ill luck.

On September 13, at an abandoned Confederate camp at Frederick, a Union corporal came across a copy of Lee's orders wrapped around a cigar packet, presumably dropped by a careless member of his staff. They described in detail the dispersal of his forces and offered McClellan a unique opportunity to destroy his opponent's army piece by piece. Even so, such good fortune did not spur the Union commander into speedy action. He was still convinced that Lee far outnumbered him. After hard fighting he eventually broke through the barrier of South Mountain and confronted Lee near the little village of Sharpsburg, across the shallow waters of Antietam Creek.

With fewer than 20,000 troops at his side and having already suffered nearly 3,000 casualties in the bitter clashes of the two previous days, Lee had at first been inclined to withdraw as speedily as possible to the safety of the Shenandoah Valley. However, encouraged by the news that Stonewall Jackson had taken Harper's Ferry and would soon be rejoining him, he decided to stay and fight, reluctant to abandon his invasion of Maryland. Although heavily outnumbered, he had, by accident rather than design, arrived at the best prescription for success in Civil War campaigning. He had seized the strategic initiative, but was now tactically on the defensive. He could wait for the enemy to come to him. Astonishingly, McClellan delayed his attack for another day, giving Lee's tired men a little more time to rest and regroup.

The outcome of the battle on September 17, although tactically a draw, was, in the wider strategic context, a defeat for the Confederacy and hence a victory of sorts for the Union. Yet Antietam could easily have gone the Rebels' way. Although outnumbered, Lee fought with his usual brilliance, helped by the unimaginative tactics of the Northerners, who, given their vastly superior numbers, surely had an opportunity to whip the Southerners once and for all.

Like most Civil War engagements, the battle was exceedingly confused — 'a great tumbling together of all heaven and earth' in the words of one Federal survivor. It was also exceedingly bloody, far worse than Shiloh or either of the Manassas battles or any of the Seven Days struggles. Indeed it proved to be the bloodiest single 24 hours of the whole war and hence, too, the bloodiest in American history. Nearly 5,000 men lost their lives and another 18,000 were severely wounded, 3,000 of whom were eventually to die. Caring for the injured so taxed the local communities that the immediate area became, according to a visitor, 'one vast hospital'.

The casualties were four times those that the United States suffered on D-Day in the Second World War. Entire units on either side were well-nigh annihilated. Losses of 50 per cent among regiments and even brigades were not uncommon — but there were 60 and 70 per cent losses too and, in the case of one Texan regiment, an 82.3 per cent loss, the highest of the whole war. One British military observer noted that: 'In about seven or eight acres of wood there is not a tree which is not full of bullets and bits of shell. It is impossible to understand how anyone could live in such a fire as there must have been here.' A Federal officer walking around the field on the following day wrote: 'No matter in what direction we turned, it was all the same shocking picture, awakening awe rather than pity, benumbing the senses rather than touching the heart, glazing the eye with horror rather than filling it with tears'.

When it was all over, it was Lee's army, bloodied but far from bowed, that had to retreat from the field, back across the Potomac to Virginia. That they were not pursued was a measure of the persistent failure — or at least inability — of the victors in Civil War battles to follow up their success and destroy the opposing army. It was also a mark of McClellan's chronic over-caution and lack of will. If, in 1861, first Manassas had been a missed opportunity for the South to strike a knockout blow, so was Antietam for the North. Lincoln recognized this and for days afterwards was pressing his army commander to harry the weary Rebels. He even went to visit him in the field to urge his cause, but it was to be nearly six weeks before McClellan felt ready to re-cross the Potomac. When he did so, it was without much conviction and he posed little threat to Lee. An exasperated Lincoln finally fired him early in November 1862.

For all its limitations, Antietam is widely regarded as the first major turning-point of the war. After a succession of setbacks, a half-victory followed by the enemy's retreat was

43–44.   *Photographs like these of the fallen at Antietam had an enormous effect on people's attitudes towards war. Until then no one had seen dead Americans after a battle*

sufficient not only to boost Northern morale but to give Lincoln the opportunity at last to issue his Emancipation Proclamation, which he did five days after the battle. Its cool reception disappointed him. It did not abolish slavery throughout the United States, but declared that all bondsmen in states and parts of states still in rebellion on January 1, 1863 'shall be then, thenceforward, and forever free'. As cynics were quick to point out, the proclamation proposed to free precisely those slaves whom the government had no immediate power to free. This was an understandable, though not entirely fair interpretation of what Lincoln had done.

Lincoln had now passed the point of no return on the question of emancipation; if the North won the war, slavery was surely doomed. Lincoln justified his decision as one taken in his capacity as commander-in-chief, on grounds of military necessity. But, if it was initiated as a way of saving the Union, freeing the slaves almost inevitably became a second war aim. The invading Northern armies would now be considered armies of liberation, which gave a moral aura to their continuing struggle. The restored Union would be a new one, not the old.

Lee's retreat from Antietam, coupled with the Emancipation Proclamation, effectively put an end to Confederate hopes of foreign mediation or intervention. Palmerston's decision to await the outcome of the next battle had been amply justified. Now, Britain, with its anti-slavery tradition, could scarcely aid or recognize the Confederacy. The South would have to fight on alone against the superior forces of the North. Henry Adams, the son and secretary of the United States minister in London, wrote to his brother with the Army of the Potomac:

> The Emancipation Proclamation has done more for us here than all our former victories and all our diplomacy. It is creating an almost convulsive reaction in our favor . . . We are much encouraged and in high spirits. If only you at home don't have disasters, we will give such a checkmate to the foreign hopes of the rebels as they have never yet had.

Antietam was memorable in another way too: it saw the advent of the war photographer. Just two days after the battle, Alexander Gardner and his assistant, James Gibson, both then working for the New York photographic gallery owned by Mathew Brady, took a series of studies of corpses which had a sensational impact on public opinion when displayed in the gallery within the month. It was the first time cameramen had been allowed near the action before its ugliest scars, the bloated bodies, had been removed. Their efforts opened the nation's eyes as no woodcuts or lithographs had hitherto done and ushered in a new dawn in the visual documentation of war, a documentation that would be far from glorifying or inspirational. A reporter from the *New York Times* wrote: 'Mr Brady has done something to bring home to us the terrible reality and earnestness of war. If he has not brought bodies and laid them in our door-yards and along streets, he has done something very like it.'

Yankees by the thousand, especially mothers and wives of those already serving in the Union forces, flocked to see these first dramatic images of death and destruction. No longer were battlefields comfortably remote and distant places. The camera was bringing

45.   As 43

them disconcertingly nearer and the reaction of many people in New York and elsewhere was to erase finally any surviving romantic notions of modern-day combat.

Photography had come of age, although because of the slowness of exposure and the need to prepare negatives minutes before the shot was taken — and also to develop them within minutes afterwards — action pictures, as we know them today, were still not possible. Most of the photographers were from the North, and mainly from the Northeast, rather than the West. Confederate cameramen soon found it difficult to obtain the necessary chemicals and their efforts were confined to the early months of the war. Nor, of course, were photographs yet reproducible in newspapers and magazines. Instead artists made woodcuts based on them, occasionally using their imagination to improve the effect. Nevertheless, media coverage of war could never be the same again and popular attitudes towards, and perceptions of, war-making would for ever be different.

7 Mounting grievances

The South was dismayed by Antietam, and outraged by the Emancipation Proclamation. Jefferson Davis depicted Lincoln's decision to free the blacks as an act of barbarism, a deliberate attempt to incite the slaves to revolt. The press painted horrific pictures of an impending race war, with mass slaughter of innocent women and children in their own homes. The Confederate Cabinet sought to alarm European conservative opinion by claiming that the North was raising the red flag of revolution. But it was all baying in the wind.

The Rebels had lost the initiative, not only on the battlefield but also politically and diplomatically. They had been outmaneuvered by the shrewder political sense of the Union leadership. To restore the balance, the South needed either fresh victories or, at the very least, the denial of any further military success to the North, in the hope that frustration and weariness with the war would sap the Union will. But time was a dangerously two-edged weapon in the hands of the South. Already the North's greater resources and numbers were making an impact. If the generalship could be found to exploit these advantages to the full, then the outlook for the Confederacy was bleak indeed.

Under stress the Southern leadership showed signs of weakness and disunity. Jefferson Davis was the target of increasing criticism, which was often sharp and cruel. Too stiff and formal to arouse popular enthusiasm, too abrasive and unbending to inspire those around him, he could not give the Confederacy the charismatic captaincy it needed. He was one of those men who seem fated to do things which make enemies rather than friends. His determination and conscientious devotion to duty too often looked like obstinacy and inflexibility. He stuck loyally to some colleagues, particularly generals, who were personal favorites, even when they had shown themselves disastrously incompetent. On the other hand, he lacked Lincoln's capacity to cooperate with able and efficient men to whom he had taken a personal dislike.

Indeed, Davis never showed Lincoln's flexibility or pragmatism, nor his instinct for what was politically prudent or expedient. He was inordinately sensitive and had a touch of self-righteousness which many construed as arrogance. He revealed the warmer side of his nature to his family and close friends, and also in the numerous letters which he wrote to mothers or wives in distress at the loss of loved ones. But, to a wider public, he remained something of an enigma, 'the sphinx of the Confederacy' as one associate dubbed him. Southern newspapers could be vitriolic in their attacks on him, and the editor of the *Charleston Mercury* dismissed him as 'this little head of a great country'. More seriously, perhaps, for the man who should have been the personal symbol of the cause, the press ignored him for quite long periods.

46. *Few Southerners had a good word to say for Jefferson Davis by this stage of the war. His colleagues were as critical as his opponents*

Like Lincoln, Jefferson Davis earned few accolades as an efficient or systematic administrator. He had a rather turbulent relationship with his Cabinet and there was a considerable turnover in its membership during the war. He interfered constantly in those departments whose business particularly interested him, above all the War Department, where his obsessive concern with every last military detail caused much friction.

Because there was no formal party organization, opposition to the administration often descended to the level of personal abuse or petty and destructive criticism. Not much prestige was attached to being a Confederate congressman and, although at first there were many men of political experience, they quickly tended to become bored and frustrated by their very limited role. Physical violence was not uncommon in debates and drunkenness quite flagrant. The lack of continuity in its membership became a feature of the Congress; few served right through its four years of life. Many hated living in Richmond, which was overcrowded and outrageously expensive, and a number left to join the army or to return home. Alexander Stephens, the Confederacy's Vice-President, spent much of the war in his own state of Georgia, from where he operated as a kind of leader of the opposition.

For Davis, the most serious opposition often came not from Congress but from the governors of the individual states. They resented what they regarded as the usurpation of many of their powers and functions by Richmond. After all they had seceded in order to retain essential rights for the states and here was Jefferson Davis's government attempting to dominate them, to create a strong central control, to form in fact a closely consolidated union, which is precisely what they had tried to get away from. In turn these governors were not averse to deflecting the protests and grievances of their own people away from themselves, towards Richmond.

Localism was a powerful force in the South, and many citizens gave their loyalty more naturally and easily to the state government than to the newly created, remote government in Richmond, which seemed to impinge on their lives only in ways that were disagreeable. State governors knew how to play on such feelings. Governor Joseph Brown of Georgia, for example, enabled 10,000 of his citizens to avoid the draft by making them second lieutenants in the state militia. Later on in the war, when Lee's soldiers were barefoot, in rags and cold at night, it turned out that the North Carolina governor, Zebulon Vance, was hoarding for his state militia nearly 100,000 uniforms as well as countless blankets and shoes.

The growing dissidence within the Confederacy accurately reflected many of the differences and divisions within Southern society. Secession had been widely, though far from universally, supported by the whites of the deep South in 1861, but opinion was always strongly divided in the upper South. When the war proved to be more protracted and costly than anyone had anticipated, old grievances came to the surface — nowhere more so than in the mountain country of Appalachia, where poor whites eked out a living from the thin soil, or from hunting and fishing. This was a world far removed from the plantation aristocracy of South Carolina or Louisiana; it must never be forgotten that in the South as a whole less than a quarter of white families owned slaves. If the feeling ever became widespread that war was being waged at appalling cost simply to protect the interests of slaveholders, then dangerous cracks in Southern morale were bound to appear.

It was the poorer, non-slave owning whites who seemed to bear the brunt of the slaughter at Shiloh, in the Seven Days, and at Antietam, and it was their families who often suffered most from food shortages and other privations. When conscription was introduced in April 1862, once again it was they who were worst affected. This was the most hated imposition of all; to be compelled by authority went very much against the American grain. However, the Confederacy had no realistic alternative; it drew on a far smaller pool of white men of fighting age than the North, and many of the volunteers who had signed on for twelve months when the war began were showing marked reluctance to re-enlist. All white males between the ages of 18 and 35 were inducted for three years or the war's duration, whichever proved the shorter. The upper age limit was raised to 45 in September 1862, and then to 50 in February 1864, when the lower limit was reduced to 17.

Conscription also aroused opposition because it was riddled with exceptions and exemptions, favoring the better off and the more influential. The immunity of teachers produced a sudden rash of new schools across the South, a region not noted for the high priority accorded to education. Draftees could also hire substitutes, and brokers and other go-betweens soon promoted a vigorous trade which drove up their price to several thousand dollars in some cases. One conscripted Virginian offered a 200-acre farm to avoid the call to arms. Newspapers carried numerous advertisements for substitutes and many men who came forward were too old or too young or in no fit state for military service. Desertion among them was widespread, and some offered themselves several times over — one as many as 20 times.

Even more disliked than substitution was the 20-Negro law, which exempted one white man for each 20 slaves on larger plantations. The argument was that they were needed to

47.   *Despite the political wrangling, morale among the Southern soldiers was high*

keep order and to deter any threat of slave insurrection while so many men were away at the front. But within no time at all some of the larger slave owners were exploiting the law to their own advantage. It was not difficult to see why the struggle was being dismissed by many Southerners as 'a rich man's war, but a poor man's fight'.

In many areas the poor simply ignored the draft and the authorities gave up the struggle of trying to implement it, though not before some officials had been killed by roving bands of draft dodgers and deserters in the remoter regions of northern Alabama and western North Carolina. At times the Confederacy had to divert troops to deal with this rebellion within a rebellion. Perhaps as many as half of those eligible for conscription avoided it, and the manpower difficulties of the Southern armies steadily worsened. Elsewhere, particularly near the front line, the military scarcely added to its popularity with farmers by requisitioning food, livestock and other supplies. A Richmond journalist wrote: 'We often hear persons say, "The Yankees cannot do us any more harm than our own soldiers have done."'

Jefferson Davis and his Cabinet had been undecided at the war's outset how best to fund it. Americans had seldom had to pay direct taxes; government had been financed from the proceeds of customs duties and land sales. Expecting the war to be brief, the Confederacy had opted for borrowing through bond sales and printing extra money. The bonds were only minimally successful and soon the issue of paper money got out of hand. The individual states joined in with their own note printing and counterfeiting also became widespread.

As the blockade tightened and the shortages got worse, prices for even the commonest goods escalated. By early 1863 tea cost $32 a pound. Even soap had soared from 10 cents a pound at the war's outset to $1.10. Soldiers at this time were paid $11 a month. Inflation was soon rampant with the Confederate dollar shrinking in value by the month. Real wages never caught up. Barter took over and a black market sprang up in most of the major cities, especially Richmond. When money had to change hands, gold or Union dollars — the famous greenbacks introduced during the war — were preferred. Corruption became commonplace and looting was not unusual. Trading with the North was not unknown, nor was it discouraged. Food riots were not as rare as the authorities tried to claim, and as the war dragged on they became more frequent and uglier.

The Southern states had seceded, and then gone to war, not only to protect slavery but to preserve a whole way of life. Ironically, the sheer scale of the conflict and the manner in which it had to be fought changed that way of life quite drastically. The Confederacy had been set up for an essentially conservative purpose, and most of its leaders were deeply conservative in outlook, but they now found themselves caught up in a revolution. The industrial and commercial values of the North, its administrative skills and centralizing tendencies, which they had long derided and deplored, were precisely what were now needed in the fight for independence. They had to organize the industrial war effort, mobilize the citizenry, interfere in unprecedented ways with individual freedoms and property rights, and centralize the decision-making process. The Southern people and their leaders never fully grasped the basic contradiction in their situation. They could not reconcile the ends for which they fought with the means necessary to win the war.

With cash crops like cotton and tobacco denied their traditional markets, many planters had to switch to food crops. Many men had gone away to fight, and women, previously thought not fitted for such work, played a greater role in running plantations and working on farms. It was white women, too, along with slave labor, who filled the war factories. One diarist remarked: 'Ladies who never worked before are hard at it making uniforms and tents.' Women also took the place of men in schools and hospitals.

Shortages in the rural areas, and the incursion of Federal troops, pushed more and more people into the towns and cities. Richmond in particular became overcrowded, as its population tripled. In the mood of the time, entertainments became more and more risqué. Those who disapproved supported a local newspaper in demanding a halt to the 'short skirts and nigger dancing, ribaldry, blasphemous mock-piety, gross buffoonery and other "piquant" and profane attractions for the carnal-minded and illiterate'. Because of conscription, many of the South's colleges and universities closed down for long periods.

For civilians, travel within the Confederacy turned into a nightmare: the railroads were poorly maintained and miles of track were destroyed in the fighting, while the trains which did run were often taken over by the military. Wagons and horses were, of course, requisitioned by the army. As men from different walks of life fought together, the social and geographical divisions of pre-war Southern society became blurred or confused. No matter which way the result now went in the war, life could never be the same again for Southerners. The South Carolinian diarist Mary Chesnut spoke for many when she wrote: 'There are nights here with the moonlight cold and ghostly when I could tear my hair and cry aloud for all that is past and gone.'

It was not only in the East that things were going badly for the Confederacy in the autumn of 1862. The situation in the West was still difficult, as the Rebels struggled to defend a very wide front with inadequate forces. On the other hand, cavalry raids by the legendary Nathan Bedford Forrest and John Hunt Morgan had cut Union supply lines, caused a good deal of chaos and confusion, and blunted the enemy's aggressive intent. Meanwhile, the new Confederate commander, Braxton Bragg, took his army from northern Mississippi, by a long rail detour via Mobile on the Gulf Coast, to Chattanooga in eastern Tennessee. By the late summer, he was preparing to launch an invasion of central Kentucky, where, like Lee in Maryland, he confidently expected many of its citizens to rally to the Confederate cause. Indeed, he took 15,000 rifles with him to arm the anticipated stampede of volunteers, but found no takers for most of them. In early September he seized Frankfort, the state capital, and toyed with the idea of installing a Confederate governor. His advance caused more than a tremor of anxiety among Northerners living beyond the Ohio River, who never expected the war to reach their doorsteps. By mid-September, prior to Antietam, the combined effects of two Confederate invasions, Lee's in Maryland and Bragg's in Kentucky, had brought Northern morale to one of its worst crises.

Fearing the loss of Louisville and even Cincinnati on the Ohio river, the Union high command rushed larger forces to the area and managed to halt the Southerners on October 8 at Perryville, some 50 miles south-east of Louisville. Although this was scarcely a decisive setback, Bragg chose to retreat to Chattanooga and his opponent made no serious attempt to pursue. At the same time Rebel efforts to re-take Corinth in northern Mississippi and re-enter western Tennessee were likewise repulsed, with particularly

48.   *A rare glimpse of life in a Southern camp early in the war. Because the necessary chemicals
      became scarce due to the blockade, few photographs were taken in the South after the first year*

heavy casualties for the Confederates, who were compelled to withdraw southwards into
Mississippi proper, the home state of Jefferson Davis.

On the eastern front during that December, Lincoln faced what he was to describe as
'yet another progress through Hell'. The new commander of the Army of the Potomac
was General Ambrose Burnside, a big, bluff, good-looking, fair-minded and amiable man,
whose reputation in the army had hither been more for bonhomie than for competence.
His fellow officers had dubbed his extravagant side-whiskers 'side-burns', a reversal
of his own name, and a description which would move into common parlance. More
impressively, he had been the inventor in the 1850s of a breech-loading rifle, which the
army was slow to adopt through a mixture of caution and concern over costs, and it did
not become the standard infantry weapon until the end of the 1860s. His courage was
never doubted, though, and he had not sought this promotion. Indeed when it had been
offered earlier, he had turned it down, pleading that he did not think he was up to it.

Urged on by Lincoln, Burnside began to move against Lee within a week of his
appointment, much to the President's initial satisfaction. Rather than tackle Lee head-on at
Warrenton along the Orange-Alexandria Railroad, Burnside preferred to transfer the bulk
of his force 40 miles eastwards to Falmouth, opposite Fredericksburg on the Rappahannock
River, midway between Washington and Richmond, while he maintained the pretense of
an attack at Warrenton. For a while Lee hesitated and, if Burnside had been able to get his

49.   *The war produced ingenious ways of wrecking railroads. Both sides did it*

troops over the river promptly, as intended, the outcome could have been very different
As it was, although his army, now nearly 120,000 strong, was in position on November 19
as planned, the pontoons to be used for bridging the Rappahannock did not arrive until the
end of the month, due to incompetence back at the base. By that time Lee was waiting for
Burnside with 73,000 troops, strongly entrenched in the low hills above Fredericksburg.

Never before in the war had so many armed men faced each other, nor would they ever
again. During the days of inaction, the soldiers of both sides fraternized freely across the
river, trading Southern tobacco for coffee and other Northern treasures, such as warm
overcoats. A Federal army greatcoat could command at least $100 on the Richmond black
market at that time. The evening before Burnside's men moved to put the pontoons in
place for the crossing of the river, which in the bitter cold of that early December was
already partially frozen, Union bands played 'The Star Spangled Banner', 'Yankee Doodle'
and even 'Dixie'. The last evoked great roars of delight from the Confederate soldiers
many of whom joined in the singing.

The next morning Federal artillery blasted the old colonial town which George
Washington had known in his youth, and some of the first troops over the river looted
what remained. Rebel skirmishers delayed the proceedings further, but by December 13
Burnside felt that he had enough forces across the river to begin his attack. Although the
Confederate line south of the town was breached for a while, the Union losses in trying
to scale Marye's Heights in the center were so enormous — 12,500 dead and seriously
wounded in just a few hours — that Burnside was dissuaded from renewing the assault
and withdrew across the river.

50. *General Burnside of sideburns fame had initially been apprenticed as a tailor before joining the army*

Recriminations soon followed, in the Army of the Potomac and beyond. Most observers agreed that to assault frontally a position like the Heights was foolish, if not downright suicidal. A member of Burnside's own staff had warned him on the eve of the battle that such a tactic would be 'murder, not warfare'. Lee's artillery commander said of the approach, 'A chicken could not live on that field when we open on it.' 'We might as well have tried to take Hell,' maintained one Federal survivor. A Confederate described it as 'butchery'; another as 'utterly hopeless'. A reporter wrote, 'It can hardly be in human nature for men to show more valor, or generals to manifest less judgement.'

For the South, Antietam appeared to have been avenged, while in the North the bogy was raised again of the invincibility of Lee and his Rebels, at least when defending their own soil. It seemed that Lincoln had once more misjudged his choice of a commander for the Army of the Potomac. Morale within the ranks sank to an all-time low and, as the extent of the casualties became known, many quietly went home without leave. Despair among the officers turned into almost open mutiny. A Congressional inquiry into the defeat found the generals in clear discord. When a delegation took their complaints directly to Lincoln, he instructed Burnside 'not to make a general movement of the army without letting me know'. Burnside himself was on the point of submitting his resignation.

Lincoln was already on the rack politically. His party had managed to retain a majority in the House of Representatives after the November elections but had suffered damaging losses in a whole swathe of states running across the North: New York, Pennsylvania, Ohio, Indiana and Illinois. The Republicans also lost the key governorships of New York and New Jersey, as well as control of the legislatures in Indiana and even Lincoln's home state of Illinois. The Democrats had been able to exploit not only feelings of war

51. *The Federals would attempt other crossings of the river below Fredericksburg and yet more pontoon bridges would need to be laid*

weariness, but the unpopularity in many quarters of the Emancipation Proclamation and of another presidential edict extending his power to suspend the writ of habeas corpus.

In December, Lincoln faced a major cabinet crisis involving relations with his own party in Congress. Bitter rivalry had broken out between Secretary of State William H. Seward and Secretary of the Treasury Salmon P. Chase, both of whom had aspirations to succeed him. Seward, a former Whig like Lincoln, was widely believed to exercise a malign influence over the president in military appointments and in frustrating the radical wing of the party. When a caucus of Republican senators confronted Lincoln with complaints about cabinet disharmony and criticisms of his prosecution of the war, he was able as usual to outmaneuver them, though the whole affair once again raised doubts over his leadership. A senator from his party even went on record that the President was 'too weak for the occasion'. Many claimed also that the administration had no clear notion of how to win the war; Lincoln's habit of frequently changing his generals scarcely inspired confidence.

When times were bad, there was a greater inclination to poke fun at the President's tall, spindly physique, his clumsy manner and less than classically handsome features. Other critics disapproved of his folksy humor and his fund of dubious stories, which looked like unseemly levity amid the sufferings of war. In 1862 a president who was not very widely known before assuming office did not have the advantage of the image-building resources of modern mass communications. Lincoln seldom left Washington, except for very occasional visits to the army, and he made hardly any public speeches as President.

His impact on the wider populace gradually gathered force by indirect means. He received so many visitors that at times the White House became a glorified reception room, and he wrote letters to all manner of people throughout the country. His preference was for dealing with individuals and small groups rather than for the dramatic gesture or the grand public occasion.

As the year drew towards its close, it appeared far from certain that Lincoln would actually go ahead with emancipation. The proclamation that he had issued in the wake of Antietam was only a preliminary statement. Still concerned about the border states and ever mindful of an anti-black backlash, he went to considerable lengths to soothe anxieties that emancipation would lead to a massive influx of freed slaves into the North, even arguing that the opposite would happen and that, once slavery was abolished, blacks in the North would choose to return to the South.

Nevertheless, when January 1, 1863 came he was as good as his word, and in addition he now gave his belated blessing to the recruitment of black troops. There were still plenty of critics to point to the proclamation's limitations and to enjoy the famous jibe of the *Spectator* in London: 'The principle asserted is not that a human being cannot justly own another, but that he cannot own him unless he is loyal to the United States.' However, as the next two years were to show, the Emancipation Proclamation acquired a force and momentum which became irresistible. Lincoln had deliberately kept the temperature as cool as possible, but the consequences were nonetheless profound. As one of his fellow Republicans maintained, it was 'a poor document but a mighty act'.

Despite emancipation, the mood in the North, and particularly in Washington, was scarcely confident at the beginning of 1863. Coming so soon after the relief of Antietam, the shock of Fredericksburg had been all the greater. The defeat seemed inexcusable as well as humiliating. Weariness with the war spread and there were even demands among some Republicans for an armistice during the coming year.

Washington's problem was that it could not escape the war. It had long been turned into a vast military camp and columns of soldiers wending their weary way through its muddy, unmacadamized streets were an everyday sight. So too were the four-horse wagons used as ambulances for the wounded, which streamed steadily, 30 or 40 of them at a time, across the bridges from the South into the District — 'the marrow of the tragedy' in the words of Walt Whitman, who, like many others at that time, helped out in the makeshift infirmaries dotted around Lincoln's city. After a bloodbath like Fredericksburg these hospitals were filled to overflowing; on occasion more than 50,000 men lay sick within the confines of the Federal capital.

The war's financial burden was bearing down heavily on many sections of the community, from New York financiers and businessmen, who had formerly relied on Southern trade, to Midwestern farmers who felt that they were exploited by the railroads or by the commercial interests of the Northeast. Although they paid for only a fraction of the war's cost, taxes rose steadily, including excise duties on a wide range of goods, and the first Federal income tax was introduced, levied at the scarcely penal rate of 3 per cent on all income above $800. Huge issues of government bonds put pressure on the financial community, although the small investor was encouraged to participate too.

The grumbles increased whenever news from the front was gloomy. Recruitment sagged, especially after the slaughter at Antietam and Fredericksburg, and the introduction of conscription seemed inevitable in the near future. Unpopular measures and military disasters combined to put a question mark against the Northern will to sustain the struggle. After almost two years of bitter conflict, neither side looked within sight of victory. As a new year dawned, it was an open question which would be exhausted first: Southern resources or Northern morale.

8 Death struggle

The West had often provided good news for Lincoln to compensate for setbacks in the East, but during the winter of 1862-3 it too brought him little comfort. The Union goal of clearing the Mississippi was still thwarted by the Confederate strongholds at Vicksburg and Port Hudson, which between them controlled a 250 mile stretch of the river. Port Hudson was just north of Baton Rouge, the Louisiana state capital, while Vicksburg, the more important of the two, was upstream about halfway between Memphis and New Orleans. It was a vital crossing-point for food and essential minerals from Texas like mercury, used in making percussion caps, as well as for other strategic goods, including weapons, that found their way from Europe via Mexico. To Jefferson Davis it was 'the nailhead that held the South's two halves together'; its loss would mean the isolation of Texas, Arkansas and the whole trans-Mississippi area of the Confederacy.

For Midwesterners including Lincoln himself, the Mississippi had long been the traditional route by which the surplus produce of the region found its way to distant markets via New Orleans. As a young man, he had himself traveled by flat-boat down river to the delta on the gulf. However, even before the Civil War, much of the trade of the Midwest had been switching to Canadian and Northeastern ports. Now its farmers were at the mercy of the Eastern railroads and complained that they were paying heavily for that dependence. Democratic politicians as usual were eager to exploit such grievances. For political as well as military reasons, therefore, Lincoln was anxious to clear the Mississippi.

Grant, restored to favor and given a field command, set out from southern Tennessee in early November 1862 down the Mississippi Central Railroad towards Jackson and Vicksburg. Not only was he harried en route by Confederate irregulars but his now lengthy supply line, stretching several hundred miles back to Columbus, Kentucky was disrupted by cavalry led by Nathan Bedford Forrest and Earl Van Dorn. For Grant the last straw came on December 20 when the Rebels completely wrecked his main supply base at Holly Springs. This convinced him that a long overland advance was too hazardous, and he switched to a push down the river from Memphis, which he entrusted initially to William Tecumseh Sherman. The approach was fraught with difficulty. The area on the east bank upstream from Vicksburg was known as the Yazoo Delta, a region of swamps, streams, bayous and tangled vegetation, while the town itself, standing on high cliffs above the river, presented a formidable obstacle. Sherman's attempt in late December to storm Chickasaw Bluffs, immediately to the north of Vicksburg, was repulsed with heavy casualties.

A few days later, further to the east in central Tennessee, a full-scale battle at Stones River ended indecisively. Despite heavy casualties, the Southern army remained intact

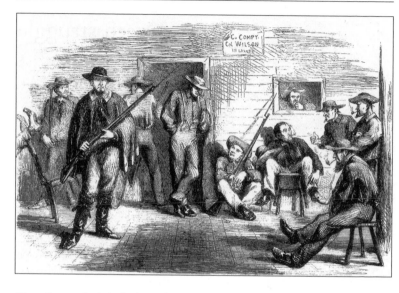

52.   *For every day in battle, the Civil War soldier spent many, many more in camp where
        boredom was a problem*

and withdrew to lick its wounds. The Northern army, too, suffered enormous losses
— up to 30 per cent of those taking part. As Lincoln wrote later, 'Had there been a
defeat instead, the nation could scarcely have lived over.' Something of a lull followed
during the ensuing months as the rival forces observed the common practice of holing
up for the winter. It was not just a question of the cold, but also that rain and mud
made movement difficult, if not impossible, at that time of the year. Roads throughout
the South, mainly dirt tracks without adequate drainage, often became quagmires
during the winter, particularly if large numbers of men had tramped over them.
Southern railroads were generally in poor shape too and, because of the long distances
involved, were extremely vulnerable to cavalry raids. On the whole, the Confederates
had the better of the cavalry war, certainly up to 1863. Their horsemanship and bold
tactics enabled them to take advantage of operating on familiar territory and among a
friendly population.

In all theaters of war, the experience of individual soldiers, North and South, alternated
between short bursts of savagery and horror on the battlefield and long periods of idleness
in camp which, in their way, were almost as hard to bear. The men whiled away their time
playing cards, writing letters home, drilling, cleaning their weapons and improving their
shelter against the rigors of the weather. Boredom and homesickness depressed morale
and raised nagging doubts about the purpose and wisdom of continuing the war.

The concentration of such large numbers of men in confined spaces also created a

53.   *Sometimes that boredom led to indiscipline when the punishment could be bizarre as well as harsh*

health problem for which the medical services of the day had no real answer. Disease was rampant in the camps and country boys in particular proved to have little resistance. Dysentery and diarrhea — known in the West as the 'Mississippi quick-step' — were very common, while epidemics of childhood illnesses, such as measles, diphtheria, scarlet fever and chicken pox, killed tens of thousands. Something like 90 per cent of today's medicines were unknown in the 1860s, and there was little idea of how to prevent the spread of infection. At least twice as many soldiers died from disease as on the field of battle.

Treatment of the wounded was equally primitive, and often more dangerous than the original injury. If a man was shot in the arm or leg and a compound fracture resulted, amputation was almost automatic. After a major battle, there were piles of arms and legs outside the surgeons' tents. For anaesthetic, the wounded would either bite on a bullet or were given a slug of whiskey. There was little or no attention to hygiene even in the few hospitals that existed — which were little more than groups of tents where men lay on the bare ground. The chances of surviving a wound were many times worse in the Civil War than in more recent conflicts such as Korea and Vietnam. It has been estimated that, whereas an American soldier in the Korean War stood only a one-in-fifty chance of dying later from a battlefield wound, half the wounded soldiers in the Civil War suffered the same fate.

Much the most effective medical care was provided, at least in the North, by non-governmental bodies like the United States Sanitary Commission, founded in 1861 and

54.   Specially built, pavilion-style hospital wards were an innovation that owed something to the experience of the British during the Crimean War

modelled on the British agency established during the Crimean War by the legendary Florence Nightingale. Its aim was also to improve the living conditions of the ordinary soldiers. It soon fell foul of the Washington bureaucracy, especially the US Army Medical Bureau, which, among other things, showed the predictable resentment of a male preserve towards many of the formidable ladies recruited by the Commission.

Lincoln himself was lukewarm towards it at first but was won over by the energy and keenness of the volunteers, who fussed and lobbied until things were done. They did not just channel the usual home-front comforts to the troops in the field but, more importantly, saw to it that the camps were cleaned up and the soldiers provided with appropriate washing facilities, something that was practically revolutionary for the time. They also inquired after men who were missing and softened the blow of the loss of a relative. Mothers and wives had previously learned of the fate of their sons and husbands only by reading it in the local newspaper or seeing the names pinned up outside a public building.

But it was as 'angels on the battlefield' that the women volunteers were best remembered. Many a soldier owed his life simply to their presence, and for every Dorothea Dix or Clara

Barton, Civil War nursing names that have rightly found their way into the history books, there were hundreds, if not thousands, of anonymous women who did similar pioneering work.

The fate of prisoners was often as hazardous as that of the wounded and in many ways it was as dangerous to be captured as to remain in combat. Not only were many of the prison camps badly sited and incompetently run but, particularly in the South, where medicines were in such short supply on account of the blockade, most prisoners were denied even the most minimal of health care. At least 56,000 were to die in the prisons of North and South. The problem was that no one had had experience of dealing with such large numbers in captivity. At first, as in previous wars, the captured were paroled — that is, allowed to go free on condition that they did not fight again — or they were exchanged for an equal number of prisoners from the other side. But as the struggle grew in bitterness and it dawned on some Northern generals, like Grant, that they should exploit their advantage in numbers, paroles and exchanges became few and far between.

The soldier's diet was fairly monotonous, whether he was a Northerner or a Southerner. Salt pork, nicknamed 'sow belly', or pickled beef, dismissed as 'salt horse', loomed large. Instead of bread the Federals had 'hardtack', tough, square-shaped biscuits made out of flour and water, known within the army as 'sheet-iron crackers'. They usually sported the initials B.C., which stood for Brigade Commissary, though the Union soldiers joked that they referred to their age. The Rebels had to make do with cornbread, likened by some to 'a pile of cow dung baked in the sun'. The Northerners, however, seldom went hungry, which was not the lot of their rivals. During the winter of 1862–3, the daily ration in Lee's army was a mere 4 ounces of bacon and 18 ounces of cornmeal, with an occasional handful of rice or black-eyed peas. Thousands suffered from scurvy, which began to die out only when spring and summer brought fresh supplies of wild vegetables.

The logistics of maintaining such large armies in the field presented massive problems. Here the Union side had the edge, not just because of its greater resources, but more particularly as a result of its better organization. Lincoln's Quartermaster-General, Montgomery Meigs, played a substantial part in the eventual Northern victory. The Southern soldiers, on the other hand, often went without shoes and blankets, tents and even uniforms, often the result of inadequate distribution rather than actual shortage. Many of Lee's men solved the problem by stripping the uniforms from those they killed or took prisoner, a practice that added to the confusion of some of the battles. Although after Manassas in July 1861 the North adopted a standard blue, the South was never so punctilious in its choice of grey. Dyes of this color soon ran out because of the blockade, and the home-made substitutes from walnut shells gave the uniforms a yellowish brown or so-called 'butternut' shade.

Even in the age of the railroad, distribution of supplies to the armies in the field depended on the horse-drawn wagon, at least for the crucial distance between the railhead and the front. Both sides needed roughly half as many animals for this task as the number of men on their muster-rolls. The wastage rate was shockingly high, with the average working-life of a horse or mule being measured in months rather than years. Any failure in the major task of finding not only the hundreds of thousands of animals required annually, but also the forage for them, could soon immobilize an entire army.

55.   *Amputations often took place in the open air under makeshift conditions. Doctors were not callous. It was just that medical knowledge was still somewhat primitive*

The early battles, like that at Manassas, did not look very different from those fought during the previous century. Yet the true nature of the fighting had changed quite dramatically, largely as a result of the introduction of the rifled musket and its bullet, the Minié ball, which increased enormously the chances of killing the enemy at a range of up to 500 yards. In contrast, the old smooth-bore musket had a maximum range of a mere 100 yards, and its effective range was far less. Furthermore, the old flintlock had been replaced by the percussion cap, which made the weapon more reliable in all weathers and raised the rate of fire. Although reloading via the muzzle was still a relatively slow process, attackers advancing over open ground were now exposed to several shots for every one previously. Thus the balance of advantage had shifted strongly in favor of the defender. Already it had discouraged cavalry charges. Cavalry had become increasingly confined to scouting and reconnaissance, and raids against supply lines.

Rifled artillery was slower in appearing on the battlefield and hence smooth-bore batteries remained the norm. Grape-shot and canister, which sprayed lead balls or pellets into the massed ranks of attackers, were used with devastating effect against troops in the open. Many thousands of lives were lost in hopeless frontal assaults before the lessons taught by the new weaponry were fully learned. Even with a substantial numerical advantage the massed infantry assault over open ground against men in well-prepared positions was now suicidal, as Fredericksburg had shown. The old saying that generals are usually a war behind in their tactics seems borne out by the experience of many engagements during the first years of the American Civil War.

56.   Nurses and doctors pose for a photograph outside a Northern hospital late in the war

Battles were particularly confused when they occurred in thickly wooded country which made nonsense of conventional tactics. The paucity of reliable maps added to the muddle and uncertainty. It was also extremely difficult to keep control of huge armies at a time when there was no field telegraph and orders had to be conveyed by messengers on horseback. Subordinate commanders were left with more discretion than many of them could prudently use. The better and braver ones led from the front, and casualties among senior officers were appallingly high. Hundreds of generals lost their lives during the Civil War; only one American general was killed in battle in eight years in Vietnam.

As the indecisive outcome of many of the battles showed, it was extremely difficult to follow up or press home a hard-won advantage. After hammering away at each other for hours or even days, the contestants would disengage, limp off to lick their wounds, and prepare to fight another day. Until almost the very end, for all the grievous bodily harm inflicted by their combined efforts, neither army had the power to annihilate the other, and the victorious side on the battlefield lacked the stamina, resources or sheer, ruthless will to follow up its success.

Given the undoubted advantages in defense, the Southern armies, in the view of some critics, attacked too often — they were on the offensive in eight of the first twelve major battles of the war. According to this school of thought, since the South's war aims were defensive, it needed only to sit back and let the North make all the running. Moreover, because it had fewer men and less resources, it could not afford to be profligate. The

115

*57.   Confederates captured in the Shenandoah Valley, May 1862, being kept in a makeshift
prison compound*

fact that the South never lost a battle where it was purely defending supports this view.
However, others argue that the smaller contestant needs to be the more daring — 'audacity,
always audacity' said Napoleon, and Robert E. Lee would surely have agreed — and must
try for a knockout blow before its more powerful opponent could muster its full strength.
Still others claim that an offensive approach was in the Southerners' make-up, a part of
their alleged Celtic heritage which made them aggressive, impatient for battle and unlikely
to wait to be hit first. As Winfield Scott put it, 'If they could not win in one wild, mad
dash, then perhaps it wasn't worth doing.'

Southerners were also said to make better fighters than soldiers; in other words they
were not particularly well disciplined and did not adjust to regimentation. Johnny Reb,
as the Confederate soldier was fondly called, was thought to be more attuned to the
outdoors, inured to hardship, more experienced in horseback riding, camping, hunting
and shooting, and hence found army life easier than Billy Yank, his Northern counterpart.
Of course there were many in the North, particularly those from the Midwest, who had
similar rural or frontier backgrounds. In many respects these two groups had more in
common with each other than either had with the Yankees from the Northeast, who
were more often town dwellers or recent immigrants anxious — or sometimes not so

58.   *An NCO's mess with the Army of the Potomac during 1863; the food was always better on the Union side*

anxious — to demonstrate their allegiance to their newly accepted homeland. It was true that there were fewer natural horsemen among the Yankees, and attempts to make up for the initial Confederate superiority in cavalry were sometimes faintly ludicrous. Some early Northern cavalrymen had to be strapped to their mounts and sought to protect themselves with cumbersome breastplates made from several layers of tin. It was also true that the usually hungry Rebels could be goaded into reckless attack by envy of Yankee knapsacks, since the Federals tended to carry better rations. But both armies had their full complement of heroes as well as their share of fugitives and deserters. If Southerners were typically bold, daring, resolute fighters, their Northern counterparts also had sterling qualities, not least tenacity and resilience in the face of the numerous setbacks of the first half of the war.

59.   By the time of the Civil War some 3,000 photographers were making a living in the United States. Many found their way into working for the armies

Because of the advent of the camera, we have a better idea of what the Civil War soldier looked like than we have of any of his predecessors. Photography was barely 20 years old when the first shots were fired at Sumter, but it had taken huge strides in those two decades. The development in 1851 of the glass-plate negative by an Englishman, Frederick Archer, meant that copies of a photograph could be made; before then a photograph, like a painting, could not be reproduced. Today it is difficult to imagine the excitement created by such a humble invention, which soon made the collecting of prints, not just of friends and relations, but also of distant places and national celebrities, a popular hobby. A new industry was born. Every town and village in North America had its local photographic studio and one of the first things a recruit did, whether he was a Rebel or a Yankee, was to have his photograph taken in his splendid new uniform before going off to the war. Fortunately, perhaps as many as a million of these images have survived.

Most camps had their photographers too, with their mobile dark-rooms usually located in the same wagon in which they lived. Because the glass-plate negative had to be damp in order to be light-sensitive, making, exposing and developing the shot all had to be carried out before the plate dried, usually a matter at most of about 10 minutes. Hence the photographers seldom strayed from base. Besides, business was good in the camps, particularly during the winter when not much else was happening. On these occasions the soldiers, and officers too, preferred to be photographed in groups with their friends; many were elaborately posed, certainly by today's standards. The cameramen had few precedents to guide them. Every frame they exposed was literally a new experience and the results often gave the impression that the war was a high-spirited game.

Such a feeling was created too by the significant part music played in the Civil War, more so than in any other war the United States has been involved in before or since. A vast outpouring of sentimental and patriotic ballads was stimulated in both North and South. Some 10,000 songs are said to have originated during the struggle, many of them equally popular among Confederates and Yankees. They spoke of home and country, of loved ones left behind and of faith in eventual victory. Their emotions were as simple as their titles: 'Cheer Boys, Cheer', 'Tenting Tonight on the Old Camp Ground', 'Vacant Chair', 'Tramp, Tramp, Tramp', 'Just Before the Battle, Mother' and 'Johnny Has Gone for a Soldier'. Some of course, like 'Marching Through Georgia', 'Bonnie Blue Flag' and 'The Battle Hymn of the Republic', have survived into the present.

In camp on an evening lusty voices would strike up a tune around the fire or inside the tent, to be echoed by others far away. Rebel sang against Federal, and on occasion they sang together. Because music met an inspirational need, the conflict acted as a catalyst in helping develop an indigenous style. Hitherto Irish, Scots, English, Italian and German influences had been so strong as to discourage any authentically American popular music. It was with the Civil War that African-American music also began to fully penetrate the national consciousness.

Both armies went into battle with brass bands blaring. At a critical moment in the Seven Days campaign during the summer of 1862, when a Northern brigade started to crumble, its commander ordered its band to strike up 'Yankee Doodle', which successfully rallied the troops, enabling them to hold out until reinforcements arrived. The casualty rate among bandsmen could be high, particularly since many of them doubled up as litter-bearers for the wounded. As well as sustaining morale on the battlefield, bands helped to relieve the monotony of camp life. Men became used to marching to the cadences of fife and drum. Military commands were communicated by the bugle call. Every regiment had its corps of musicians and sometimes the individual companies had their own bands too. A single camp could have between 30 and 40 different bands.

Lincoln felt that the numbers were getting out of hand within the Union army and curtailed them after July 1862. Jefferson Davis was not so mean, though natural attrition, coupled with a shortage of musical instruments in the South, took its toll on Rebel bands. Lee went on record as saying that he could not imagine an army without music, while Grant disliked bands so much that he would go to great lengths to avoid having to listen to them.

Grant had spent a frustrating winter trying, without success, to get his army on dry ground close enough to Vicksburg for an assault from the east when spring came. Having learned from his earlier experience that the long overland route from the northeast was

60.   *The underhand men of war: scouts and guides of the Army of the Potomac after Antietam.*
The North relied less on local people for these duties than did the South

too difficult and too dangerous, he experimented with various schemes on the river itself, even endeavoring to cut a canal to bypass the town's menacing batteries, as well as seeking a way through the labyrinth of tributaries and channels in the Yazoo Delta north of Vicksburg. It was all to no avail. His gunboats either got stuck or were nearly trapped by the Confederates hounding them. Such was the plight of one of these expeditions that the naval officer in charge suffered what was officially described as 'an aberration of mind'.

In the end Grant decided to march his 33,000 men past Vicksburg on the opposite bank, while his remaining gunboats and transports, with their decks and funnels protected by bales of hay and cotton or sacks of grain, ran the gauntlet of the Rebel batteries located on the bluffs above. A few were sunk. and many damaged, but most got through. Grant was now able to ferry his troops unmolested across the river 35 miles south of the town, while Sherman distracted its garrison with a show of force from the north. The Confederates were also confused by the remarkable Union cavalry raid commanded by Colonel Benjamin Grierson, who in two weeks covered 600 miles from southern Tennessee across the heart of Mississippi to end at Baton Rouge in Louisiana. He led the pursuing Rebels a merry dance, causing much havoc, burning bridges, cutting telegraph lines, destroying large sections of three important railroads and taking hundreds of prisoners.

61.   *The drum corps of the 93rd New York Infantry Regiment in Virginia during the summer of 1863; soldiers marched to the beat of fife and drum*

Announcing that his army forthwith would live off the land until Vicksburg was captured, Grant cut himself loose from his supply lines in early May 1863 and, having commandeered every wagon, buggy, carriage and farm cart for miles around, pressed his now 44,000-strong army towards Jackson, the Mississippi capital. It fell on May 14 and two days later, having first set fire to most of the city and uprooted the rail tracks passing through it to prevent any Rebels threatening his rear, he turned westwards towards his goal. At Champion Hill, halfway between Jackson and Vicksburg, he encountered a part of the latter's garrison which had been sent out to meet him and drove it back in the bloodiest battle so far of his campaign. More than 1,000 men on both sides lost their lives and nearly 6,000 were wounded.

While the Confederate high command disputed whether Vicksburg should be defended at all costs or whether it was more important to avoid the danger of a large force being bottled up there, Grant had thrust his army between his opponents and prevented them from acting in any coordinated way. Fending off the Rebels to his rear, he now moved on the town which had been his objective for so long. Within a few days a Southern army of over 30,000 men was penned inside the river-port's formidable fortifications: trenches and earthworks sited on a ridge that ran in a 7-mile arc around Vicksburg from north to

62.   *Vicksburg, like Natchez and the other Mississippi river ports, had grown rich with*
       steamboats regularly calling. It was also an important rail-crossing point

south, resting on the Mississippi at each end. No Union force had yet confronted such impressive defenses.

Thinking the Confederates were already beaten, Grant attacked straightaway, but was thrown back with heavy losses. He tried again a few days later with the same result. In these two sorties he suffered as many casualties as in the previous three weeks. By now his supplies were extremely low and his troops almost rebelliously hungry as well as tired. Replenishment and regrouping became a necessity. Having seen to it that the town was completely surrounded and his gunboats in place to cut off any relief by the river, Grant settled down to a siege. 'This is a death struggle,' his colleague Sherman confided to his wife.

Vicksburg's garrison and citizens now had to face daily bombardments not only from Grant's field artillery but also from gunboats stationed in the river. Soon most of the civilians were spending their days as well as their nights living in caves burrowed into the hillsides. At one time there were more than 500 of these caves, many comfortably furnished and some even subdivided to house several families. Miraculously, only about 10 civilians lost their lives in the siege and less than 50 were wounded. What kept them going was the hope that they would somehow be relieved by the Rebel force gathering at Jackson.

Grant was wary of this possibility, too, and maintained two lines of defense. He feared also that the garrison might be tempted to break out, but the enthusiasm of some Confederate officers for such a move was not shared by their commander, General John Pemberton. As the days of the siege wore on Pemberton became more and more demoralized and less and less inclined to take any action on his own behalf, leaving the initiative to Grant as well as the Confederate army in Grant's rear or to the authorities in Richmond. He now had little communication with either, although a few couriers did manage to find their way through the lines and some even back again. Their replies were meant to sustain the garrison's morale, with hints of relief on the way, and also to stiffen their commander's will with pleas to resist to the bitter end. But Pemberton was more concerned with relief than with resistance, while the force which he expected to provide it champed at the bit, lacking the nerve and the strength to challenge Grant.

Grant's campaign leading up to the siege of Vicksburg was one of the boldest and most remarkable of the war. The man who had been the target of criticism for his drinking habits, for his unpreparedness at Shiloh and, more recently, for his apparently futile schemes on the Mississippi, now emerged as a new national hero, at a time when the North badly needed one. The fickleness of headline and editorial writers was as shameless then as now. Letters home from some of Grant's soldiers had helped to build up his reputation and politicians, including the President himself, fell over each other to applaud a general who knew how to fight and to win. Whereas his demands for reinforcements had earlier fallen on deaf ears, now Grant's every request was granted. Soon he had some 70,000 men to maintain his cordon around Vicksburg and to deter any challenge to his rear. What Lincoln and the Northern public desperately wanted now was a general with the same grit and determination to face Lee in northern Virginia.

9 Confederate high tide

Morale in the Army of the Potomac had never been lower than during the winter of 1862–3, when it faced Lee's Confederates across the Rappahannock after the Fredericksburg debacle. Desertions ran at 200 a day during January alone. Burnside tried one final attacking move, aimed at outflanking both the town and the now dreaded Marye's Heights, but his troops became bogged down, literally, in the deep mud. After two frustrating days in late January, he called a halt and withdrew into winter quarters. Dismayed by this further humiliation, Lincoln replaced him with one of his subordinate commanders — or, as some would have it, one of his most insubordinate commanders — and strongest critics, Joseph Hooker. It is claimed that, like his predecessor, Hooker added a new word to the English language, though a less salubrious one than Burnside's. It is said that his alleged predilection for prostitutes resulted in his name becoming associated with them ever after.

Hooker was generally well liked by his troops and his regard for their welfare made him even more popular. Improvements in living conditions and an increase in rations reduced the level of sickness in the army, where dysentery and scurvy had been taking a heavy toll. Better arrangements for leave and for pay, which was six months in arrears in some cases, lifted morale and cut the desertion rate. Lincoln was persuaded to sanction an amnesty for deserters and as a result many rejoined the service. Discipline, which had become slack under Burnside, was tightened up. More attention to weapons training, drill and sporting activities helped to relieve boredom and reduce opportunities for mischief-making. Hooker also regrouped his regiments into new corps and divisions, which were given distinctive badges for identification in an attempt to boost esprit de corps; such badges were eventually to become standard throughout the United States army. He unified the cavalry and set up a Bureau of Military Information to prepare intelligence reports. All these efforts to make the Army of the Potomac more manageable were much needed now that its strength had grown to nearly 120,000 — almost twice the size of the opposing Confederate force.

Lee's army had had a very hard winter. Food was scarce and the men did what they could to eke out their skimpy diet by foraging for wild vegetables and roots. Virtually everything was in short supply, including shoes, blankets and warm clothing. Disease swept through the ranks, but morale remained extraordinarily high and loyalty to Lee unquestioned. The soldiers had busied themselves building an elaborate set of earthworks and trenches fronting the Rappahannock, knowing that once the weather improved the Federals would inevitably be moving against them.

As usual, Lincoln was eager for his army commander to attack, but Hooker was wary of

63.   *Cockily dressed and brimful of confidence, cavalrymen always thought themselves an elite. The Federal horsemen were no exception and their performance was improving as the war went on*

repeating Burnside's mistakes. He reconnoitered a number of undefended fords upstream from Fredericksburg and, while giving the impression that another frontal assault was intended, in late April he got the bulk of his force across the river unchallenged. They were to rendezvous at a country crossroads called Chancellorsville, some 10 miles west of Fredericksburg.

Well aware of what Hooker was doing but outnumbered by almost two to one, Lee was in a quandary about how best to deal with this threat to his left flank. Many of his staff were all for withdrawing nearer Richmond before they were cut off but as usual Lee was reluctant to retreat. Leaving barely a sixth of his men to defend Fredericksburg, he moved the rest to face the Federals on his left and to his rear.

Hooker had been hoping for a bloodless victory and seemed momentarily disconcerted by this turn of events. Instead of attacking the Confederates with his vastly superior force before they could take up any positions, he yielded the initiative to Lee by going on to the defensive himself. His troops were further handicapped by their unfamiliarity with the area where they were to fight.

The region around Chancellorsville was known as 'The Wilderness', since it consisted mainly of dense woods and tangled undergrowth, with few roads. It was perfect fighting country for small units and Lee could scarcely have chosen a better battlefield for his inferior force if he had tried. The Federals could not assert their greater numbers and the power of their formidable artillery. Worse still, Hooker had sent his cavalry on a raid aimed at severing Lee's supply lines and communication links with Richmond. At other times this might have been all to the good but on this occasion it meant that he was without any means of determining Lee's dispositions, let alone fathoming his intentions. In military parlance he was blind. Lee still had his cavalry, who quickly found the gaps in Hooker's defenses, particularly those on his right flank.

Ever daring, Lee split his army yet again, despatching Stonewall Jackson with nearly two-thirds of the troops on a 14-mile march via forest roads around the right flank of the Union forces. At one time Jackson's column of infantrymen filled virtually the whole stretch. Since they were moving in broad daylight it was impossible for them to conceal their presence entirely and Hooker inevitably got wind of it. However, he thought they were retreating to Richmond and, rather than harry them, preferred to let them go unmolested, convinced that the outcome could be only to his advantage. Not all his colleagues shared his optimism.

Their worst fears were confirmed when, on the early evening of May 2 while most of the Federal soldiers were eating or cleaning their equipment, 28,000 Rebels came surging out of the woods behind them to cut through the Union right flank as though it was soft putty. Panic-stricken, many of the Northern troops fled to the rear, abandoning their weapons. The retreat soon turned into a rout. Some, however, offered strong resistance and the Confederate advance was slowed down as nightfall approached.

The next morning Hooker desperately tried to regroup his demoralized forces. Although he still outnumbered Lee, and Lee's army, like Gaul, was now divided into three parts, he appeared incapable of seizing the initiative. Lee, in his position, would almost certainly have counter-attacked to throw the opposition off balance, but Hooker preferred simply to defend. It seemed as if he knew that he was beaten before he started and acted accordingly. His morale was scarcely improved by being badly shaken up when a cannon-ball struck a pillar against which he happened to be leaning. Nevertheless the fighting was especially bitter and vicious that day as the Rebels eagerly sought a breakthrough and the Federals desperately tried to prevent one.

Lee had been concerned for his own rear, since the group he had left to defend

64.   The Confederate dead littered Marye's Heights above Fredericksburg in May 1863

Fredericksburg had been overwhelmed that very morning and the daunting Marye's Heights, which had seen so many Union dead the previous December, were now in Northern hands after being stormed at the point of the bayonet. But, almost incredibly, Hooker stood by and did nothing while Lee moved a portion of his army to deal with this threat behind him. In fierce fighting during May 4 the Federals advancing from Marye's Heights were driven back across the Rappahannock. The next day, Hooker and the main army also withdrew, leaving the field to Lee. Union casualties were 17,000, while Confederate losses were proportionately higher at 13,000.

Described by many as Lee's 'greatest masterpiece', the victory at Chancellorsville owed much to Hooker's failings, though it also saw Lee at his most daring and aggressive. In the end it was a somewhat hollow success for him, for on May 10 Stonewall Jackson died. He had been accidentally shot by one of his own side the week before, while reconnoitering in front of his lines on the night of his great outflanking movement. The wound had led to his left arm being amputated and pneumonia had set in, from which he never recovered.

65. *Robert E. Lee never referred to
     the North as the enemy and
     rebuked colleagues for saying
     rude things about Lincoln*

Many were to say that the South, too, never recovered from Jackson's death, because Lee had grown to rely on him and was never again to find such a loyal or dependable subordinate commander to whom he could entrust the bold, flanking movements which had become his trademark. When word reached the Rebel army 'a great sob' swept over it, according to one former colleague. Jackson's body was borne to Richmond where it lay in state in the Capitol. On the day of his funeral all shops shut in the city and crowds wept openly in the streets.

In the North Lincoln took the Chancellorsville humiliation particularly badly.   'My God! my God! what will the country say?' was his reaction when told. News of it came before that of Grant's successes at Jackson and Champion Hill, and it provided damaging ammunition for the critics of the President's leadership whose barbs had grown ever more bitter that winter and spring. The North still had the numbers and resources but its will to sustain the struggle looked less than rock-solid.

In the South, the victory at Chancellorsville inspired the kind of elation which encourages rashness. Lee, anxious to maintain the momentum generated by his army's success, could now do little wrong in the eyes of most Confederates. Even Jefferson Davis and his Cabinet were somewhat in awe of him. Besides, they had many other pressing problems on their minds, ranging from rampant inflation, crippling shortages and increasing dissidence on the

66. *Most slaves were brought to the United States from West Africa on British ships. Ports like Bristol grew rich on the infamous trade*

67. *With its vivid colours and simple message,* Uncle Tom's Cabin *was a popular choice for that most Victorian of family pastimes, the lantern-slide reading*

68. *Tearful departures became the norm in North and South, and print-makers were encouraged to cater to every patriotic and pathetic sentiment. This lithograph by Currier and Ives is entitled* Off to the War

69.*Early euphoria in the North and talk of marching against Dixie made recruitment fairly easy*

ATTENTION, TO SAVE YOUR BOUNTY!

SECOND REGIMENT

EMPIRE BRIGADE!

Col. P. J. CLAASSEN, Commanding.

☞ FIRST REGIMENT IN THE FIELD UNDER THE NEW CALL.

WANTED, 25 MEN

Between the ages of 18 and 45 years, to fill up one of the best Companies now forming, under officers who have seen active service.

Clothing, Subsistence and Comfortable Quarters provided on enlistment.

PAY FROM $13 TO $23 PER MONTH,

TO DATE FROM DAY OF ENLISTMENT.

$50 BOUNTY GIVEN BY THE STATE.

$25 BOUNTY GIVEN BY THE U. S. GOVERNMENT.

TO BE PAID AS SOON AS MUSTERED INTO SERVICE.

☞ $100 BOUNTY WHEN THE WAR IS OVER!

☞ It is intended to make this one of the best Companies in the Brigade or service, and no labor will be spared to do so. The Officers are experienced men, having been over one year in one of the First Regiments in the service.

CAPTAIN J. H. STINER, LATE OF HAWKINS' ZOUAVES.

70. … *but, as the war wore on, replacement of losses in the ranks became ever more difficult. Cash incentives were resorted to and many hundreds of millions of dollars were paid out in such bounties. Whoever organized a regiment got to be its Colonel. Other officers were usually elected*

71. *Washington was certainly vulnerable after Manassas, but no one on the Southern side had given a thought before the battle to what they should do if they won*

72. *Stonewall Jackson and Robert E. Lee were the two Southern heroes. Jackson got his nickname at Manassas, but the colleague who gave him it did not survive the battle. Jackson was not to survive the war*

73. *Round one of the clash of the ironclads:* Monitor *v* Merrimac *on 9 March 1862. It proved inconclusive and there were few repeat matches*

74. *The taking of Island Number Ten in April 1862 by river gunboats was a sharp reminder to the Confederates of how vulnerable they now were in the West*

75. *Artillery may no longer have been the king of battles, but it still played a lethal role in the war, as here at the battle of Malvern Hill during the Richmond campaigns*

76. *Dashing cavalry charges are one of the fondest images of the American Civil War. The Confederates had the better of the cavalry war. Their horsemanship and bold tactics enabled them to take advantage of operating on familiar territory and among a friendly population*

77. *Burnside Bridge saw much of the fiercest fighting on America's bloodiest day. Antietam Creek ran red with the blood for days afterwards. A Kurz and Allison lithograph*

78. *'Hell's Half Acre' was how some described the battle of Stones River*

79. Gettysburg was the Confederates' highwater mark. Thereafter it was downhill all the way for them. A Currier and Ives lithograph

80. The Kearsage's *sinking of the Confederate commerce raider* Alabama *ended Southern hopes of a European salvation*

81. *Storming Morris Island's Fort Wagner in July 1863 was, for the Negro regiment involved, a baptism of fire. But their performance helped to make blacks more acceptable in the Union army*

82. *During the battle for the Wilderness in May 1864 many of the soldiers found bodies unburied from the fighting there the previous summer*

83. Grant had meant Cold Harbor to be the culmination of his 1864 campaign but for many Federal soldiers it was their final battle. The casualties were the worst of the war

84. The Chattanooga–Atlanta railroad ran through Resaca which made it a prime target for General Sherman and his northern troops intent on destroying the Southern heartland. A Kurz and Allison lithograph

85. From the top of Kennesaw Mountain the Georgian city of Atlanta, of Gone with the Wind *fame, was clearly visible In their eagerness to take this great prize the northerners suffered 3,000 casualties in just a few hours on 27 June 1864. A Kurz and Allison lithograph*

86. General Sherman directing the bombardment of Atlanta. Short of numbers for a siege, he intended to intimidate it into surrendering. Thure de Thulstrop is the artist

87. *James McPherson, the commander of the Army of the Tennessee, was killed during one of the climactic battles for Atlanta, as this Kurz and Allison lithograph depicts, though he was not leading his men into the thick of battle at the time as is suggested. The print-makers were not above indulging in artistic licence*

88. *Fort Fisher dominated the main entrance to Wilmington's harbour on North Carolina's coast. A home for Southern blockade-runners, it held out for nearly four years before being finally subdued on 14 January 1865 following a bombardment and assault by land*

89. Just as they had marched into battle shoulder to shoulder, so were they buried shoulder to shoulder. Collecting and reinterring the remains of those who had died was a haunting task for some after Appomattox. Inevitably the winning side spent more time and effort doing so

90. Many of the South's plantation houses passed into new ownership. Some were even bought by Yankees

91–99 Re-enacting Civil War battles is one of the most popular weekend pastimes in America today. Some would go so far as to say it is the nation's fastest growing leisure pursuit

home front to the near collapse of the Rebel position in the West and the vulnerability of much of the coast, particularly in the Carolinas, to Northern incursions.

As spring gave way to summer the political and military leadership was locked in serious debate about its strategic priorities. There were those who argued that Chancellorsville had won a breathing space in the East which could allow a part of Lee's army to be sent West in a bid to restore the situation there, either by relieving Vicksburg or by a drive into central Tennessee, which might indirectly achieve the same objective. Lee and his supporters preferred to use the Chancellorsville success as the springboard for a bold attacking move which might snap the frayed nerves of the North, encourage Democratic opposition to the war, perhaps even rekindle British and French interest in recognition of the Confederacy — and, through a combination of these pressures, bring Lincoln to the negotiating table.

To a man like Lee, ever prepared to gamble, another invasion of the North, with the chance of a startling victory on Lincoln's doorstep which might just achieve all these goals, was too tempting a prospect to resist. He had his sights firmly fixed on a new crossing of the Potomac and a move to outflank Washington, perhaps to threaten Philadelphia, Baltimore and even New York. He felt that he could rely on the rich farming lands of Pennsylvania to provide food for his troops and forage for their horses, which would take the pressure off embattled Virginia. As a Virginian first and foremost, he sometimes had a restricted view of broader Confederate strategy. However, his reputation was such that Richmond gave him virtually a free hand.

Lee and his staff spent the rest of May and early June gathering together 70–80,000 men. Hooker had surprisingly retained his command after the ignominy of Chancellorsville, largely because Lincoln had no sure successor in mind and could not risk admitting his mistaken appointment so soon. Suspecting that something was afoot, Hooker sent his newly emboldened cavalry, who had been smarting ever since their somewhat hapless role at Chancellorsville, to reconnoiter the Rebel positions in northern Virginia. The Confederate horsemen under Jeb Stuart were caught unawares and, in what turned out to be the biggest cavalry battle of the whole war, received a bloody nose at Brandy Station on June 9, although the Federals were forced to withdraw across the Rappahannock. Stuart's determination to counter this blow to his prestige was to cause Lee problems with his cavalry in the coming campaign.

Once again the invasion route was by way of the Shenandoah Valley and, anxious not to waste time, Lee set out the day after the Brandy Station mishap. His cavalry, needing time to reorganize, did not catch up with him for at least a week. First Lee had to deal with a Federal garrison some 5,000 strong at Winchester, which he surprised and disposed of on June 15. The very next day his army began crossing into Maryland and within the week they were in Pennsylvania. By June 28 Lee's vanguard had reached the Susquehanna River, across which lay Harrisburg, the state capital of Pennsylvania, nearly 100 miles north of Washington. The plan was to capture it, destroy the rail links with Baltimore and the West, and push on towards Philadelphia. In fact it was to be the most northerly point reached by Lee's forces during the war.

Hooker meanwhile had been largely inactive. His reaction to news of Lee's move north was to ask Lincoln for permission to march south on Richmond. The President promptly

100. *Jeb Stuart leading his horsemen on a scouting expedition. Vain and devil-may-care, he was almost as big a hero in the South as Lee, but unlike Lee he began to worry unduly about his reputation*

vetoed the proposal, arguing that the destruction of the Confederacy's army should be Hooker's goal, rather than the capture of its capital. Without much sense of urgency, Hooker then transferred the bulk of his force west of Washington, where he thought the Rebel forces might be aimed. But he was reluctant to tackle them, complaining that he was outnumbered and undersupplied. This by now all too familiar refrain exasperated Lincoln, who sacked him on June 28 — the very day Lee's advance guard reached the Susquehanna. On being told of his appointment, his replacement, General George Meade, exclaimed, 'Well I've been tried and condemned without a hearing, and I suppose I shall have to go to execution'. Hooker was so relieved to be losing his command that he left even before briefing Meade on the state of his force, let alone giving any hint of how to cope with Lee's threat.

Meade had served under Hooker as a corps commander and had been one of the few Union generals to distinguish themselves at Chancellorsville. Before that his bravery and determination had not gone unnoticed at Fredericksburg, where it had been his division that had breached Stonewall Jackson's line. In appearance he was not particularly impressive. Gangling, lean and somewhat somber-looking, he had a seemingly gentle disposition which cloaked an extremely violent temper. However, he was capable of moving fast if need be and was not a man to avoid a difficult decision, which was a change for the luckless Army of the Potomac. He had the additional advantage for Lincoln of being a Pennsylvanian and hence likely to be especially keen to rid his home state of an invader. Within 24 hours of his appointment he had got his troops marching in the general direction of the Rebel concentrations, prepared to give battle.

As Lee's army advanced into Pennsylvania the Confederate commander had made no effort to try to win friends among the Northern populace. His troops were free to forage for food wherever they could find it, there was some looting and many of the towns they passed through were required to pay tribute in the form of produce and clothing. It was a search for footwear, desperately needed by the ill-shod Southern soldiers, that brought them to a small Pennsylvanian market town by the name of Gettysburg, hitherto safely remote from the front line, where it was rumored that there was a supply of shoes.

Although his advance had been almost unmolested, Lee had plenty of cause for concern. His army was strung out over a wide area and he had little idea of his opponent's movements. Now on enemy soil, he could not rely on obtaining accurate information from the local population and his cavalry, which should have been supplying such intelligence as well as protecting his own advance, was completely out of contact. Acting on a flimsy pretext provided by Lee, but more out of a desire to avenge the wound to his pride inflicted at Brandy Station, Jeb Stuart had taken the bulk and the best of his horsemen on a wild-goose chase away to the east of the main thrust. His aim was to disrupt the Union army's communications and create confusion in its rear, but in fact he caused more confusion for Lee than Meade or Lincoln. When at last Lee discovered that Meade was north of the Potomac and moving towards him, it was almost too late, for the gap between the armies was shrinking fast. He scrambled to gather together his widely dispersed forces and chose as their point of concentration the area around Cashtown, some 8 miles west of Gettysburg, that, he felt, had the makings of a good defensive position.

Meade's route had happened to take the Union army close to Gettysburg, and on July 1, when a group of Confederate infantrymen made their way from Cashtown into Gettysburg in search of shoes, they ran into the Federal cavalry screen just west of the town. Thus began the most important battle of the Civil War and perhaps the most crucial in American history. What opened as a skirmish by the end involved some 160,000 troops.

Lee had been uncertain just where Meade was concentrating. Now he rushed his men to the scene, getting 25,000 or so there the same day, while the Union force still numbered less than 20,000. He himself arrived during the afternoon in time to see the Northerners driven from the town, after much fierce fighting, on to a gentle ridge to the south near the local cemetery. He urged his generals to dislodge them from there without delay, but they hesitated and by the time they started to move the Federals had dug themselves in and brought up enough reinforcements with artillery to discourage any further advance before darkness fell. There were many in the Southern camp then, and even more later, who were to say that if only Stonewall Jackson had still been alive the Gettysburg battle would have been over and won that first evening.

By the next morning the Union troops had strengthened their position to such an extent that any attack on it now was a very doubtful proposition. Meade, too, had arrived by this time, and within the day he was expecting to have nearly 100,000 troops in position along

101. *James Longstreet became Lee's closest colleague after the death of Stonewall Jackson. His dispute with Lee over how Gettysburg was fought never soured their relationship, though others sought to argue his case forcibly later*

the Cemetery Hill and Ridge at Gettysburg. Lee's closest colleague, General Longstreet, deemed the line nearly impregnable and argued that it should be left alone or outflanked from the east so as to sever its links with Washington and thus force Meade to attack the Confederate army. But Lee was convinced of his army's invincibility and in any case, without cavalry, he could not consider such a sweeping move as Longstreet was recommending.

Lee decided on an assault, though against the southern end of Meade's line where he thought it was less well defended. All day long bitter fighting — some of the bitterest of the whole war — raged at places now forever etched in the American memory: Little Round Top, Devil's Den, the Wheat Field, the Peach Orchard. Although the Rebel soldiers showed great valor and extraordinary determination, they could not shift the Northerners and by nightfall they retired to regroup and count their casualties, which had already been considerable.

That evening Longstreet again tried to dissuade Lee from continuing his attack against such a strong position but Lee believed that the Union soldiers were almost beaten. He sensed, he said, that their morale was sagging. Indeed, Meade had consulted his corps commanders as to whether they should withdraw. One final push, Lee hoped, and his opponents would collapse like a pack of cards. The great victory which he had come north to secure would then be his, for Washington would be vulnerable and, unlike Beauregard at the first battle of Manassas, he would follow up his success to the very gates of the White House. He determined to strike where Meade would least expect it — in the center

102. 'A Harvest of Death' was how the photographer captioned this. The corpses are Northern soldiers who fell at the Peach Orchard on the second day of Gettysburg and their boots seem to have been already taken by the Rebels who had occupied this spot. The somewhat ghostly burial party completes the macabre scene

of his line — and for the attack he would use the fresh troops of General George Pickett's division, mostly Virginians like Lee himself, who had hitherto been guarding the rear. The die was cast for what is widely regarded as the military climax of the war.

All the morning of July 3 the Confederates prepared for their do-or-die frontal assault. Stuart's cavalry had at long last returned from their fruitless sortie and Lee had immediately sent them on a foray behind the Federal position on Cemetery Hill to attempt a diversion. But they were repulsed by a detachment of Northern horsemen led by the 23-year-old General George Custer.

Longstreet had gathered nearly 170 guns with which to intimidate the Union infantrymen lodged along Cemetery Hill and force a path for the attacking Rebels. Just after 1 p.m. they opened up in the noisiest and heaviest barrage of the war. In the words of one eyewitness, 'The air was all murderous iron.' Federal batteries fired back but after a while appeared to give up. Lee was convinced that they had been knocked out, whereas they were simply saving ammunition. After two hours the Rebel guns gave way too, as the long, tightly packed lines of Southern foot-soldiers emerged silently from the woods opposite Cemetery Hill. Pickett's famous charge was about to begin.

Without so much as a murmur, let alone a yell, the 13,000 Confederates picked their way calmly over the gently sloping, wide, open field in one of the most splendid sights of the war.

103. *A photograph of Lincoln taken by Mathew Brady before the Gettysburg Address. Brady used to relish his self-styled title of 'Mr Lincoln's Cameraman'*

Many of the Northerners facing them admitted afterwards that they had appeared awesome and irresistible — though to anyone today, looking from Cemetery Hill across the distance over which they had to advance, it would seem an act of folly on the grand scale. As they neared their goal, the clump of oak trees atop Cemetery Hill, the very center of Meade's line, the Federal artillery suddenly blasted forth to scythe through the serried Rebel ranks, while volleys from the rifles of the Union troops crouching behind the little stone wall below the hill's crest tore into the grey-clad groups. The noise and carnage were appalling.

The battle raged for another hour. Much of the fighting was hand to hand and, as ammunition ran out, men used their rifles as clubs. The few Virginians who did make it to the copse were cut down in their brief moment of glory. Soon the remainder were falling back, despite the efforts of their officers to persuade them to press on. Less than half made it home again — nearly 7,500 of them were left on the field. All 13 colonels in the division were killed or wounded and of the three brigade commanders, two were already dead and the third severely wounded.

Lee rode out to meet the survivors. They included Pickett, whom he greeted with the words, 'Upon my shoulders rests the blame. The men and officers of your command have written the name of Virginia as high today as it has ever been written before.' To another colleague he said, 'It is I who have lost this fight and you must help me out of it the best way you can.' He even had a remark for an observer from the British army: 'This has been a sad day for us, Colonel, a sad day, but we can't always expect to win victories.' When he got back to his headquarters he gave vent to his real feelings. 'Too bad, too bad, oh too bad.' He knew that he had lost his gamble in invading the North. The military pretensions of the Confederacy had reached and passed their high-water mark.

The next day, July 4, rain hindered the burial parties that were busy all over the battlefield. Lee had already faced the inevitable. Abandoning his dead, he had begun to withdraw to Virginia, sending his wounded and his slowest wagons on ahead. Today, when it takes only a matter of hours to drive from Gettysburg to Richmond, it is difficult to appreciate the plight of the Johnny Rebs in 1863, making their weary way on dirt tracks, through mountain passes and over swollen rivers, ill-shod, sore-footed, hungry, tired, battered and, above all, bitterly disappointed.

For his part, Meade, a naturally cautious man still adjusting to the responsibilities of his new command, did not attempt a counter-attack at Gettysburg and showed little heart for an energetic pursuit of Lee. Although he had reserves who had not fought in the battle, he was very conscious of the heavy casualties his army had suffered — 23,000 in three days, more than a quarter of those engaged. Lee's were higher still — 28,000 or nearly two-fifths of his force — and in addition he was almost out of ammunition. Federal cavalry occasionally harassed the retreating Southerners but there was no sustained pressure. Even when Lee was at his most vulnerable, on the tenth day as his army was re-crossing the Potomac, Meade grossly overestimated the strength of the Confederates' thinly held defensive line and decided against an attack. Once again, a great battle had exhausted the victors almost as much as the vanquished, and once again the sweet taste of victory soon turned sour because of the failure to follow it up. Lincoln shared this feeling of disappointment to the full; in a letter to Meade, which was finally never sent, he wrote that if Lee had been pursued and caught the war would have been ended. 'As it is,' he went on bitterly, 'the war will be prolonged indefinitely.'

The President's anger was somewhat assuaged by news from the West of the final capture of Vicksburg and Port Hudson. In one of those curious coincidences of the war, at the very moment that Pickett was beginning his fateful charge at Gettysburg on July 3, Vicksburg's commander, John Pemberton, was meeting with Ulysses Grant to discuss surrender terms. All hope of relief had gone and both the garrison and the civilian population had been reduced to eating mule meat and fricasseed cat or rat steaks. About 30,000 Confederates were taken prisoner, though most of them were paroled and went home, never to fight again. Four days later the 16,000-strong garrison at Port Hudson laid

Address delivered at the dedication of the cemetery at Gettysburg.

Four score and seven years ago our fathers brought forth on this continent, a new nation, conceived in Liberty, and dedicated to the proposition that all men are created equal.

Now we are engaged in a great civil war, testing whether that nation, or any nation so conceived and so dedicated, can long endure. We are met on a great battlefield of that war. We have come to dedicate a portion of that field, as a final resting place for those who here gave their lives that that nation might live. It is altogether fitting and proper that we should do this.

But, in a larger sense, we can not dedicate— we can not consecrate— we can not hallow— this ground. The brave men, living and dead, who struggled here, have consecrated it, far above our poor power to add or detract. The world will little note, nor long remember what we say here, but it can never forget what they did here. It is for us the living, rather, to be dedicated here to the unfinished work which they who fought here have thus far so nobly advanced. It is rather for us to be here dedicated to the great task remaining before us— that from these honored dead we take increased devotion to that cause for which they gave the last full measure of devotion— that we here highly resolve that these dead shall not have died in vain— that this nation, under God, shall have a new birth of freedom— and that government of the people,

by the people, for the people, shall not perish from the earth.

Abraham Lincoln.

November 19, 1863.

104. Lincoln took just two minutes to deliver the Gettysburg Address November 19, 1863. Many in his audience thought it inadequate for the occasion: the dedication of the military cemetery there

down its arms too. The Mississippi had now been cleared of Rebels. As Lincoln himself put it: 'The Father of Waters again goes unvexed to the sea.'

What was equally important for Lincoln was the growing conviction that in Grant he now had an aggressive general who might prove a match for Lee. 'Grant is my man,' he said, 'and I am his the rest of the war.' Church bells rang out all over the North at the dual victories and in many cities the militia fired off 100-gun salutes. For Jefferson Davis it was 'the darkest hour of our political existence'. A colleague confided to his diary: 'The Confederacy totters to its destruction.' Certainly a page had been turned in the destiny of the South. But the war was far from over yet.

The Gettysburg and Vicksburg victories, happening simultaneously, are often regarded as the decisive encounters of the Civil War. Yet the conflict still had almost half its course to run. It was unlikely that the Confederacy would ever be able to mount another offensive on the scale of Lee's invasion in the summer of 1863; outright military victory was now probably beyond its capacity. But such outright victory had never been the requisite of Southern success. If the Rebels could stave off military defeat, they might gain what they wanted by other means. War weariness, frustration and internal dissension in the North might yet tip the balance in favor of the South's independence — and in 1864 Lincoln and the Republican Party would face a presidential election.

During the heady days of July 1863, excited Northerners again speculated that the war would be over by Christmas. Just four months later, when Lincoln made one of his rare excursions beyond Washington to attend the dedication of the military cemetery at Gettysburg, the fortunes of the North had once more receded. Lee and Meade were watching each other warily in northern Virginia, not many miles from where their armies had been at the beginning of the year. Vast expenditure of effort, resources and, above all, blood seemed to have ended in stalemate.

At Gettysburg that November, Lincoln spoke second, after the main orator of the occasion had delivered his formal two-hour address. Lincoln's speech lasted little more than two minutes; many of his audience scarcely heard him and much of the press thought his paltry few words unequal to the occasion. But those words have become an indelible part of the American political tradition. In seeking to define the war aims of the Union, Lincoln arrived at a definition of democracy itself. He had consistently taken the view that the cause of the Union was the cause of democracy everywhere. He urged the Northern people to dedicate themselves to the unfinished work which the Gettysburg dead had so nobly advanced and thus to ensure that 'government of the people, by the people, for the people, shall not perish from the earth' — from the earth, be it noted, and not just from the United States. Abraham Lincoln never had any doubt about the universal significance of what was happening at Gettysburg and on all the other battlefields of the Civil War.

10 Tightening the squeeze

The anticlimax which had soon followed the euphoria induced in the North by Gettysburg and Vicksburg was to last for some time. The two armies in Virginia settled for caution and dug themselves in for the winter. Having accomplished his mission to clear the Mississippi, Grant turned his thoughts to an attack on Mobile on the Gulf Coast, a center of Confederate blockade-running, but received neither the forces nor the encouragement for such a venture. A series of amphibious operations during the summer and autumn against Charleston, another blockade-running port as well as the infamous symbol of secession in many Northern eyes, all ended in costly failure. The central front in Tennessee, where a decisive move by either side might have tilted the balance of advantage in Virginia or Mississippi, had been quiet for so long that it came as something of a surprise when a Northern offensive gathered momentum during the autumn. It was not until the closing weeks of the year, however, that this campaign produced a clear Union success.

During such periods of frustration and disappointment, when an end of the war seemed as far away as ever, Northern morale was put severely to the test. The Union home front was plagued by many of the problems that beset the South, though seldom to the same degree. Inflation, profiteering, sectional grievances, political backbiting and dissension, uneven and unfair distribution of the war's burdens, conscription and the deep resentment that its implementation aroused, all posed a threat to the continuing commitment to the struggle by Northerners and depressed morale among large groups of the population.

Although modest by comparison with what was happening in the South, inflation in the North was outstripping the wage raises of most workers. As usual it was the poor who felt the pinch worst, while many merchants and manufacturers were making handsome profits from war contracts as well as benefiting from the boom that was gathering momentum in much of the economy. The wartime boom had its distinctly seamy side. Reports of racketeering and corruption in handling government contracts were commonplace and contained a large measure of truth. Profiteers and cheats flaunted their sudden, ill-gotten wealth and there sprang up what the newspapers dubbed the 'shoddy aristocracy'. During the autumn of 1863 the *New York Herald* complained bitterly:

> The world has seen its iron age, its silver age, its golden age and its brazen age. This is the age of shoddy . . . Their professions and occupations are pure shoddy. They are shoddy brokers in Wall Street, or shoddy manufacturers of shoddy goods, or shoddy contractors for shoddy articles for a shoddy government. Six days a week they are shoddy businessmen. On the seventh day they are shoddy Christians.

105. *The Civil War was the first media war. Northern newspapers sent scores of journalists to cover every battle. This team of the* New York Herald *even had their own wagon. Not every general welcomed their presence of course*

The number of millionaires in New York and other major cities grew by leaps and bounds. Many of the great financial and industrial giants of later days were set on the path to wealth and power by the Civil War and many of the great American family fortunes began at this time. Andrew Carnegie, John D. Rockefeller, Marshall Field, Jay Gould,   J. Pierpont Morgan and others all exploited in their own ways the business opportunities that the war offered and never forgot the lessons that it taught them, not least the advantages of efficient organization and the economies of large-scale enterprise. Industry was encouraged by government to think in national terms as seldom before; one consequence was the establishment for the first time of nationwide business and trade associations.

There were also other encouraging signs. Fortuitous discoveries of oil in northwestern Pennsylvania and of gold and silver in Nevada and Colorado made little difference to the war effort but were impressive evidence of the potential for growth of the Union economy, even under the pressures of war. The productivity of Northern and especially Northwestern farmers was such that, in addition to feeding the Federal armies, they were able to double exports of grain to Europe to compensate for bad harvests there. This not only helped the balance of payments, hit by the loss of cotton exports, but also made up for the denial of Southern markets. American pork and bacon were in much demand

and as a result Chicago was launched on its career as the great center of American meat-packing and processing. The 'Porkopolis of the West' quadrupled its output during the war, while the population of the city doubled in a few years. Canned fruits and vegetables, and even condensed milk, met the needs of the Northern armies and production soared.

Perhaps the best indication of faith in the future was that Congress found the time and the inclination, in the midst of bloody struggle, to pass major economic and social legislation which may have been of little or no immediate help in waging the war but was of immense consequence for later generations. In some cases these were measures which had long been held up by Southern obstruction, for example, the Homestead Act, passed in May 1862, under which genuine settlers could acquire 160 acres of public lands free of charge simply by working them for five years. Some 15,000 families were to benefit in this way, to the tune of $2\frac{1}{2}$ million acres, mostly in the West, by the war's end in 1865. The College Land Grant Act of 1862 led directly to the founding of such distinguished institutions of higher learning in the East as Cornell, Rutgers, Brown and the Massachusetts Institute of Technology, as well as most of the state universities of the West. The Pacific Railroad Act of the same year paved the way for the realisation of the great dream of a transcontinental railroad, while the National Banking Acts of 1863 and 1864 established a framework which lasted half a century until the inauguration of the Federal Reserve system during Woodrow Wilson's presidency.

Of all the causes of turmoil and discontent on the home front, none was more serious than the draft. The Confederacy had resorted to conscription in April 1862 but the Union, with its much larger pool of manpower, was able to defer it for almost a year. Some individual states had introduced their own versions of the draft in 1862 but Congress did not pass its Enrolment Act until March 3, 1863. The measure was prompted not only by a slump in recruiting after such costly battles as Antietam and Fredericksburg but also by concern over the expiry of earlier enlistments, particularly two-year volunteers who had joined up at the start of the war. In addition, the ranks of the armies in the field were thinning because of desertion.

The Enrolment Act made every able-bodied male in the Union between the ages of 20 and 45 liable for call up. As in the South, substitution was permitted, and little or no stigma was attached to it. Moreover anyone could escape the draft by paying $300, about half the average annual wage of an artisan. This practice, known as 'commutation', was resented by poorer workers as an unfair privilege that favoured the better off, and in the run-up to the election of 1864 the Republican majority in Congress was persuaded to drop it except in the case of conscientious objectors. Lincoln argued that commutation actually served to make the option of avoiding military service open to a wider section of the community; without it, he said, the price of buying a substitute would be very much higher! The Andrew Carnegies, John D. Rockefellers and Jay Goulds bought themselves out of war service in this way while they pursued their business careers.

As a direct means of raising large numbers of men, the draft failed. Indirectly however its great achievement was to encourage more men to volunteer since, by doing so, they could choose their own regiment and could take advantage of the substantial bounties on offer. Bounties and the draft became the carrot and the stick of the new recruitment policy. Conscription was unpopular in principle, and even more so in practice, on account of the

106. *The street in New York City where this lynching occurred in July 1863 was, ironically, called Charleston*

real or alleged unfairness in its enforcement. It led to violent protests in various towns and cities, particularly in the Midwest, and some draft officials were murdered. But the worst rioting — indeed, some of the worst street violence in American history — took place in New York City in July 1863, just 10 days after the great Union victory at Gettysburg. It is estimated that over 100 people died in the riots, but some of the wilder rumors at the time put the casualties at several hundred, if not indeed several thousand. The disturbances began as a protest against the first draft under the new law but they quickly turned into an ugly race riot in which at least a dozen blacks were senselessly lynched by the mob. Democratic politicians had been whipping up opposition to the draft for some time, linking it with emancipation and playing upon fears that men who were drafted might return to find their jobs taken by black workers. The resentment towards blacks in many working-class and immigrant communities had been inflamed by recent strikes in which employers had used blacks as strike-breakers.

The New York violence was sparked off when the first names called under the draft included many which were unmistakably Irish, such as O'Reilly, McGuire, O'Shaughnessy and McManus. This was too much for men in the Irish community, already unenthusiastic about the war. They set fire to the draft office and then rampaged through the city, burning public buildings and the homes of prominent Republicans, seizing weapons from the armory and attacking blacks whom they found on the streets. The rioting lasted for several days and it took the recall of units from the Army of the

107. *Timber from Lookout Mountain was used to rebuild the wagon bridge over the Tennessee River at Chattanooga*

Potomac finally to quell it. Most of the casualties occurred when rioters were shot down by soldiers and feelings continued to run high. Many of the bodies were buried secretly in the graveyard of the old St Patrick's Cathedral in lower Manhattan. For the rest of the war, many Irish Americans remained convinced that they were being forced to shoulder an unfair burden in a conflict that was no longer being fought just to save the Union but was being prolonged to free the slaves, who would then become a threat to their jobs and future prospects. Anti-black feeling on the one side and anti-Irish feeling on the other were part of the bitter legacy of the Civil War in New York and in other cities too.

The turbulence on the home front contrasted with a period of quiescence on the battlefield. The one campaign of major significance in the second half of 1863 took place in Tennessee. In this crucial theater, where each side hoped for an opportunity to drive a wedge between its opponent's positions in Virginia and Mississippi, very little had happened since the Stones River battle at the beginning of the year. The two armies sat facing each other at a distance of 30 miles or so in central Tennessee. Braxton Bragg, the local Confederate commander, felt that his considerable numerical inferiority ruled out any possibility of him affording an offensive, while Southern cavalry played enough havoc with Union supply lines to subdue the aggressive instincts, which had never been very conspicuous, of the Northern commander, William S. Rosecrans.

Even Lincoln failed to prod him into action and was on the point of replacing him when at last, in late June, Rosecrans began an advance. Within a matter of days he had surprised everyone, including himself, by skilfully maneuvering Bragg out of his defensive positions in middle Tennessee and forcing him back towards Chattanooga, which stood on a vital east-west rail link where the Tennessee River cut a gap through the formidable barrier of the mountains to the north and south. Chattanooga's capture would threaten further division of the Confederacy and provide a springboard to penetrate northern Georgia, in the direction of Atlanta, now one of the key communication and manufacturing centers of the South. Rosecrans's success coincided with Gettysburg and Vicksburg, and he always complained that his own achievement was undervalued because it was not 'written in blood'. Perhaps made wary by his easy initial success and certainly concerned for his lengthening supply lines, Rosecrans resisted Lincoln's pleas to press ahead, preferring first to build up his forces. He also wanted to synchronize his next move with the advance of the newly formed Army of the Ohio from Kentucky towards Knoxville in eastern Tennessee, so as to protect his left flank. The advance did not happen until August, and Knoxville fell on September 3. By this time, Rosecrans too was advancing, leaving part of his army in front of Chattanooga while the rest swept through two mountain passes to the south to outflank Bragg's forces there. The Confederates evacuated the city but, by contriving to make their withdrawal look like a disorderly retreat, baited a trap into which Rosecrans rushed headlong. Bragg was now in a position to attack separately one or more of the three groups of the Union army which, because of the difficulties of the terrain, were strung out over a wide area with little communication between them. In addition, he was about to be reinforced by two divisions under Longstreet, detached for the occasion from Lee's army in Virginia and sent on an extraordinary 10-day rail journey by a roundabout route of almost 1,000 miles, involving 16 transfers from one line to another.

Having missed earlier opportunities to strike at the divided Federal forces, Bragg might have been well advised to wait until Longstreet's men had all arrived and recovered from their arduous trip. He would then have enjoyed the rare luxury for a Confederate commander of near parity with his opponent. Meanwhile Rosecrans had got wind of the trap set for him and managed to gather most of his troops 12 miles south of Chattanooga, along Chickamauga Creek, a name which in Cherokee has the ominous meaning of 'river of blood'. The ensuing battle on September 19 and 20 produced some of the most savage as well as the most chaotic fighting of the war. Much of it took place in thick woods amid tangled underbrush. Communication was difficult and coordinating the movements of large numbers of men almost impossible.

The first day's fighting was bloody but inconclusive. However, at a crucial moment on the second day, a confused order from Rosecrans, all too literally obeyed by a subordinate commander, left a gap in the Union line just at a point where a Confederate attack was about to be launched. The Northern defenses were breached, their forces split and a part of them, including Rosecrans, humiliatingly routed. Only the determined action of another general, George H. Thomas — thereafter known as the 'Rock of Chickamauga' — prevented total disaster and allowed the Union army to withdraw to the safety of Chattanooga.

The defeat plunged the North once more into despondency while, after the setbacks of midsummer, it provided a cause for some rejoicing in the South. Confederate casualties, however, were proportionately as well as numerically higher than the Union's — more than 18,000 as against 16,000 — which represented in total almost 30 per cent of those taking part. The carnage among senior officers was particularly heavy on both sides. For the Rebels, with their dwindling pool of manpower, such losses were now virtually irreplaceable, whereas Federal resources of men and material seemed inexhaustible. Once again there was no vigorous pursuit of the retreating army, for this was one more battle where the victor was as disorganized as the vanquished. Many in the South sensed another missed opportunity, especially when Braxton Bragg appeared content to sit and wait for the Union army in Chattanooga to be starved into submission. Wrangling among the Confederate generals became so serious that Jefferson Davis himself made the long journey to visit the army, only to stick by Bragg even after hearing numerous complaints of inadequacies levelled against him.

Bragg's army dominated the high ground around Chattanooga. His main position was on the formidable Missionary Ridge to the east but he also had troops on the massive Lookout Mountain to the south which commanded the major supply route into the city from the west along the line of the Tennessee River. Attempts were made to bring food and ammunition to the Union forces by tracks through the mountains to the north but such a supply line could not meet the army's needs and in any case the wagon convoys faced harassment from Rebel cavalry. For a time, starvation or surrender appeared the garrison's almost certain fate, for Rosecrans showed no inclination to fight his way out. However, Lincoln, always concerned about east Tennessee, was determined to hold Chattanooga. He now put Grant in overall command of the western armies and replaced Rosecrans with George H. Thomas. At the same time troops were transferred from Virginia; two corps of the Army of the Potomac, under Hooker, were carried by rail to Tennessee and further reinforcements, led by Sherman, made their way from Mississippi.

Within days of Grant's arrival in the area in late October, the siege of Chattanooga was lifted, not by any stroke of genius but by the kind of application, determination and dynamism that generals like Rosecrans so conspicuously lacked. Grant was aided and abetted by Bragg's failure to ensure that his grip on the western approaches to the city was really secure. The Confederate commander made things even worse for himself by detaching part of his army for a futile move against Knoxville to the north, just at the time Grant was preparing to go on to the offensive. His plan was not to make a direct assault on Bragg's central position on Missionary Ridge but to attack the two ends of his line.

On November 24, Hooker's men scaled Lookout Mountain and drove off the outnumbered Rebels in an almost bloodless, though daring, encounter amid the swirling mists, which gained the romantic name of the 'Battle Above The Clouds'. But on the following day Hooker was slow to move against the southern end of Missionary Ridge, while Sherman was being frustrated in his attempts to dislodge the Confederates at the northern end. To help them both Grant ordered Thomas to mount a diversion against the center of the Confederate line. What happened next defied all the lessons of previous Civil War battles on the suicidal risks of frontal assaults. Coming under heavy fire at the foot of the ridge, Thomas's men began to charge up its steep face. The Rebel guns could not be sufficiently depressed to shoot at them as they scrambled up the hill. They kept going and, in one of the most dramatic moments of the war, swept the Southerners in panic from what had been thought an impregnable position.

108. *Unloading bales of cotton from blockade-runners in the Bahamas during 1864. Nassau,*
     then British, was one of the many ports where trading was conducted between North and
     South

Chickamauga had been avenged in truly remarkable fashion by a general whose victory was the product of an irresistible combination of resolution and sheer luck. This time the victors did pursue the vanquished but the Confederates fought back valiantly and managed to regroup on a line some 25 miles to the south, albeit within Georgia, before the weather deteriorated and both sides holed up for the winter. Even his close friendship with Jefferson Davis could not save Braxton Bragg after such a disaster and he was replaced by Joseph E. Johnston. More importantly for the outcome of the war, Chattanooga finally established Grant's reputation as the North's most aggressive and efficient general. He was soon destined for even greater responsibilities. Meanwhile, during the winter, Chattanooga was turned into a massive supply base and staging post for the next advance towards Atlanta. Freight trains trundled into the town, once bridges had been repaired, tunnels redug and road-beds relaid. Huge numbers of fresh horses had to be found and forage gathered to feed them. Such were the North's resources that demands on this scale could now be taken in its stride.

For the South, it was a different story. By the winter of 1863 it seemed to be losing the war on the home front as well as on the battlefield. Morale within its armies was sagging. Although the muster rolls recorded their strength at 465, 000, only 278,000 were actually available for duty. Some of the remainder were temporarily absent, many were sick, still

109.   Blacks were put to work for the Northern armies almost as soon as they crossed the lines. This group are teamsters with supply wagons

more thousands had deserted. A large number had not been paid for months and most were on only half rations. Morale among civilians was no better. Shortages of all kinds, and particularly food shortages, added to the depression. Bread was being baked out of rice flour; tea was brewed from sage, holly or blackberry leaves; coffee made from yams, peanuts or okra seeds; whiskey distilled from anything that would ferment; sea-water boiled to extract salt; sunflower oil substituted for butter and lard, and sorghum for sugar.

Inflation had long since got out of hand. Whereas wages had merely risen threefold, prices in the Confederacy were 28 times what they had been three years before; by March 1864 they would be 41 times higher and at the war's end a staggering 92 times higher. Within four months during the winter of 1863 the price of flour, for instance, quadrupled in Richmond. In such conditions, the black market inevitably flourished.

Trading with the enemy was now quite flagrant. The authorities of both sides had given up any pretense of discouraging it, let alone preventing it. On balance the South probably benefited more than the North and by condoning such trading the Union leadership may have helped to prolong the war. Lincoln was well aware of the trade but was desperately anxious to acquire supplies of cotton wherever they could be found. In the South the loss of Kentucky and Tennessee, the main pork-producing states in the Confederacy, led to severe food shortages and for long spells Lee's army depended heavily on salt pork and bacon bought through the lines. Although he strongly disapproved of the practice, Lee had to accept its existence.

Whereas Southern cotton and Southern tobacco were most in demand in the North, almost everything was needed in the South. When traders could make an instant 1,000 or so per cent profit by moving goods across the lines, they were going to find ways of doing business. Some of the methods used were ingenious, such as Southern belles concealing medicines within their crinolines; others were macabre — coffins meant for Confederate corpses were loaded instead with rifles and ammunition; occasionally they were just blatant, when front-line officers were bribed to turn a blind eye to it all.

As the South dipped ever more deeply into its manpower pool, it grew more dependent on its slave labor force which, ironically, came to play a vital role in the Confederate war effort. Large numbers of workers in the armaments factories were black and many slaves had been impressed into service as military laborers to dig trenches, build fortifications, drive wagon-teams, cook, clean and indeed do almost anything short of firing a gun. A lively debate developed both in the army and outside it over the question of actually enlisting slaves in the Confederate army — with or without the promise of freedom after the war. The nature of the peculiar institution was inevitably changing quite radically. More and more slaves were living away from the plantations and the traditional pattern of slave control, and were enjoying far greater mobility and freedom than they had experienced before. Some were being paid wages and were finding their own lodgings in the towns. Harassment and discrimination were still the norm and slave-codes by and large had not been relaxed but such slaves were no longer under the beady eye of the master or overseer. On the plantation itself, discipline was often less rigid simply because there were fewer able-bodied white males around to enforce it; many plantations were now managed by women or older men. But also, realizing that their bondsmen might be much more easily tempted to run away, owners prudently tried to avoid antagonizing them. In many cases, slaves in their turn were letting their masters know just what they were prepared to tolerate.

Even so, under the circumstances it is perhaps surprising that there were no large-scale slave uprisings, though the possibility was a constant threat and the Confederate leadership had to look over its shoulder to guard against the potential enemy within. Most slaves were far from revolutionary in their attitudes and behavior and were apprehensive of risking their families in any sort of trouble. Particularly after Lincoln's Emancipation Proclamation of September 1862, many realized that time was probably on their side and preferred simply to wait and see what would happen. Those who were more impatient for freedom could always walk off the plantation and cross the Union lines — an option that became more and more feasible as the war was brought nearer to the main centers of slave population.

The attitudes of many Southern whites towards their peculiar institution were confused and complicated by their wartime experience and this added to the internal tensions of the Confederacy itself. Mary Chesnut from South Carolina confided to her diary how much she now hated slavery:

We are human beings of the nineteenth century and slavery has to go, of course. All that has been gained by it goes to the North and to Negroes. The slave owners, when they are good men and women, are the martyrs.

There was a movement during the war to reform slavery. Seeing the bloody conflict as a judgement not on the peculiar institution itself but on unjust features of the system, the reformers pleaded for greater respect for slave marriage and family life, and more attention to be given to slave religion and education.

In the North, it was only after the terrible losses at Antietam and elsewhere that the idea of recruiting black troops began to attract wider support. The leaders of the free black community had been pressing for such action since the war's outset, arguing that once former slaves had fought for their country they would not be denied eventual full citizenship. In the words of the black abolitionist Frederick Douglass,

Once let the black man get upon his person the brass letters, US; let him get an eagle on his button, and a musket on his shoulder and bullets in his pocket, and there is no power on earth which can deny that he has earned the right to citizenship.

Some whites had long opposed the recruitment of blacks as a slur on the capability of whites to fight their own battles. 'This is a government of white men, made by white men for white men, to be administered, protected, defended, and maintained by white men,' was how one Democratic congressman had put it. Iowa's Governor Kirkwood bluntly stated the opposite argument in his comment that before the war was over he wanted to see 'some dead niggers as well as dead white men'. Lincoln himself had previously expressed doubts publicly about the blacks' military value and he approached the whole subject with great circumspection.

Despite various local initiatives in the first year or so of the war, the recruitment of black regiments did not amount to much until the second Emancipation Proclamation in January 1863. Progress was slow at first. Only two regiments were in existence by the spring of 1863 but there were 60 in all by the end of that year and 80 more in 1864. Eventually almost 200,000 blacks fought on the Union side, about a tenth of the total strength, and nearly 3,000 of them were killed in action. Their contribution, while seldom spectacular, was still notable and was sufficient to cause many Northern whites to revise their opinion of their black brethren. Yet the black troops suffered all manner of discrimination. They were at first not paid the same as their white counterparts — the 54th and 55th Massachusetts regiments, having been promised equal pay on enlistment, refused all pay for two years until the matter was settled in their favor. Nor did black soldiers have the same opportunities for promotion: less than 100 ever became officers and even then none ranked higher than captain. When Frederick Douglass took such complaints to Lincoln, he was told that blacks should be pleased that they were able to fight at all. When they did fight, they also faced the threat from the Confederate leadership to execute any captured black officers and to return ordinary black soldiers to slavery. There were many stories of atrocities allegedly committed against black troops but the worst recorded incident was at

110. More and more black regiments were mustered as the war drew to its climax. Mixed units were, of course, unthinkable in the climate of opinion then. Abolitionists were convinced that once blacks had donned Union uniforms political and social rights would follow

Fort Pillow in Tennessee in April 1864 when a number were slaughtered in cold blood by Rebel cavalry after they had surrendered.

Yet for all the inadequacies and injustices in its implementation, the raising of black regiments was one of the most remarkable, even revolutionary, developments of the whole war. In the racial climate of 1860, it would have been unthinkable to the great majority of white Americans that thousands of blacks should be put into uniform and armed against other white Americans. By 1865, those black soldiers were accepted by most and welcomed by many. That they still encountered discrimination served to show that four years of war might change many attitudes but could not eradicate dyed-in-the-wool prejudice.

Military service was only the most conspicuous of the many ways in which former slaves contributed to the process of their own liberation. Many thousands crossed into the Federal lines in pursuit of their freedom and even greater numbers welcomed the Northern armies as they advanced further into the South. The Union government and army faced formidable problems in coping with the numbers of slaves or ex-slaves now under their control, both in terms of meeting their basic need for food and shelter, and in considering their longer-term future. Often their treatment was not as sensitive as it should have been, nor their reception as warm as it might have been. Some blacks were driven to the sad conclusion that there was not much difference between freedom and slavery. Crammed into improvised camps, they were vulnerable to disease and white Yankee predators. A great number died before enjoying the fruits of emancipation more than a few were parted from their miserable possessions and had such unhappy experiences at the hands of their Northern 'liberators' that it affected their attitudes to the new Union for the rest of their lives.

Those who stayed on the plantations often found themselves put to work for a new master who could be every bit as tyrannical — and in his attitude to black women, every bit as lascivious — as the old. But there were also many compassionate and sincere overseers and officials involved in dealing with the freedmen. What the former slaves cried out for was land on which they could settle and from which they could derive a livelihood, but Lincoln, like most Northerners, was not yet ready for anything so radical as a major redistribution of property. Their other plea, for education, was met to some extent, mainly by missionaries and voluntary aid societies, much of whose teaching was geared to imparting the free-labor ethic. The question of giving the freedman the vote was, as yet, scarcely on the agenda of practical politics.

However, 1863 had seen a dramatic change in attitude towards the blacks in the North. At the beginning of the year, following the formal proclamation of emancipation, there had been increased desertions among many Midwestern regiments, particularly by men from areas like southern Illinois, in Lincoln's home state, who refused to fight 'to free the Negroes and enslave the whites'. During the elections for state legislatures held that spring and early summer, Republicans had been under considerable pressure but by the fall, wherever emancipation was an issue in such elections, the party seeking to exploit the race issue, the Democrats, received a drubbing. A Midwestern editorial writer declared in December that, if Lincoln's Emancipation Proclamation had been put to a vote the year before, 'there is little doubt that the voice of a majority would have been against it. And yet not a year has passed before it is approved by an overwhelming majority.' Perhaps the most compelling comment was that confided in his diary by a Baltimore freed slave:

> This year has brought about many changes that at the beginning were or would have been thought impossible. The close of the year finds me a soldier for the cause of my race. May God bless the cause, and enable me in the coming year to forward it on.

11 Further deadlock

Many in the South had known from the start that any attempt to out-produce or overpower the North was futile and that the answer to Northern strength and numbers lay in Southern resilience and resourcefulness. The important thing was to keep the struggle going until the North decided that it had had enough and could not win. Meantime, ingenuity and innovation must be sought to offset Northern superiority in manpower and productive capacity.

Nowhere was such inventiveness more clearly displayed than in the war at sea, where those responsible for Confederate naval policy were ready to resort to the unconventional and the experimental in a bid to counter the Union's formidable advantages. This had led to the improvisation of their first ironclad, the *Merrimac*, and to their pioneering use of floating mines, or torpedoes as they were then called, in rivers and coastal waters. By the war's end some 43 Federal vessels, including four powerful Monitors, had been sunk or damaged in this way.

The same bold approach led to experiments with submarines cranked by hand. After a series of costly disasters, which earned it the nickname of 'the peripatetic coffin', the minuscule Confederate submarine *Hunley* sank the Federal gunboat *Housatonic* with a torpedo just outside Charleston harbor on February 17, 1864. This, the first submarine 'kill' anywhere, was suicidal as well as successful, since the *Hunley*'s eight-man crew perished with its victim.

The South had better luck with its custom-built commerce raiders aimed at sweeping Northern shipping from the seas. Most of them were built in British shipyards and caused a series of bitter diplomatic disputes between London and Washington, particularly as they often carried a large complement of British officers and crew. The two most successful, the *Alabama* and the *Florida*, both products of Birkenhead on the Mersey, between them captured, burned or sank nearly 200 Union merchant vessels before they met their end in the summer and fall of 1864. The *Alabama*'s quite spectacular demise was during a gun-fight with the Federal sloop *Kearsarge* off Cherbourg in full view of French shore-watchers one Sunday morning in mid-June — trainloads of sightseers had come down from Paris especially for the occasion. The *Florida* came to a more inglorious end; she was captured by a Union warship while at anchor in the Brazilian port of Bahia in October and sank after a collision while being towed northwards.

The commerce raiders were certainly successful in driving Union ships from the high seas, though perhaps not exactly in the way originally planned. Many Northern merchant vessels simply passed into other ownership, principally British, or Northern cargoes were carried in non-Northern ships, again principally British ones. Indeed the main beneficiary

111.   Union ships were being fitted with heavier and heavier guns for siege activities. This is a 13-inch mortar mounted on a schooner based on Richmond's James River during 1864

of the exploits of the commerce raiders was not the cause of Southern independence but rather British maritime interests. Like the blockade-runners, they operated more often than not from British-controlled ports like Nassau in the Bahamas and St George in Bermuda as well as occasionally from havens elsewhere in the Caribbean and the Atlantic.

Naval strategy and diplomacy went hand in hand so far as the Confederacy was concerned. The exploits of its commerce raiders were meant not only to embarrass the North but to bring maximum publicity to the South and if possible to embroil one or two neutrals in the conflict. However, the diplomatic struggle almost got out of hand with the furor over the building at Birkenhead during 1863 of the Laird rams, which were well-armed ironclads, intended to be the most powerful afloat. These were clearly a different proposition from the commerce raiders and could not possibly be passed off as anything other than warships. What with talk of them being used to hold New York to ransom they assumed in Southern eyes almost magical powers, as well as offering more realistic prospects of smashing the blockading vessels off the Confederate coast, which might just tilt the balance of the war their way in the nick of time. Such was the pressure of protest on the British government that in the end it bought the rams for the Royal Navy, though not before the spying and counter-spying exploits of both sides in the streets and pubs of Merseyside and Clydeside, as well as the clubs and bars of Westminster itself, had reached quite ludicrous proportions. Even the United States minister in London, the normally cautious Charles Francis Adams, was moved to warn the British government in stark terms of the implication of any decision to release the Rams. 'It would be superfluous in me,' he wrote to the British foreign secretary, 'to point out to your Lordship that this is war.'

Thereafter the Confederates switched their shipbuilding efforts to France, where for a time it looked as though they might be more successful. In the end, however, they fell victim to Napoleon III's prevarications. He had enough problems of his own elsewhere in Europe as well as in Mexico, which he had unwisely invaded in 1862 on the pretext of collecting debts — not just his but those of other powers including Britain and Spain — although his motives had more to do with illusions of imperial grandeur. His Mexican venture had already brought him into conflict with the Union and, as with other colonial expeditions of this sort, the difficulty was to extricate himself without loss of face.

As the blockade became tighter, the Confederacy went into the blockade-running business itself. Previously this had been in the hands of private enterprise, though the Richmond government had always been the runners' best customer, but in 1863 the Confederacy began to acquire ships of its own, as well as commandeering half the outbound cargo space on existing vessels and claiming first option on half the incoming cargo. By this time Charleston, Wilmington, Mobile and Galveston, Texas, were the main blockade-running centers left within the Confederacy. Since Charleston enjoyed the advantage of being only a short voyage to and from Nassau and Bermuda, it was much favored by blockade-runners and hence became a prime target for Federal attention. After an attempted assault by land during the summer of 1862 had ended in total disaster, the North expended much effort throughout 1863 and 1864 in seaborne assaults on Charleston. In April 1863 a fleet of Union ironclads received a terrible mauling from the guns of Sumter and other forts while trying unsuccessfully to penetrate the harbor. However, in July, Federal troops secured a beach-head at enormous cost on Morris Island to the south of Sumter. From there they pounded away at Fort Wagner, but a desperate assault failed to capture it. The attacking force included the 54th Massachusetts, a black regiment which fought bravely and incurred heavy casualties. One of its number won the Congressional Medal of Honor, the first black to do so, and the performance of the troops was a landmark in winning recognition of the contribution of blacks to the war effort.

For a while even the city of Charleston itself was shelled, to the jubilation of the Northern press, for, as the symbol of secession and the birthplace of the rebellion, it had long been a focus of Northern fury. Scruples about endangering the civilian population had faded as people became inured to the war's rising horrors. The Union assaults succeeded at least in putting paid to Charleston's contribution to blockade-running, which thereafter was centered on Wilmington in North Carolina and Mobile, Alabama; even at this late stage in the war, two out of three runners were still getting through. The Union had long had its eyes on Wilmington but all attempts to increase its precarious foothold on North Carolina's shores, secured during the early months of the conflict, came to nought in 1863 and 1864.

Early 1864 was a frustrating time for the Union generally. A raid into Florida was thwarted in February. Sherman's foray the same month in southern Mississippi came unstuck at the hands of Confederate cavalry under Nathan Bedford Forrest, who had gone on to harry Federal garrisons throughout Tennessee and even Kentucky. The only relief from

112–114.   By the summer of 1863 the war had returned to Charleston, though this time it was the   Northern guns that did the bombarding

the stalemate in Virginia came from an escapade by the Union cavalry, which took them close to Richmond but then ended in failure. Contrary to other impressions, it seemed that there was still a lot of life left in the Confederacy. Morale remained high among the front-line Southern troops, helped by a religious revival that winter. Although the Rebel armies were declining in numbers, they were now composed mainly of battle-hardened veterans, prepared to see the struggle through, come what may. The North, on the other hand, was once more facing recruiting problems. Re-enlistment was at a low ebb and, in a bid to increase numbers, all manner of bounties and other inducements were offered, which resulted in officers complaining of the low standard of many of the replacements.

One hopeful sign for the Union, however, was that at long last it found the right structure and the right man for its military high command. In March 1864 Lincoln promoted Grant to lieutenant-general, the first to hold that rank since George Washington, and put him in overall charge of the Federal armies East and West, which by then mustered well over half a million men. Intended perhaps to be the President's main military figure in Washington, Grant preferred instead to make his headquarters in the field, alongside the existing commander of the Army of the Potomac, George Meade. His aim was to utilize the North's greater numbers and resources to the full by squeezing the Confederacy hard, going for its armies relentlessly, giving them no chance to regroup or to recover, in the belief that sooner rather than later they would collapse. He was resolved, too, to hit them on as many fronts as possible and, with this in mind, was determined that the eastern and western campaigns should be coordinated and synchronized, something that Lincoln, for all his persistent prodding, had hitherto been unable to achieve.

Grant's grand plan was for the Army of the Potomac to maintain pitiless pressure on Lee, while two smaller armies pressed in on his flanks from the Shenandoah Valley and up the James River from Fort Monroe — the latter an echo of McClellan's earlier Peninsula campaign. It was meant to be a pincer movement, though Lincoln described it in more colloquial terms as 'those not skinning can hold a leg'. Meanwhile, Sherman, who had succeeded Grant in the West, would strike against the second main Confederate army under Joseph Johnston, drive him back to Atlanta and then press on to destroy the capacity and the will of the Rebels to continue the war.

Once again, even the best-laid plans were not followed. Sherman was meant to be helped by a move along the Gulf Coast to Mobile from New Orleans but this force was diverted at the last minute by Lincoln for an abortive advance towards Texas, intended both as a warning to Napoleon III in Mexico and as a raid on the rich cotton supplies of the region. It achieved neither goal and only extricated itself somewhat ignominiously. Similarly, the force that was supposed to threaten Lee's rear by way of the James River was thwarted in early May 7 miles short of the Confederate capital and boxed itself into a position where it was easily contained. Worse still for Grant, the Rebels in the Shenandoah Valley, although outnumbered, routed the Federals there in a battle at New Market on May 15 which is remembered warmly by Southerners for a brave attack on an artillery position by several hundred teenage cadets from a local military school.

The main assault was to be against Lee near the same spot where Hooker had come to grief at his hands the year before at Chancellorsville. On May 4, after many months of virtual inactivity, Meade's troops, now numbering more than 120,000 compared with Lee's force of barely 60,000, began crossing the Rapidan tributary of the Rappahannock River, a mere 60 miles from the Confederate capital. The hope, and the expectation, was that this would be the final campaign of the war. Grant had assured both his troops and the President that there would be no turning back.

His aim was to threaten Lee's eastern flank, cut him off from Richmond and the south, and force him out of his entrenchments to do battle in the open. The plan almost worked but Lee read Grant's intentions accurately and the first clash occurred not in open country, but in that area of thick forest and tangled undergrowth known as the Wilderness, which had been the scene of such bitter encounters between Federals and Confederates 12 months previously. Once again the North's superiority in men and cannon would be nullified.

As before, the fighting was confused, some of the Union troops even firing on their own side. The thickets were so impenetrable in many places that the soldiers could barely see around them and some became so disoriented that they wandered away lost. In such conditions the commanders found it difficult to keep firm control over their men. Moreover, because the brush was so dry and the brambles so brittle, they caught fire easily and the flames and smoke added to the chaos. Many of the wounded were burned to death before help could reach them and scorched corpses littered the woods.

115. *Grant, never noted for his personal appearance, was once described as 'an ordinary scrubby-looking man with a slightly seedy look, as if he was out of office on half-pay'*

Much of the fighting was close, with bayonets being used as spears and rifle-butts as clubs; bodies were later found pierced by ramrods like arrows. Such was the intensity of the firing that many of the rifles became too hot to hold and some even blew up in the faces of the soldiers as cartridges ignited spontaneously. The battle became a grim, desperate nightmare, vividly remembered by the participants. As one of them wrote: 'It was as though Christian men had turned to fiends, and hell itself has usurped the place of earth.'

At the end of the first day, however, Meade appeared to have the upper hand but in the violent struggles of the following 24 hours the initiative slipped away from him. Between

116. *A remarkable photograph of a gathering of Grant with his generals on May 21, 1864, a few days after the battle of Spotsylvania. Grant is leaning over Meade's shoulder looking at a map. The pews from the nearby Massaponax Church were brought out for the occasion. The photographer captioned it 'A Council of War'*

them the two sides suffered in just two days 28,000 casualties, a sixth of those taking part. The Federals lost more numerically, though not proportionately. It was yet another battlefield stalemate. Lee had not been dislodged nor outflanked. Before, when this had occurred, the Army of the Potomac had simply retreated back to its starting point and many of the Northern veterans expected this to happen now. But next morning, without waiting to bury all his dead, let alone clear the field of everyone wounded, Grant ordered the army to move forward. This surprised many, and seemed to delight most, who felt that at long last they had a commander who meant business.

Grant's objective was still to threaten Lee's eastern flank and to try to get between him and his supply lines, while utilizing the coastal rivers for his own replenishment. The logistics of moving such a large army were now a major challenge. This time Grant moved southeast and concentrated his force at a crossroads known as Spotsylvania Court House, some 12 miles southwest of Fredericksburg, and that much nearer to Richmond, indeed controlling the shortest route to the Confederate capital.

Lee, however, anticipated his move and won the race to Spotsylvania by the narrowest of margins. When Grant's troops arrived, they found two Confederate divisions already dug in and waiting for them. Instead of a breakthrough, Grant now faced another slogging match as both sides prepared their lines of trenches and breastworks. Such tactics were becoming the norm, with a spade and axe as important for the infantryman as his rifle and bayonet. Every time Grant tried to move around Lee's position, he ran into yet another set of such earth-fortifications, each a little more impressive than the one before.

Eventually the Federals came up against a network of especially strong entrenchments which were dubbed, because of their shape, 'the Mule Shoe'. Located on the edge of thick woods, they would have to be assaulted across an open field in the face of intense cannon fire. At the apex of this line was a group of earthworks that came to be known as 'Bloody Angle' on account of the particularly vicious fighting that took place there. So frenzied was the firing at times that trees riddled through by the fusillades fell down and added to the confusion, while corpses were found later that had been cut in two by the hail of bullets.

Spotsylvania saw some of the most savage encounters of the whole war. Much of the fighting was hand to hand, with rifles being brandished like cudgels, and officers aiming their pistols at point-blank range. The constant rain contributed to the frenzy as the dead and the wounded alike were trampled into the mud and the blood from their compressed bodies stained the rifle pits red. The Confederates fought grimly on while yet another set of entrenchments was dug a mere half mile to the rear.

When nightfall on May 12 brought the noisome carnage to a close, some 14,000 bodies lay within a few hundred yards of each other and in all the casualties at Spotsylvania amounted to nearly 30,000. During the darkness the bands of both armies struck up, the Confederates first playing 'The Dead March' from Handel's Saul and then inevitably 'Bonnie Blue Flag' and 'Dixie', while the Union musicians responded with 'Nearer My God to Thee' and, equally inevitably, 'The Star Spangled Banner' and 'Home Sweet Home'.

Although he had failed to puncture Lee's line, Grant persisted for a week or so in trying to maneuver the Rebels out of their positions by steadily moving forward around their right flank, seeking to unhinge them, to side-step their defenses and find a weakness. Lee was there to meet his every gambit, to counter each sally. He had never before had to deal with such a determined opponent as Grant. Lincoln as ever was anxious for news and in the midst of all the campaigning Grant found time to telegraph him that he would 'fight it out on this line if it takes all summer'. Such language caught the mood in the North and newspaper headline-writers spread the glad phrase from coast to coast.

Even while the assault on the Mule Shoe salient was only just beginning, Grant had sent his 10,000-strong cavalry, under their new commander, the 33-year-old Philip Sheridan, on a spectacular raid through Lee's rear which brought them to the very gates of Richmond. Sheridan had distinguished himself in the storming of Chattanooga's Missionary Ridge the previous November but had hitherto been considered more of an infantryman. His foray caused alarm among the citizens of the Confederate capital and troops were hastily assembled to block his path. He destroyed vital Rebel supplies, especially of food destined for the front line, cut important telegraph wires and ripped up miles of irreplaceable rail-track. Of equal significance perhaps, his troops killed the legendary Jeb Stuart, leader for so long of Lee's cavalry, at the battle of Yellow Tavern, a few miles from Richmond. When told of the news, Lee took it particularly badly. 'I can scarcely think of him without weeping,' he confessed to one of his officers.

Although tired and weary himself, and suffering from an attack of diarrhea, Lee was not to be outwitted. He still met every maneuver of Grant's with one of his own, refusing to commit his troops to the decisive, open battle away from their trenches that the Union generals eagerly sought. Following the Spotsylvania bloodbath, his near-exhausted, perpetually hungry soldiers foot-slogged it the 20 miles or so southwards to a new set of defenses quickly prepared along the North Anna River. Here they foiled yet another attempt by the Northerners to outflank them, sustaining further losses, although the fighting was never on the scale of the Wilderness or Spotsylvania.

After spending almost five days trying to dislodge the Rebels from their strong positions along the river bank, Grant once more moved his army southeast around the right of Lee's flank across the Pamunkey River, to the swampy Totopotomoy Creek, a mere 10 miles from Richmond, which he reached late on May 29. Here he was again foiled by Lee's quick response and late on May 31 he moved yet further southwards to an isolated crossroads called Cold Harbor, so named because the inn there did not provide hot meals. It was due east of the Confederate capital, less than 9 miles away and close to the Chickahominy River, scene of fiery battles during McClellan's campaigns two years earlier.

While the Southerners frantically prepared a new line of defenses, Grant threw his tired troops against them but was again rebuffed. He was now so near to Richmond, yet still thwarted by Lee at every turn. He determined on one more all-out attack. Rain forced its postponement by a crucial 24 hours during which the Confederate fortifications were massively strengthened. As June 3 dawned, many of the Union veterans, seeing the well-placed trenches and the imposing earthworks, as well as the massed Confederate infantry and cannon spread behind them, feared the worst. Some even attached name-tags to their uniforms so that their corpses could be more easily identified.

The assault was to be one of the most costly of the war. Within barely half an hour Grant suffered 7,000 casualties, a seventh of his remaining force, and nearly five times those of the Confederates, whom he outnumbered; it was the fastest rate of killing in any of the Civil War battles. Bodies were stacked up in front of the Rebel trenches like so much cordwood and the firing was so severe that Lee later remarked that it had sounded 'like sheets ripping in the wind'. Once again Cold Harbor showed the futility of direct, frontal attacks on strong defensive positions. It was aptly said that 'this was not war, but murder'.

When some of the Union generals tried to persuade their men to renew the assault, the orders were met with sullen refusal and after a flurry of threats, few officers tried to persist. It was several hours before Meade and Grant realized the severity of their defeat; neither bothered to go and look for himself. Little attempt was made to rescue the wounded, since neither side would tacitly admit defeat by seeking a truce for the purpose. Desultory firing

117.   *Confederate losses during the May 1864 struggles were less than those of the Union, but the South was losing the flower of its manhood which could never be replaced*

continued for the next three days and it was only on June 7 that burial teams were allowed on the field, by which time the corpses were nearly unrecognizable.

Bitter recriminations followed. The South had won one of its easiest victories, while the North had suffered one of its heaviest and most pointless defeats. Grant's determination had turned into a mindless desperation which betrayed him into his bloodiest mistake. He acquired the reputation of being 'Butcher Grant', ironically from the lips of many of the same people who had recently been praising him to the skies. There were those who thought that, while he might be good enough to take on the Braxton Braggs of this world, he was no match for Robert E. Lee. Within certain circles in the North, especially among the veterans of the Army of the Potomac, Lee was beginning to attract to himself that same aura of invincibility as Rommel had with the British armies in the Libyan desert in 1941 and 1942.

In fact, Grant's campaign had not been just a crude head-bashing confrontation but a relentless, inventive search for an effective opening, which had been continually foiled by

118. *Work parties had the gruesome task after Cold Harbor of collecting the remains for reburial. Identification was virtually impossible*

a resourceful and skillful defense. Each phase had ended in bloody stalemate, though the margin between success and failure had more than once been a matter of hours or minutes — or even a few feet. Inevitably there was a great feeling of disappointment, especially after such a hopeful start to the spring. When the casualty lists for the whole campaign were published, morale in the North plummeted. Even before Cold Harbor, Grant had been losing an average of nearly 2,000 men a day for almost a month. The Army of the Potomac in fact lost 55,000 men, virtually half its strength, and its officers corps, particularly the senior ranks, had been very severely hit. Some regiments were close to mutiny.

Lee had not, of course, escaped unhurt. He had suffered 30,000 casualties, which he could not replace, but his army still retained the will to resist. They had lost some ground but gained time. More importantly, whereas Lee's reputation was intact and untarnished, his foe's prestige had been dimmed. Few stopped to consider, though, that Lee was running out of room, that he was now pushed up against the gates of his capital, in danger of being besieged there, a fate which he had always sought to avoid. For all his skill in escaping defeat, he had not been able to send the Union forces reeling homewards. Grant was still pressing him hard, secure in the knowledge that, while decisive battlefield success still eluded him, the overall strategic situation continued in his favor.

Smarting after the debacle at Cold Harbor, Grant again moved southwards, transferring his army across the James River in a bold and brilliantly executed operation. Once more, he glimpsed the possibility of bringing the war to a speedy end by positioning his army where it would leave Lee only two unpalatable options; to come out and fight in the open or stay cooped up in the capital's defenses. For at least three days in mid-June, while Lee's cavalry had been distracted so that he temporarily had no idea exactly what Grant was up

119. As 118

to and hence had delayed concentrating his forces to meet the threat, the thinly manned defenses of Petersburg, a key railroad junction some 20 miles south of Richmond and the main link with the remaining heartland of the Confederacy, were in no condition to resist a major Union assault. However, the blow never fell because of the incompetence and procrastination of some of Grant's subordinates and the lack of immediate direction from the commander himself, still supervising the crossing of the James. It was one of the biggest missed opportunities of the war. Petersburg not only survived those three days in June but nine more months of siege.

Frustration and a sense of lost chances affected the fickle Northern electorate. Lincoln, who was up for re-election later that year, became steadily convinced as the summer wore on that he could not win. He had even had problems in securing the nomination as the Republican candidate. The prevailing tradition was for presidents to serve only one term: none had been elected to a second term since 1832 and no incumbent had been renominated by his party since 1840. Nor was Lincoln short of rivals for the office,

120. Grant's crossing of the broad James River during June 1864 with his full army was one of the great logistic operations of the war and yet further evidence, if any now still had doubts, of the North's edge in such matters. This bridge was strong enough for cannon and loaded wagons

even within his own Cabinet. But he had managed to outwit them a little more easily than Lee had outwitted Grant, not least because he had built up considerable support for himself within the grass roots of his party's organization through skillful manipulation of patronage.

When, within a few days of Cold Harbor, the Republican national convention met in Baltimore, few opposed Lincoln's renomination. To broaden its appeal, the Republican Party renamed itself the National Union Party and nominated a so-called War Democrat from Tennessee, Andrew Johnson, for vice-president. For platform it rejected any compromise with the South and endorsed a constitutional amendment to abolish slavery. Lincoln's war policies to date were by and large backed, though with less than total enthusiasm, and the contentious issue of the 'reconstruction' of the Southern states was discreetly avoided. A bitter battle was raging within the Republican Party between those who supported Lincoln's moderate, essentially pragmatic approach, designed to promote the war effort as well as his own political prospects, and those who preferred a more radical and doctrinaire course of action which would impose much stiffer conditions on the Rebel states.

During that summer of 1864, Northern public opinion was not running in Lincoln's favor, particularly after the casualty figures in the Wilderness, Spotsylvania and Cold Harbor battles were released in mid-June. The Confederate leadership seemed to be succeeding in its aim of making Grant's self-styled final offensive so costly that the despairing voters in the North would seek a new president less disinclined than Lincoln to consider a negotiated peace. Many Democrats eagerly seized the opportunity to condemn the Republicans for their willingness to shed the last drop of white blood in what they saw as a struggle unnecessarily and unashamedly prolonged in order to free the blacks. Clearly the coming election campaign was going to be every bit as bitterly contested and as crucial as the fighting on the battlefield.

12 Total war

If June 1864 was an exasperating month for Grant and Lincoln, July threatened to be worse, since it began with a humiliation which boded ill for Northern morale. The attempt to drive the Rebels from the Shenandoah Valley had failed; worse still, the retreat of the Federal forces there left wide open the now classic route for a Confederate incursion into the North and put Washington itself at risk. Nor did Lee waste time in taking advantage of this opportunity. On July 5 he sent Jubal A. Early with a force of nearly 15,000 Southerners across the Potomac into Maryland. In little more than a week they were at the gates of the Federal capital, whose defenses were only thinly manned because Grant had denuded the garrison for his spring offensive. Lincoln himself came under fire when he went to watch the action.

When troops from Grant's army around Petersburg were rushed back to the capital, Early was dissuaded from attempting to enter the city. With his small force, he could not have held Washington, though even a temporary occupation, coupled with an ignominious flight of Lincoln and his Cabinet from their seat of government, or a destructive foray through the outskirts, would surely have had a devastating effect on Northern public opinion. However, Early withdrew, relatively un-harassed, back to the valley, contenting himself with extorting financial 'tribute' from various towns en route and putting property to the torch, including the home of Montgomery Blair, Lincoln's Postmaster-General, at Silver Spring, Maryland. Other of his men later that same month made further mischievous sorties, ranging as far north as Chambersburg, Pennsylvania, most of which they razed to the ground.

Stung by these persistent, damaging raids, Grant now entrusted to Philip Sheridan the task of eliminating the threat from the Shenandoah Valley once and for all. His orders were to lay waste this fertile region of Virginia, a prime source of food for Lee's army, so that, as Sheridan graphically put it, 'crows flying over it for the balance of the season will have to carry their provender with them'.

Elsewhere that July the Union forces were being foiled. Among Grant's troops around Richmond and Petersburg there had been a distinct reluctance since Cold Harbor to attack trenches and earthworks. Some assaults had faltered out of sheer insubordination by ordinary soldiers and senior officers alike. Even so, the Union suffered a further 11,000 casualties in just four days of fighting at Petersburg — nearly three times as many as the Rebels did. The war of attrition was not necessarily going the North's way. Grant's commanders were tired in mind as well as in spirit and were making even more mistakes than usual. His army was weakened, too, when thousands of veterans chose not to re-enlist that summer when their terms of duty expired. He now had to settle for a siege which, like Lee, he had sought to avoid.

121. Sherman and Grant conferring. They had been close to each other during the earlier campaigns in the West. 'He stood by me when I was crazy and I stood by him when he was drunk', was how Sherman once summed up their relationship

The frustrations of such a situation were epitomized in the attempt during late July to blow a hole in the now massive Confederate defenses at Petersburg by means of an underground mine shaft filled with four tons of gunpowder. Its very construction was a notable technical feat, since it ran more than 500 feet, required ventilation holes that the Rebels would not notice and above all had to be dug secretly. A group of former Pennsylvanian coal miners had put the idea forward and in the end carried it out. The explosion blew an enormous hole in the Confederate line and initially caused the confusion hoped for among the defenders, but the opportunity to exploit this advantage was bungled by the Northerners due to a mixture of bad leadership, faulty planning and blatant cowardice on the part of at least two Union generals, who were later cashiered. It resulted in huge loss of life on the Northern side, as volley after volley poured into men who were scrambling helplessly in the vast crater. Grant, who had at first been sceptical about the project, had come to set much store by it and was bitterly disappointed with the outcome. 'Such opportunity for carrying fortifications I have never seen, and do not expect again to have,' he reported to Washington. The crater remains to this day as a sad reminder of the debacle. For the rest of 1864 the slow, remorseless grind of siege warfare continued day after day, month after month, around Petersburg and Richmond.

If Grant himself, and Sheridan too through his exploits in the Shenandoah Valley, came to be considered as stern exponents of total war, the Civil War general most associated

122. Atlanta's railroad station. The end of the line for Sherman. A vital transport centre for the Confederacy

with that approach is William Tecumseh Sherman. He had succeeded Grant in the West and now sought to apply his brand of all-out, sustained pressure on the Confederate troops and civilians in Georgia. Sherman had begun his campaign at the same time as Grant and Meade had moved against Lee in early May. His force was only marginally smaller than that of the Army of the Potomac but his tactics were totally different. Although he outnumbered his opponent, Joseph Johnston, by almost two to one, Sherman did not immediately seek any confrontation with him, preferring each time to maneuver him out of his set positions by skillful flanking movements. Since both armies were being replenished by rail, indeed different sections of the same railroad, control — or rather protection — of that vital route was the key to the campaign. Johnston's supplies came from Atlanta, which at the beginning of the campaign was some 90 miles distant, whereas Sherman's came from Chattanooga, 25 miles away. As the months wore on, Sherman paid the price of success in his longer, more vulnerable supply line.

Sherman would not allow civilians, especially newspaper reporters, to use the railroads. Even when his soldiers went on leave, they could not go by train. Luxuries were barred and the troops were issued with only three days' rations at a time, which were expected to last five. His staff were discouraged from having large tents and numerous pack-mules.

Above all he was determined to keep his army slim for the coming battles, where he felt maneuverability and speed would be of the essence.

The terrain of northern Georgia was vastly different from that of eastern Virginia — steep mountains and deep gorges compared with slow-moving rivers and gently sloping countryside. The former offered far better defensive opportunities than the latter and Johnston, if not noted for his aggression, was a worthy opponent in a war of maneuver.

Sherman's force was made up of three armies. By far the largest, the so-called Army of the Cumberland, under George H. Thomas of Chickamauga and Missionary Ridge fame, amounted to nearly two-thirds of the total. The Army of the Tennessee, Sherman's previous command, now led by James B. McPherson, had about a quarter of the troops, while the remainder formed the Army of the Ohio commanded by John M. Schofield.

Ever since the defeats at Missionary Ridge and Lookout Mountain the previous November, the Confederates had been ensconced along a precipitous pass, aptly named Rocky Face Ridge, near Dalton and some 30 miles south of Chattanooga. Although to assault it head on would be madness, Sherman feinted as if to do so with Thomas's army, while McPherson's force found a gap in the mountains further south, through which they crossed on May 9 with the aim of cutting the railroad at Resaca, some 20 miles in Johnston's rear, and thereby trapping him. However, it so happened that reinforcements were passing through Resaca at the time, destined for Dalton, and their presence was enough to deter McPherson from proceeding. This bitterly disappointed Sherman, since he felt that he could have bagged the Rebels there and then, and thus ended the campaign almost before it had started. Not to be outdone, he switched the bulk of Thomas's army to back up McPherson but Johnston got wind of it and withdrew his whole force safely from Dalton, down the railroad to Resaca, in time to confront the Federals in strength from positions that had previously been prepared, making good use of higher ground.

After a few days of skirmishing here, the same tactic of outflanking was successfully pursued, and again at Cassville, some 30 miles nearer Atlanta, when Johnston dropped back there on May 19. It was also repeated at Allatoona Pass, another 12 miles down the railroad. So far, in sharp contrast to events in the East, there had been hardly any heavy fighting but much maneuvering and quick improvising of fortifications.

For a while in late May Sherman broke away from the route the railroad was following towards Atlanta and almost got behind Johnston's lines at Dallas, Georgia — a mere 30 miles from Atlanta — but he was halted in thick woods reminiscent of many encounters further east. For the first time there were several days of sustained fighting around a Methodist church called New Hope, which was soon nicknamed 'Hell-Hole' by the Northerners, who suffered heavy casualties there. Sudden rainstorms delayed Sherman's progress even more, making the dirt roads impassable and forcing him back on to the route of the railroad itself.

By mid-June the sides were confronting each other on the last range of hills before Atlanta, where the single track of the Western and Atlantic Railroad makes a wide sweep around the base of the Kennesaw Mountain. From the top of the mountain the town was clearly visible. By that stage of the war Atlanta had become almost as much a symbol of the Confederate cause as Richmond. It was also one of the most important manufacturing centers left in Rebel hands, as well as a vital rail junction linking the deep South with the

123.   The siege of Atlanta, 1864

124.   The siege of Atlanta, 1864

125. *The siege of Atlanta, 1864*

126. *The siege of Atlanta, 1864*

Carolinas and Virginia — hence Grant's eagerness for Sherman to capture it without delay.

Perhaps the knowledge that his goal was almost in sight made Sherman impatient, since for once he chose not to try to get around Johnston's strong positions on the mountain but instead to attack head on, possibly in the hope of catching the Confederates unawares. But they were waiting for the luckless Northerners and in a matter of hours on June 27 they inflicted more than 3, 000 casualties on them, for a mere 600 of their own. It was almost as if Cold Harbor had never happened.

Luckily for Sherman, the disaster did not receive anything like the immediate publicity such happenings were apt to attract on the eastern front. Ironically, too, at the very moment of the suicidal assault one of his subordinate commanders, John M. Schofield was in the process of successfully outflanking the mountain while its defenders were momentarily distracted by the events to their front. The lesson was not lost on Sherman, who promptly returned to his previous tactics of maneuver and feint, which again worked, with the result that by July 10 Johnston had been forced behind Peachtree Creek, the last line of defenses before Atlanta, now a mere 5 miles away. Panic seized its citizens and those who could began to leave, jamming the roads and crowding the trains going east and south, a scene which those familiar with *Gone with the Wind* will vividly recall.

Although he had delayed Sherman's advance for more than two months and had suffered only minimal casualties, Johnston, never a personal favorite of the Confederate leader, found little support from Jefferson Davis or his advisers. They feared that he would surrender Atlanta, too, without much of a fight and he was replaced on July 17 by one of his youngest subordinate commanders, John Bell Hood. Thirty-three years old, Hood had already lost an arm and a leg in previous battles and needed to be strapped in his saddle while riding. He had a superb battlefield record but lacked the intelligence and judgement for higher command. Hood could simply have deployed his troops within the formidable defenses of Atlanta, which had been more than a year in the making, largely with slave labor. But, true to his aggressive nature, he took the offensive at once.

As Sherman moved to close the ring round the city and to cut off its rail links, Hood launched three separate attacks in eight days, from July 20 to 28. In one battle, Sherman's young protégé, James McPherson, was killed but all three engagements ended in costly and futile Rebel defeats. In the week and a half since taking command he had lost 18,000 men, nearly three times the Union toll and more than twice as many as Johnston had lost in 10 weeks. This was too much for many of the remaining Southern soldiers who started deserting in droves. Civilian morale was already low and took another dip once Sherman began bombarding the city in deadly earnest in early August. When Hood complained that innocent women and children were being killed, Sherman merely increased the rate of shelling.

Even though it seemed but a matter of time before Atlanta must fall, Lincoln, with an election in the offing, was desperate for a dramatic success on the battlefield and did not feel that time was on his side. Grant was stymied in front of Petersburg, a further half million recruits were being sought and the price of gold had risen to fresh heights, which upset Wall Street and was accelerating inflation. Northern public opinion was showing all the signs of chronic war-weariness. The Republicans were beginning to fall out with each

27.   The siege of Atlanta, 1864

other; some were even calling for Lincoln to renounce his nomination and for another stronger candidate to be sought. The Democrats were sensing possible victory at the polls, while Richmond felt that, if only its armies could hang on, such a success might bring them their independence at this eleventh hour.

Lincoln's opponents were making the most of every failure or setback on the battlefield and the lengthening casualty lists were a godsend to the editorial writers of the Democratic press. Sherman to date had lost only 25,000 men in the three months of his campaign, which had brought him 90 miles to the gates of Atlanta, and during that time he had inflicted 28,000 casualties on the Confederates but his efforts were not yet considered enough of a success to tip the balance Lincoln's way. During August the President became convinced that he would not win the election and told his Cabinet so.

The candidate chosen by the Democrats to fight Lincoln was George B. McClellan, the former commander of the Army of the Potomac who had been sacked by the President in late 1862 following his record of failures and missed opportunities, culminating in Lee's 'escape' after Antietam. The Democratic party platform described the war as a failure and called for a halt to hostilities with a view to convening a peace conference of all the states. The Republicans tried to link the Democrats with all manner of treasonous activity, citing alleged conspiracies concerning Confederate attempts to blow up Union gunboats or to liberate Southern prisoners of war, which were claimed to be financed by Democratic

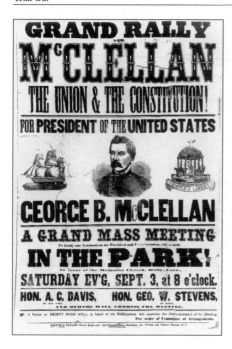

128. *George B. McClellan was Lincoln's luckless opponent, though he never seemed to have his heart in the fight. There were others who were quick to point out that that had been his problem as a general too*

sympathizers in the North. Similarly, Rebel gold was said to be behind many of the re-election campaigns of Democratic candidates. Some McClellan supporters were even accused of running guns to the South or supplying them with medicines and food. There was rarely more than a slender grain of truth in these stories, which were symptomatic of Republican desperation.

However, even before McClellan had secured the Democratic nomination — in fact on the very day Lincoln had told his Cabinet of his doubts regarding his re-election — the President got the dramatic success he had been hoping and waiting for, though it came from an unexpected quarter. On August 23 Admiral David Farragut, of New Orleans fame, captured Mobile Bay on Alabama's Gulf Coast to put an end to its role as a center for Confederate blockade-running. Farragut had been trying for some time to achieve this goal and had assembled an impressive fleet for the purpose, made up of four ironclads and 14 wooden warships, together with some 5,500 soldiers. In early August he had at long last felt able to move against the Rebel port's considerable defenses, consisting of three massive forts, numerous minefields and other underwater obstructions, as well as a squadron of four gunboats, including the newly built, giant ironclad *Tennessee*.

The assault began badly for the Union since almost immediately one of their ironclads hit a mine and blew up. Farragut, lashed high up in the rigging of his flagship *Hartford* in order to have a view of the battle over all the smoke from the guns belching below,

129.   David Farragut was everything that a hero needed to be: dashing and successful. Here he is aboard his flagship USS Hartford with Captain Drayton in Mobile Bay, August 1864

persisted in sailing his vessels through the minefield. His order to his fleet has become as famous as any that Nelson issued during the Battle of Trafalgar: 'Damn the torpedoes [i.e. mines]! Full speed ahead!' As a result the fleet safely — or perhaps luckily — negotiated the minefields and, once inside the bay, was able to eliminate the Confederate squadron, including the giant ironclad *Tennessee*, which was fought to a standstill. Subduing the forts, however, was to take until August 23.

Two days later Sherman launched his final assault on Atlanta, concentrating his main force against Hood's remaining rail links with the south. There were more heavy casualties, especially on the Confederate side, as Hood tried in vain to resist the ever-tightening encirclement. During the night of September 1–2, realizing that, if he left it any longer, abject surrender would be staring him in the face, he slipped out of the city with 30,000 of his men, after burning what remained of their stores. The blaze lasted several hours and the tremors from the exploding shells could be felt for miles around.

The next morning, while he left the actual taking of Atlanta to one of his subordinates, Sherman telegraphed the news that Lincoln had been eagerly awaiting. The President promptly proclaimed a day of national thanksgiving together with the firing of 100-gun salutes in all major cities throughout the North. Atlanta, coming on top of Mobile Bay,

130. *The remains of Fort Morgan, the biggest of the forts guarding the approaches to Mobile Bay, after its bombardment by the Union fleet*

revived Lincoln's re-election prospects — and there was an unseemly scramble to climb aboard his campaign bandwagon. The differences with his colleagues were for the time being forgotten and Lincoln as usual was magnanimous towards them. The double victory exhilarated the North. Although they might be weary of the fighting and concerned for the losses, Northerners felt that they had now at least gained something for their pains.

By mid-October, despite some tough opposition from Jubal Early, Sheridan had driven the Confederates from the Shenandoah Valley and gone on to ravage the area as promised. The local civilian population in western Virginia witnessed a totality of destruction hitherto without parallel during the conflict. Sheridan reported that, when his job was complete, 'the Valley, from Winchester up to Staunton, ninety-two miles, will have little in it for man or beast'. Rebel guerrillas tried to resist but they only encouraged the Union soldiers to still further extremes of retribution. The indirect sufferers were Lee's troops, who had long relied on the area for food and forage.

By the time the North went to the polls in early November, the outcome of the election was hardly in doubt. It had been a bitter and fiercely contested campaign, with the Republicans accusing the Democrats of treachery and the Democrats charging the Republicans with 'nigger-loving' and Lincoln with executive tyranny. The Republicans had the edge in party organization and their propaganda machine worked impressively. Lincoln in his turn exploited the power of government patronage for all that it was worth;

31. Atlanta's business centre was put to the torch by Sherman's men before they left on their march to the sea

those companies which had army contracts or aspired to obtain them were left in little doubt of the importance of a contribution to campaign funds.

When the results became known on November 8, Lincoln had received 55 per cent of the popular vote, and won an overwhelming majority in the electoral college (helped of course by the non-participation of most of the Southern states). Only New Jersey, Kentucky and Delaware went Democratic. The Republicans swept Congress and regained control of every state legislature lost two years earlier. In a period when electoral margins were usually very narrow, Lincoln and his party had won an emphatic victory. For the first time soldiers on active duty had been allowed to vote. Many states permitted absentee voting but, for those that did not, leave was arranged so that the troops could go home and record their ballots. Lincoln described them as 'voting bayonets', and he was proved right, for 78 per cent of them voted for him. In some states, especially New York and Connecticut, as well as perhaps Maryland and Indiana, they may well have tipped the balance his way.

The most remarkable feature of the election is that it took place at all. Its happening in the midst of a bloody and bitter civil war bore eloquent testimony to the vigor of American democracy, all the more since this was no ritual process, nor forgone conclusion, but a serious challenge to the incumbent war leader. Almost as astonishing was the fact that, for all the irregularities here and there, and the looming presence of troops at the polls, it was for the most part a normal election, conducted in very much a peacetime way. Its consequences and its outcome were enormous — and, in one sense, heavily ironic, as

177

132.   *Ripping up railtracks became an industry in itself at Atlanta. Sherman insisted that it should be done so thoroughly that the rails and ties could not be re-used*

Lincoln the staunch Republican would be succeeded, when his second term had scarcely begun, by the maverick figure of the Southern War Democrat, Andrew Johnson, who was nominated as the vice-presidential candidate in order to broaden the appeal of the ticket. But the 1864 election virtually guaranteed the future of the Republican Party, still barely a decade old, and helped to set American politics in the mold of the two-party system of Republicans and Democrats where it has remained ever since.

Lincoln's electoral victory ended the one remaining realistic hope for Southern independence. It is impossible to know what would have happened if McClellan had won at the polls but such a result would have indicated a degree of war-weariness on the part of the North which might well have led to compromise through negotiation rather than Confederate surrender on the battlefield. Now only a military solution was left and there could no longer be any serious doubt of the outcome.

Soon after capturing Atlanta, Sherman determined to evacuate the city's civilians and turn it over entirely to the military. Both the mayor and General Hood protested vehemently. In trying to explain to them the reasons for his action, Sherman said, 'War is cruelty and you cannot refine it; the crueller it is, the sooner it will be over.' He had long resolved that the struggle must be pursued relentlessly, regardless of its effect on man or boy, woman or child, soldier or civilian. For him, a war of this kind was not waged between armies but between peoples; in fighting a nation you were fighting its entire citizen body, and in order to defeat a nation, you needed to defeat not only its soldiers but also its civilians. To this end, it was necessary to destroy the opposing nation's factories and farms, railroads and harbors, bridges and cities, to deprive the civilians of the means of livelihood as well as the soldiers of the wherewithal to resist. Above all the will of soldier and civilian alike to sustain the struggle must be broken. 'We cannot change the hearts of those people of the South,' Sherman maintained, 'but we can make them so sick of war that generations would pass away before they would again appeal to it.'

Sherman now pleaded with both Grant and Lincoln to let him put this concept of war into practice by marching his army first southwards through Georgia to the sea and then northwards through the Carolinas to join up with the Army of the Potomac outside Petersburg, all the while living off the land and destroying what was not needed by his troops. He argued that the impact would be even greater psychologically than materially, since it would demonstrate to the Richmond regime and the Southern people just who held effective power in the South.

Washington had feared letting Sherman move very far from his Atlanta base while Confederate cavalry were able to threaten his long supply line, stretching back to Chattanooga and beyond, over hundreds of miles of vulnerable rail-track. But now he was proposing to release himself from these problems. There were still Rebel forces roaming loose in the South, and Hood was already harassing Sherman's supply lines and planning a counter-attack, which would eventually carry him all the way back to central Tennessee. Sherman intended to assign a part of his force to contain this threat, while the bulk of it joined him on his march. His arguments won the day with both Grant and Lincoln.

Just a week after the President's re-election, having set fire to everything of military value in Atlanta, which included warehouses, factories, public buildings and railroad installations, Sherman and his 62,000 men set off for Savannah on the Atlantic coast 285 miles away, determined, as he put it, to 'make Georgia howl!' A band played 'John Brown's Body'. The South's final agony was about to begin.

13 Conclusion at Appomattox

The fall of Atlanta and, still more, Lincoln's re-election drove further nails into the coffin of Confederate hopes. The more realistic Southerners understood that, short of a miracle, defeat for Lincoln and the Republicans at the polls in November 1864 had been their last chance. Now they could only look back gloomily on what seemed a series of missed opportunities throughout the war. The failure to go for a knock-out punch after the victory at Manassas in July 1861 had been the first. Then there had been the inability to secure British and French recognition, on which so much was thought to depend. The lack of a noteworthy military success on Northern soil in 1862 had opened the way to the Emancipation Proclamation, and the setbacks at Gettysburg and Vicksburg in 1863 had rammed home the lessons that the South could not expect to obtain its independence on the battlefield. The remaining hope had lain in the erosion of the Northern will to fight and win, and the electoral defeat of the Union leadership, which might have created one last opportunity. Now that too was gone.

Desertions from the Confederate armies rose dramatically after November 1864, a measure of the disheartening effects of the news from the battlefront and the polling stations. Letters from wives to their husbands still in the field became ever more pitiful. Inflation was making a nonsense — or a nightmare — of life at home. Prices of foodstuffs and everyday necessities were increasing almost by the hour, giving an air of unreality to ordinary living. Law and order were breaking down in many places and the fear of slave insurrection was once again rearing its head among Southern planters. There was a rash of rumors, usually unfounded, about atrocities by blacks against their former owners in some of the areas recently occupied by Union troops. Much of the South faced economic ruin, not just as a direct result of the fighting but also because livestock and forage had been appropriated by the armies of both sides, fences had been torn down for firewood and houses taken apart to make winter shelters. Famine and plague loomed as grim, and by no means remote, prospects. Such a situation could not go on much longer, and increasing numbers of ordinary Southerners were coming to the simple conclusion that the war must be brought to an end.

There had always been peace movements in the South but they had been confined largely to the hill areas of eastern Tennessee, western North Carolina and northern Georgia and Alabama. Elsewhere they had never attracted much public support. Even before Lincoln's re-election, however, initiatives to end the war were being openly discussed in Richmond. Jefferson Davis's vice-president, Alexander Stephens, was calling for peace at almost any price, convinced that a settlement through negotiation was the only way to salvage something from the crumbling ruins of the Confederacy. But such aspirations

133. *Columbia's Capitol, victim of the orgy of destruction that befell South Carolina's state capital on the night of February 17, 1865 when Sherman's troops entered the city. He did not win friends in the South for himself when later he said of the burning: 'Though I never ordered it and never wished it, I have never shed any tears over the event, because I believe that it hastened what we all fought for, the end of the war.' An officer in his army was to add a further comment: 'South Carolina may have been the cause of the whole thing, but she has had an awful punishment'*

were dashed by Davis's insistence on the South's independence and the preservation of slavery as indispensable conditions in any negotiations.

North Carolina had never been wholeheartedly secessionist and influential groups within the state were now proposing a convention or referendum to decide whether to return to the Union on the basis of retaining the state's previous rights, but again this hardly offered a serious framework for negotiations with the North. There were voices in Georgia, too, ready to argue that the state should secede from the Confederacy and declare its own independence. After Atlanta's fall, Georgia's governor, Joseph E. Brown, granted 30 days' leave to the 10,000-strong state militia in order to prevent General Hood taking them out of the state. Brown also threatened to recall all Georgian troops from Lee's army around Richmond and Petersburg so that they might defend their home ground. The governors of both Alabama and Mississippi followed suit in banning their militias from leaving their states. On his own initiative, Sherman invited Georgia's governor and Alexander Stephens to Atlanta for talks on a separate peace for the state, but they declined on the grounds that he was not a constitutionally designated commissioner. Although Republicans had hitherto been insisting on unconditional surrender, Northern war-weariness was such that a less uncompromising approach to the South was not ruled out, at least until Atlanta fell. If the Democrats had succeeded at the polls that November they were committed to seeking a negotiated solution to the conflict.

Peace movements notwithstanding, the Confederacy was disintegrating politically during the autumn of 1864. From its original 11 states it was effectively reduced to just the two Carolinas and parts of Virginia and Georgia. The area beyond the Mississippi had long since been cut off, and Rebel authority was not recognized in many districts still far from Union lines, for example, along the Gulf Coast in Alabama and Louisiana. Never notable for its solidarity, the Southern leadership had now split and petty feuding was commonplace, particularly within the Cabinet.

Lincoln seemed to dash hopes of a compromise peace short of military surrender when, soon after his re-election, he told Congress that no attempt at negotiation with Jefferson Davis could result in any good. 'He would accept nothing short of severance of the Union — precisely what we will not and cannot give.' It was an issue which could only be tried by war and decided by victory. By this time Sherman was making steady progress in his march across Georgia to the sea. He met little opposition, since Hood had taken the bulk of the Confederate forces on a long, futile counter-thrust through northern Georgia and into Tennessee. For a while there was the unusual spectacle of two opposing armies virtually ignoring each other and advancing in opposite directions. Apart from the Georgia militia and a few thousand Rebel cavalry, Sherman's 62,000-strong army had the state to itself and they could well have covered the 285 miles from Atlanta to Savannah faster than they did. Speedy arrival at their destination was not, however, their main goal. Averaging only about 10 miles a day, they were cutting a swathe through the middle of Georgia, along a front sometimes 50 or even 100 miles wide.

The destruction they wrought has become part of the legend of the Civil War. Sherman's own men were methodical and generally well disciplined but on the flanks of the army much more wanton pillaging and plundering was carried out by stragglers, deserters and looters from both sides, as well as by locals seizing the opportunity to settle old scores. Ironically the Confederate cavalry and the state militia contributed to the devastation, since they had been urged by Jefferson Davis to 'destroy all roads in Sherman's front, flank, and rear', to strip from his path all 'Negroes, horses, cattle and provisions' and 'burn what you cannot carry' so that his army 'will soon starve in your midst'. Far from starving, Sherman's army lived quite well off the country. They also had in tow a growing body of freed slaves, eventually numbering up to 25,000, who acted as additional scavengers but also posed considerable logistical and other problems.

Sherman's aim was to eliminate Georgia's contribution to the Confederate war effort — and in this he was undoubtedly successful. The intention was not only to cause material devastation but also to undermine the will to fight both in Georgia and elsewhere. Certainly this was the effect on the civilian population in Sherman's path and also on many Georgian soldiers at the front in Virginia or Tennessee who took off for home to find out for themselves what had happened to their families. Whether or not

134.   Grant brought up his big guns to besiege Petersburg, including the giant 13-inch mortar
Dictator which was mounted on a reinforced rail flat-car. Its 200lb shells could be fired for
two and a half miles

the latter result had been in Sherman's mind, it was one way in which his march had a crippling effect on Lee's capacity to sustain the struggle.

On December 13, Sherman reached the coast and made contact with Union ships offshore. Eight days later, Savannah itself fell and he wired Washington to offer the city to the President as a Christmas present. As if the success of Sherman's march across the Confederate heartland was not enough, mid-December also brought news of another Rebel disaster. Hood's desperate, doomed move into Tennessee had carried him to the gates of the state capital, Nashville, where he was outnumbered and dangerously exposed. With characteristic thoroughness, George H. Thomas, the 'Rock of Chickamauga', prepared to crush Hood's tired and depleted force and at the battle of Nashville on December 15 and 16 he destroyed the opposing army with a completeness previously unmatched in the Civil War. The remnants of Hood's army deserted or otherwise melted away; they were never again a recognizable fighting force. The annihilation of an army and the destruction of a key state's capacity to wage war were terrible twin blows to the Confederacy as 1864 drew to a close.

At the beginning of 1865, although the Confederate army's official strength was 400,000, in practice it numbered less than half that. The rest were absent without leave or unavailable

135. A special railroad was built to supply Petersburg by Union army construction gangs

for other reasons. The desertion rate soared during the early months of the new year, averaging more than 5,000 a week, and the remaining troops were in appalling condition. Rations were short, footwear scarce and fresh clothing a rare luxury. Some supplies were still getting through the blockade but they dried up in mid-January when the Federals closed the last main port still open to blockade-runners, Wilmington, on North Carolina's coast. Many in the South, including Alexander Stephens, saw this as the beginning of the end. It intensified the South's sense of isolation, almost of imprisonment, and in effect imposed a time limit on further resistance. In many communities, local self-sufficiency was now the only way to survive. A complete breakdown in confidence in the Confederate currency, due to rampant inflation, led people to return to barter as the only practical method of trading. This highlighted the air of unreality which increasingly pervaded the Confederacy. No modern state could continue for long by resorting on any scale to such primitive means of doing business. The Confederate Treasury even began appealing for Southern belles to contribute their jewellery and other valuables to help pay for the war effort.

Backed by Jefferson Davis, Stephens met with Lincoln in early February to seek some common ground that might lead to peace — the first face-to-face discussion of possible terms between leaders of the two sides. Initially the President had deputed his secretary of state, William Seward, to see Stephens and his two colleagues but decided at the last minute to attend himself. The encounter took place on board ship in Hampton Roads on February 3. Lincoln insisted on reunion as the essential condition of peace, while the Confederates were still talking of independence. Slavery was mentioned but the talk as a whole was brief and unproductive, and Stephens went away empty-handed, to resign himself to the Confederacy's demise. Within the month, however, Lincoln seemed to be extending an olive branch in his second inaugural address when he spoke about malice toward none and charity for all. But he went on to stress the need to complete the task before the nation, namely of eradicating the evil of slavery, and there was little comfort for the South in his acceptance of God's will that 'every drop of blood drawn with the lash shall be paid by another drawn with the sword'.

In late January, Congress had already passed the Thirteenth Amendment to the constitution abolishing slavery once and for all, and its ratification by the states went ahead during the rest of the year. There were signs of changing times in the presence of blacks at White House receptions and in the appearance of the first black lawyer before the Supreme Court. But racial attitudes in the North were still highly ambivalent. Proposals to integrate public transport in various Northern cities were meeting stiff resistance, and there was very limited support for any notion of giving blacks the vote.

For his part Jefferson Davis still closed his eyes to the parlous state of his cause and chose to continue the fight, although for all practical purposes his government's writ did not now extend much beyond his own capital and its immediate environs. Moreover, Lee was pleading for more soldiers to man the defenses of Petersburg and Richmond. Since there were not enough volunteers and the draft was being universally evaded, Davis was persuaded to agree to an amnesty for deserters and in one last attempt to scrape the bottom of the manpower barrel, the government began to call in 14- to 18-year-olds and men in their fifties.

In early February Sherman set out on the second of his great marches, this time northwards from Savannah through the Carolinas towards the rear of Lee's defenses at Petersburg. It was one of the most remarkable logistical exercises in the history of modern warfare and had an even more devastating effect than his first march from Atlanta to the sea, although on this occasion he met rather more opposition and the weather, too, was against him. Once again Sherman's aim was not simply to destroy the Confederacy's capacity for waging war, but rather to cripple the will of Southerners in general to continue the fight. There was also an element of revenge as his troops moved into South Carolina, breeding-ground of secession, where the first shots had been fired on the Union flag at Fort Sumter nearly four years before. Sherman felt this himself when he telegraphed Lincoln: 'The truth is the whole army is burning with an insatiable desire to wreak vengeance upon South Carolina.' More towns and property were put to the torch in South Carolina by Sherman's men than anywhere else and the state capital, Columbia, came in for particularly harsh treatment. Half of the city was levelled, despite attempts to limit the looting and the burning; newly released Union prisoners added to the confusion. The

136.   One of the last Confederate soldiers to die at Petersburg

retreating Confederate cavalry also carried a large share of the blame, since they had sought to set fire to the vast quantities of cotton bales remaining in the city. Whatever may be said with the wisdom of hindsight about the proper distribution of blame for the destruction, generations of Southerners would never forgive Sherman for the burning of Columbia.

Charleston itself capitulated on February 18. The colonel of a black regiment took the formal surrender, while his troops lustily sang 'John Brown's Body' to the great delight of the local black population. Many of the city's buildings were destroyed in the fires started by the retreating Confederates but few in the North shed a tear at the news, regarding it as no more than the just deserts of the birthplace of the rebellion.

By mid-March Sherman was well into North Carolina and within the week he had linked up with a Union force, which had come ashore on the coast under his subordinate commander John Schofield. In many ways his 400-mile march through the Carolinas in just seven weeks was even more impressive than his previous one through Georgia. It made a mockery of the prognostications of 1861 that a country the size of the Confederacy — as big as Russia, which had defied Napoleon 50 years before — could not be subjugated. The devastation in the Carolinas was more widespread and blatant than that in Georgia and few houses of the rich, especially the slaveholding aristocracy, escaped the depredations of Sherman's remorseless troops.

Even now Jefferson Davis was determined to persist in the struggle. Belatedly, on February 6, Lee had been made general-in-chief of the Confederate armies. It was remarkable that the appointment had not been made earlier — perhaps a measure of Davis's conceit and, at the same time, lack of realism — but it was far too tardy. One of Lee's first acts was to give firm if reluctant support to the proposal, long debated in the Confederate Congress and in the Cabinet, to enlist slaves in the armed forces. The measure was finally passed in mid-March. It opened up the prospect of freedom as the reward for military service, although it came too late to have any real effect. In an ironic twist a struggle begun in defense of slavery was now to be waged by those same slaves on behalf of their masters. That it was prepared to yield on this issue showed how desperate the Confederacy had become. The South after all had gone to war to protect its way of life, which was based on slavery. Many Southerners were appalled at the decision, arguing that it was against everything for which the Confederacy stood. One critic spoke for many when he declared that 'it would tear the vitals of society'. In fact very few black soldiers were actually recruited, and none actually fought against the Union.

The final *coup de grâce* was delivered by Grant rather than Sherman. Ever since June 1864 he had been besieging Petersburg, barely 20 miles from the Confederate capital. For a while the ravages of the spring and summer campaigning reduced the effective strength of the Army of the Potomac to little more than 40,000 men, most of whom were ill-trained, undisciplined, inexperienced and poorly motivated. With the end of the war in sight, few were anxious to volunteer and the bulk of the new recruits were bounty jumpers, paid substitutes and reluctant draftees. Many of the better officers had been killed or wounded and, as the quality of leadership declined, the upper echelons were forever at loggerheads with each other.

An attack during August 1864 had been halted just 7 miles short of Richmond but a move to cut Lee's rail link to the south from Petersburg had been more successful, albeit at terrible cost, and the squeeze on Lee's army was tightened by another notch. Not to be outdone, the Confederate cavalry made a daring raid on Grant's main supply base at City Point on the James River during mid-September and managed to snatch nearly 2,500 head of cattle and herd them back to their lines. The meat afforded enough rations to last Lee's whole army almost six weeks. The Federals again pressed forward towards Richmond during October and got to within 3 miles of it before being stopped. Lee even tried a counter-attack against Grant's positions but his opportunities for such offensive actions were becoming fewer. Before the rains and cold of winter stopped all aggressive movements, Grant made one last attempt to get around to the west of Petersburg and cut its rail-link there to the rest of the Confederacy. For a time it seemed that he might just succeed but he was thwarted at great cost to both sides.

Although Grant chafed at the boredom and frustration of the long winter months holed up outside Petersburg, he knew full well that the plight of Lee and his men was even worse. Perpetually hungry, ill- clothed and badly shod, prone to all manner of disease or infection from pneumonia to scurvy, they were less than eager for the better weather and the renewal of fighting. Morale was helped by a surge of religious enthusiasm, in which Lee himself shared. His army's effective strength dwindled as the winter progressed and was down to barely 28,000 by the beginning of March. February had seen nearly 3,000 men desert, most heading for home, but increasing numbers were making their way into the Union lines where the food was plentiful and creature comforts more available.

At one point during January, Lee's army had rations left for only two days, while fodder for the horses had virtually run out. Ammunition, too, was extremely low and return

137.   A thousand buildings were destroyed in the blaze, including the whole of Richmond's commercial district. Some of the embers smouldered for another two months

firing had to be kept to an absolute minimum. Large-scale offensives were now out of the question for him and on March 2 Lee in fact sounded out Grant regarding the possibility of peace terms, but he was turned down on Lincoln's orders.

The Confederates were already thinly stretched around the defenses of Petersburg and Richmond, and Grant was determined to extend them even more by lengthening his lines to the west. Realizing this, Lee tried to break out of the vice by getting in an attack before Grant was ready. For a while he managed to breach the Federal positions and to threaten the Union supply base at City Point, but he no longer had the numbers to follow up his success. Grant countered, not by meeting him head on, but by hitting the western end of his defenses and by sending Sheridan's cavalry still further west on April 1 to cut Lee's escape route to the south-west as well as his remaining supply line. Lee was now in severe danger of being boxed in at Petersburg, which he could not afford. All day long on April 2 he managed to resist Grant's attempts to trap him, while the bulk of his force withdrew westwards.

With the loss of Petersburg, Richmond was no longer tenable. Jefferson Davis and his government fled south-westwards, taking what they could with them and leaving orders for ammunition dumps and other military installations to be blown up. The fires got out of hand and parts of the former Confederate capital were destroyed, while looters had a field day. Lee had been hoping to join up with Joe Johnston's forces in North Carolina,

138.   As 137

who were confronting Sherman, but that alternative was no longer open to him. With barely 30,000 men, he headed westwards towards the mountains, merely delaying the inevitable.

The first Union soldiers entered Richmond in the early hours of April 3. Ironically, but not inappropriately, many of them were black. Lincoln himself visited the city the following day, without formality or fuss, walking unprotected through its ruins, though for a while he was escorted by a unit of black cavalrymen. The only smiling faces were the former slaves still living there, some of whom greeted the President with great enthusiasm, even kneeling at his feet. For the white citizens, the collapse had come so quickly that they were stunned, but the sight of Abraham Lincoln strolling in the company of black soldiers through the streets of what had been the Confederate capital rammed home the meaning of the dramatic events of recent days.

Grant, meanwhile, was determined to prevent Lee reaching the mountains and caught up with him on April 6 at Sayler's Creek some 50 miles west of Richmond, where the Confederate rearguard was given a severe mauling and nearly 8,000 stragglers, almost a third of Lee's force, were captured. Others had already slipped off home or had thrown away their weapons and walked into the Union lines seeking food.

139. *Federal soldiers pose outside Appomattox Court House on the day of surrender, four years exactly after the first shots were fired at Fort Sumter*

140. *Courteous as always, Lee raised no objection to being photographed by a Northerner on his return to Richmond after the surrender*

141.   *Tragedy at the moment of success. Lincoln is struck down by John Wilkes Booth at the Ford Theatre, Washington, on April 14, 1865*

Lee wasted the next day on an abortive search for supplies, which, although promised, never reached him amid the chaos of the final days of the Confederacy. Two trainloads of rations had, however, been sent to Appomattox further to the west and when Lee set out in that direction, he found that Sheridan's cavalry had got there first. On the morning of April 9, Palm Sunday, he prepared to do battle for them, but discovered that he was completely surrounded. Realizing that to persist would probably mean the sacrifice of most of his men, he decided that there was nothing left for him to do 'but to go and see General Grant, and I would rather die a thousand deaths'.

Some of his subordinates suggested that they try to break out individually to the mountains nearby to continue the struggle as guerrillas. Lee would have none of this, arguing that it would not produce independence for the South, which was the only justification for maintaining the fight, and that further conflict would most probably lead to the region's total destruction. He sent word through the lines that he was prepared to discuss terms with Grant.

They met later that same day in the nearby hamlet of Appomattox Court House, at the home of one Wilmer McLean who, in order to get away from the war, had moved there from Manassas following the battle in 1861 when his house had been taken over by the Confederates as a military headquarters. Lee, dressed in his best uniform, and Grant, still wearing his campaign clothes, shook hands in the living-room and chatted about common experiences in the Mexican War.

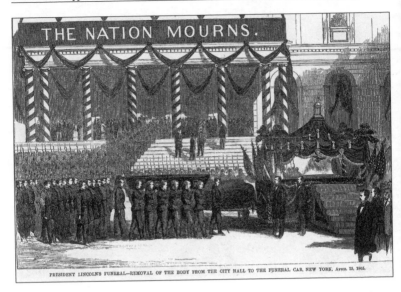

PRESIDENT LINCOLN'S FUNERAL—REMOVAL OF THE BODY FROM THE CITY HALL TO THE FUNERAL CAR, NEW YORK, APRIL 25, 1865.

142.   The joy of victory soon gave way to anger in the North, though Lincoln was buried with great dignity

For all the previous talk of unconditional surrender, Grant was anxious to offer reasonable terms which would halt the fighting in Virginia and bring the four-year-old war to a rapid close. As he mentioned later, he felt 'sad and depressed' at 'the downfall of a foe who had fought so long and valiantly, and had suffered so much for a cause, though that cause was, I believe, one of the worst for which a people ever fought'. The agreement was that, provided they left behind their weapons and promised not to continue the struggle under any circumstances, Lee's 13,000 men should be allowed to go home with their horses and mules; for some it would mean a trek of several hundred miles back to Texas or Arkansas or Louisiana, lasting many weeks and having to scrounge for food *en route*.

In a gesture reflecting the mood of the moment, Grant sent double rations to relieve the hunger of Lee's dispirited men. Most found it hard to believe how simply their long and bitter struggle had been concluded. But Northerners as well as Southerners were only too keen to see the war end and relief rather than joy was the immediate reaction. Lincoln set the tone by ordering the bands in Washington celebrating the news to play 'Dixie' as often as 'Yankee Doodle Dandy'. He said it had always been one of his favorite tunes.

As the impact of the day's events began to sink in, caution gave way to more riotous festivities, particularly among the veterans of the Army of the Potomac camped in the hills around Appomattox. Elsewhere in the North the jubilation was equally unrestrained. Lee ended his part in the war as he had performed it throughout, with dignity and honor,

43.   *The victory parade took place on May 23 and 24, 1865 down Washington's Pennsylvania Avenue with the newly completed Capitol dome as a suitable backdrop. Many had wanted to cancel it, arguing that it was inappropriate after the death of Lincoln, but others felt the nation needed some uplift from its grief. The Army of the Potomac marched on the first day and Sherman's men on the second*

and considerable courage. His conduct in defeat, along with his redoubtable reputation as a warrior, ensured him a place in the pantheon of American national heroes and it is somewhat ironic that the military leader of the greatest rebellion against the authority of the United States should have a more assured place there than the supreme commander of the Union forces which crushed that rebellion. Grant's qualities of generalship were at least as remarkable as Lee's, and certainly more recognizably modern — and he was notably free from rancor or vengeance in his moment of glory. But his downbeat style limited his popular appeal and his later record as president tarnished his status as a national hero.

On April 12, three days after Lee formally surrendered in Wilmer McLean's house and four years to the day since the first shots were fired at Fort Sumter, his army laid down its weapons at Appomattox. Lee had meanwhile returned to Richmond to see his two sons, while Grant was back at his military headquarters on the James River. He and his wife were due to join the President and Mrs Lincoln for an evening at the theater on Good Friday, April 14, but decided against it.

The play, an English comedy called *Our American Cousin*, had no particular claim to distinction, but the real drama was not acted out on stage. During the performance at Ford's Theater in Washington a failed and mentally deranged actor, John Wilkes Booth, entered the presidential box and shot Lincoln in the back of the head. The President was carried to a house across the street where he died early next morning. Booth, a man of strong Confederate sympathies, was seeking almost single-handedly to reverse the verdict of the Civil War. He was tracked down and shot, while four of his fellow conspirators were tried and hanged, and four more received life sentences, some of them on dubious evidence. As with the assassination of John F. Kennedy a century later, many Americans insisted that there must have been some wider and deeper plot hatched by the nation's enemies, but no evidence to support such claims was ever uncovered.

Plunging from joy into grief and rage in such a few days, the North still managed to recover its equilibrium remarkably quickly. Within weeks, the last flickering flames of the war were extinguished as the remaining Confederate armies surrendered and Jefferson Davis was captured. The Union soldiers had their victory parades and then went home. The great volunteer army, which had once totalled almost a million men, was dismantled in a matter of months. Meanwhile the long journey of the murdered president back to his final resting-place at Springfield, Illinois, drew the country together and began the process of transforming the flesh-and-blood political leader who had been no stranger to controversy into the legendary national hero, savior and martyr. In the months and years to come, the nation would miss his political skills at least as much as his moral vision. Apart from the poignancy that, having achieved such a dramatic victory, he was now to be denied partaking of its fruits, his loss left millions of his fellow citizens apprehensive about the future. The war might be over but the peace still remained to be won.

14 Waging the peace

For all the hatred and cries for vengeance that Lincoln's murder aroused in loyal Northerners, the ending of the most bloody conflict in American history passed off with remarkably little recrimination or reprisal. Jefferson Davis was never brought to trial and spent only two years in custody. Apart from the executions of the four Booth accomplices, only one other hanging took place, that of the commandant of the Andersonville prisoner-of-war camp in Georgia, Henry Wirz, who was made the scapegoat for the deficiencies in the Confederate treatment of Union captives.

Yet 620,000 soldiers had died — 360,000 Union and 260,000 Confederate — almost as many as in all the other wars in which the United States has ever participated. Virtually every family had been touched, through the loss of a relative or friend, and for decades afterwards veterans who were missing an arm or a leg were a familiar sight throughout the land. The South suffered particularly — the proportion of its population killed and severely wounded was very much greater; it lost a quarter of its white manhood during the struggle. As Mary Chesnut pointed out in her *Diary from Dixie*, Southern women had to get used to a new definition of male beauty, since in many communities within the former Confederacy whole men hardly existed any more. Many women living in villages and hamlets in the South remained spinsters because so few men returned from the war and the simple fact was that there were not enough local men to go round.

In many different ways the war changed the United States radically. It settled once and for all its indivisibility. The effect of the four-year struggle, and then of the three constitutional amendments which followed it, was to shift the balance of the federal system very much in favor of the center as against the individual states. The Union was transformed into a nation, and, while still retaining their local and state loyalties, Americans acquired a stronger sense of their national identity. Many businesses now operated on a scale which made state boundaries almost irrelevant, and the demands of wartime finance had shaped the framework of a national banking system and currency. Although the Federal income tax was abandoned soon after the war, new precedents had been set in the financial relationship between the central government and the individual citizen.

But the greatest impact of the war lay in the ending of slavery and with it the huge upheaval in the Southern way of life. The participation of black soldiers in the war had a considerable effect on attitudes towards black people in the North. At the very least, the idea of persuading freed slaves to leave the United States and set up colonies elsewhere was no longer tenable after so many blacks had fought to save the Union. On the other hand, even in the North, blacks still faced discrimination, segregation and denial of

144. *John Wilkes Booth, self-appointed avenger of the South's defeat. His action was, however, a source of embarrassment in the South*

political rights. When the war ended, only six Northern states had granted blacks the vote, and, in referendums during the autumn of 1865 in Connecticut, Wisconsin and Minnesota, the vote went against black suffrage.

If the North could expect to get 'back to normalcy' quite quickly, and was impatient to do so, the story was very different in the South. Although some areas were relatively unscathed, large parts of the South were in ruins. Bridges had been destroyed, railroad track uprooted, farms and public buildings burnt, plantations abandoned, cattle scattered and crops devastated. But the effect was greater on the people — wives were husbandless, children fatherless, lives had been broken. Familiar authority had collapsed and people took the law into their own hands. Deserters and former guerrillas, having ceased to steal from the enemy, now robbed defenseless widows. Poverty was commonplace, disease rampant, and refugees were everywhere. Above all there was the inescapable evidence of defeat in the continuing presence of four million newly freed slaves who, it was feared, might be tempted to wreak some sort of vengeance on their former masters. In fact most of the former slaves were far more concerned about where they were going to obtain their livelihoods than seeking to settle old scores and there was very little violence on the part of the Southern blacks.

145. *Henry Wirz, commandant of the infamous Andersonville prison camp, was duly hanged in the yard of the Old Capitol Prison in Washington on November 10, 1865 after a trial which left much to be desired*

Morale in the South was shattered. A once proud people had gambled everything and lost. As a region it lay prostrate at the feet of its conqueror and decisions regarding its future were no longer in its hands but in those of the hated Yankee. The Northern army moved into the South as an occupying force. Military courts tried offenders, while bureaucrats sent from Washington attempted to minister to immediate needs, in some cases working through local whites who had remained loyal to the Union. The latter came to be nicknamed scalawags by other Southerners, and those Northerners who bought their way into Southern properties or businesses were dubbed 'carpetbaggers' — not terms of endearment, nor intended to be.

It was ironic that the man who had to oversee the aftermath of the war was a Southern Democrat from Tennessee, albeit a Democrat who had opposed secession and supported the war. Andrew Johnson had been chosen as Lincoln's running-mate in 1864 precisely because he seemed to balance the ticket. Once the election had been won under the new name of the National Union Party, the Republicans soon reverted to their former title. Johnson had served his purpose and little was expected of him as a vice-president. When

146.   *In the immediate aftermath of the war freed blacks in Southern cities like Richmond could*
      walk tall, but the question was for how long

he disgraced himself at the March 1865 inauguration by getting drunk, it was generally regarded as no more than a minor scandal.

   Johnson, like Lincoln, was a man of humble origins, the son of a tavern porter who had become apprenticed to a tailor after his father's early death in order to help his mother bring up her young family. He had married the daughter of a shoemaker, from whom he learned to read and write. As well as being self-taught, he was self-made. At one stage he had farmed and had owned a few slaves. A natural orator, he had worked his way up the political ladder to become governor of Tennessee before the war. At the time of Sumter he had been a senator, indeed the only senator from a Rebel state to remain in Washington, and in 1862 Lincoln had made him military governor of occupied Tennessee.

147. *Cities in the South, such as Charleston, were to take a while to recover*

Johnson believed in states' rights, small-scale farming and small business, and above all in the least government possible. A champion of the Southern yeoman class, he detested the slave owners but had little time for blacks. He had accepted emancipation as a way of defeating the secessionists but his racial prejudices were those of the most narrow-minded border-state or Midwestern farmer. Unlike Lincoln, he was not flexible in his thinking, nor politically adroit. Hitherto he had not concerned himself with the vagaries of Northern opinion. He had no reputation as a conciliator, nor as a man of much vision.

Lincoln had not, of course, left one, clear plan for the so-called reconstruction of the South, including the way in which the former Rebel states were to be readmitted to the Union. He had been determined that the slaves should be freed and that those who had led the South into secession should be denied political power, but he had not committed himself to giving votes to the blacks, nor to redistributing land in their favor. All along he had been anxious to preserve the Union but by the end of the war he was well aware that the Union thus saved was a Union transformed.

Johnson had to feel his way into the problem, although he did not have much time in which to do so. It was a matter of urgency to establish acceptable, firm, loyal state governments as soon as possible in the South. Unwilling to call Congress into special session before its regular meeting at the end of the year, he preferred meanwhile to rule by executive decree. In late May he offered an amnesty, which included the restoration of their civil and political rights together with the restitution of their property, apart from slaves, to those whites in the South who would take an oath of allegiance to the United

148.   Many families were on the move in the South, refugees in search of a better future

States. Certain groups of people, such as former Confederate officials and army officers above the rank of colonel, were not eligible, but they could seek individual pardons from the President himself. By the late summer Johnson was issuing about 100 such pardons a day and some 13,000 or so were granted by the end of the year.

The President also appointed provisional governors for the former rebel states with the task of arranging elections for conventions to draft new constitutions. Only those who had taken the oath of allegiance and who qualified under existing state constitutions could vote or stand as candidates. This deliberate device to rule out black participation alarmed many Republicans and abolitionists, and dismayed the blacks themselves. Nor was there any hint of land reform that might give the former slaves the 'forty acres and a mule' which was the great aspiration of so many of them. The restitution of property to former Confederates would anyway now make this difficult, if not impossible. Confiscation of lands, even those held by people who until recently had been trying with all their might to kill or maim Northerners, was still too much for moderate, let alone conservative, Republicans.

Taking their cue from Johnson's apparent leniency, many Southern political leaders very quickly regained their previous arrogant self-confidence and prepared to obstruct Northern attempts at reform in their states. When the first Congressional elections were held under the new constitutions, among those chosen were some notable Rebels, including the Confederacy's vice-president, Alexander Stephens, as well as a number of generals and colonels from Lee's army. Those elected to the state legislatures were almost entirely prominent ex-Confederates and planters. Having failed to storm the Capitol by military means, the South was apparently having more success by constitutional methods. One of the further ironies of the situation was that emancipation had increased the South's overall representation in Congress by at least a dozen or so seats in the House of Representatives. Slaves had previously counted as only three-fifths of a person in assessing numbers for apportioning seats in the House. Now freed blacks counted as whole men, though if Southern whites had their way they would still be denied a vote.

Johnson further antagonized Northerners when in August he allowed Mississippi's new governor to recruit Confederate veterans for his state militia on the grounds that they were needed to combat increasing disorder, particularly among the freed blacks. The Union general in charge of the occupation forces there protested to Washington, but was snubbed, to the great dismay of Republicans and the immense delight of Southerners.

When Congress eventually met in December 1865, the Republican majority prevented the Southern representatives from taking their seats. Only Congress, not the President, had the power to decide who was eligible for membership of the legislature. Johnson additionally annoyed many Northerners when he insisted that land confiscated during the war by generals such as Sherman for cultivation by freed blacks should be returned to its former owners. Attempts by Congress to overrule the President on this matter failed.

Land was a central issue in the post-war South. Those fortunate blacks who could afford to buy some found that whites usually refused to sell. In fact most of the Southern states quickly enacted laws making it difficult for blacks to own or rent land. One of the first priorities of the new state legislatures was to draw up regulations governing the status of blacks to replace the old slave codes and, although some of these 'black codes' were harsher than others, they all had the same aim of subjecting the ex-slaves to white domination and circumscribing their social, economic and political ambitions. Mississippi's code, for instance, gave the courts such wide powers in defining a vagrant that almost any unemployed black could be fined and handed over to a planter to work out payment of his punishment for being poor. South Carolina's code even talked in terms of 'masters' and 'servants' as though the Emancipation Proclamation had never happened. Some codes forbade blacks to leave their place of work without permission, and most required them to obtain special licenses to engage in a wide variety of skilled trades. When Republicans protested, Southerners simply pointed out that blacks in most Northern states were still barred from serving on juries, banned from marrying whites, segregated in their education and subjected to many other forms of discrimination.

Many freed slaves ended up working for wages, often for their previous masters, some of whom insisted on retaining their former overseers who were not above 'disciplining' their labor force in the old manner with whippings. When blacks showed reluctance to work under such conditions, plantation owners interpreted this as confirmation of what they regarded as the inherent laziness of their former slaves. It was very difficult for blacks to secure remedies for their complaints through the courts, which were still in the hands of whites; nor could they serve on juries. Republicans in Congress sought to ease the problem by establishing, through the Freedmen's Bureau, a parallel set of courts to which blacks could take their complaints, although the Republicans needed to override a presidential veto before securing passage of the law.

In the depressed state of the Southern economy after the Civil War, ready cash was in short supply. Recently freed slaves could not afford to buy land; ex-planters and other landowners could not afford to pay wages. Share cropping became widespread as a means of establishing a new relationship between the owner of the land and the tiller of the soil which did not initially involve the payment of money. The landowner provided the small farmer, black or white, with a patch of land and the tools and seed to cultivate it, in return for a share of the resultant crop. However, very often both parties were soon in debt to the local merchant, to whom much of the crop was mortgaged in advance. Not only did the burden of debt become crushing, but the system was open to abuse and many blacks were exploited shamelessly. A small number were more fortunate and became farm tenants, paying rent for the land in the normal way. However, the share cropping system lasted in the South until the 1930s and was a perpetual focus of complaint between black and white.

Despite all the problems, black living standards in the South generally rose in the period after Appomattox but those for whites remained below pre-war levels and returned to them only towards the end of the century. From the 1870s onwards, some blacks were able to buy land and by 1880 one in five black farm operators owned at least some land, but they often became targets of violence and intimidation.

Although the antebellum plantation aristocracy had lost much of its old power, many of its members were regaining political and social influence. There was also a newer mercantile class emerging in the South, a number of whom, like some of the 'carpetbaggers' from the North, had bought up plantations, and were anxious for new economic opportunities. The name 'carpetbagger' arose from the fact that the only 'property qualification' they had was the baggage they brought with them, usually carried in a travelling bag made of carpet. The term has of course became a scornful one for political candidates and the like without local connections.

The social upheaval of the war and its aftermath touched all groups and classes within the former Confederacy. Second only in importance to land ownership, in the eyes of freed blacks, was education. Many white Southerners opposed educating blacks on the grounds that it threatened white supremacy. Much of the educational effort was in the hands of Northerners, due not only to a shortage of Southern white teachers but also to the reluctance of some of the latter to have anything to do with black pupils. Northern teachers became a target for intimidation and many of them returned home, so that by the end of the decade only one in eight black children of school age was receiving any formal education. However, the percentage for white children was not much higher. Literacy was still low among blacks but real progress was made: whereas only one out of 10 was literate at the war's end, by the close of the century it was around one in two.

Schools in the North began to be desegregated soon after the war. Massachusetts already boasted such a system and it was joined in 1866 and 1867 by Rhode Island and Connecticut. Michigan, Minnesota, Iowa and Kansas followed suit within the next few years. Although in theory Louisiana, South Carolina and Florida had integrated schools, in practice theirs, like the rest of the South, were totally segregated, despite the efforts of Northern administrators to encourage white and black children to attend the same schools. The amount spent on education in the South was less than a third of that in the North. Moreover, funding for all-white schools was appreciably greater than that for purely black ones, a disparity that increased considerably during the following century.

During 1866, Johnson became more and more intransigent, and whatever chance there may have been of some accommodation between him and the Republicans in Congress rapidly disappeared. He vetoed not only a measure extending and enlarging the Freedmen's Bureau but also the first civil rights bill in American history, which was intended to guarantee certain elementary rights to the former slaves. The Republicans found the requisite two-thirds majority in both houses to override these vetoes — the first time in American history that major legislation had been carried over a presidential veto. Congress then approved the Fourteenth Amendment to the Constitution, which, among various other provisions, defined United States citizenship for the first time — and in a way that included all the freed slaves — and offered protection of the basic rights of the citizen against interference by the states. This Amendment, acceptance of which became one of the conditions for the reconstruction of the former rebel states, was to provide the legal basis for much of the work of the civil rights movement a century later.

Northern opinion in 1866 was further incensed by increasing violence against white Republicans as well as blacks in the South — violence that led to at least 46 deaths in Memphis in May and a further 40 deaths in New Orleans two months later. In both instances, white policemen stood by and did nothing to prevent the killings. When the mid-term elections came around in the autumn, Johnson campaigned against the Republicans, but his efforts were counter-productive. They won a landslide victory which not only assured their two-thirds majority in both houses of Congress, but also gave them control of the governorship and legislature of every Northern state.

The chasm between the President and the congressional majority was now unbridgeable. Early in 1867, Congress passed a series of measures laying down a new and much more rigorous reconstruction program for the Southern states. The South was divided into five districts, each under a military governor to oversee the process of making new state constitutions, which were required to provide for universal male suffrage, including votes for black males. Meanwhile, the Republicans were enacting a series of measures to trim the President's powers, which Johnson resisted every inch of the way. In their exasperation, they resorted, perhaps unwisely, to the procedure of impeachment, which had never before been attempted in the case of a president. Partly because the prosecution was mismanaged, Johnson escaped by the narrowest of margins when the crucial vote was taken in May 1868. A two-thirds majority of the Senate was required for a guilty verdict, and this was missed by a single vote. The experience was sufficiently chastening for Johnson that during the rest of his term of office he behaved with much more restraint.

Meanwhile, when the time came in September 1867 for black and white voters in the South to register, more blacks did so than whites and in five states, namely Mississippi, Louisiana, Florida, Alabama and South Carolina, black voters were in the majority. This was largely because more than a tenth of potential white voters had been barred by the new reconstruction legislation and about another quarter had not bothered to register.

149. *After Lincoln's death the nation's affairs were in the hands of the untried Andrew Johnson*

These electorates now voted on delegates to attend state conventions to amend existing constitutions with a view to them being accepted by Congress and hence the states in question being readmitted to the Union.

It was during further elections to ratify these new constitutions that there first appeared in some states a secret organization of white cloaked and hooded night-riding terrorists by the name of Ku Klux Klan. Pledged to oppose racial equality, their members included former Confederate soldiers, many of them officers, among them more than a score of generals and colonels — Nathan Bedford Forrest was for a while the Klan's 'Grand Wizard'. They attempted, with undoubted success, to intimidate both white and black voters, and did so without much harassment from most white state officials.

Nevertheless, in June 1868 seven of the states previously in rebellion were formally readmitted to the Union, while Texas, Virginia and Mississippi followed during the next year. Tennessee had already been readmitted. At long last it seemed that, four years after Appomattox and eight years since Fort Sumter, the Civil War was really over. The tragedy was that so much time and energy in those four years had been devoted to feuding between President and Congress to the detriment of the interests of the country as a whole and of the freed slaves in particular.

If a genuine opportunity ever existed for a reconstruction policy which would provide both a measure of justice to black Americans and a tough but not unreasonable settlement for the defeated South, it was almost certainly in 1865, in the immediate aftermath of the war. Prostrated by defeat, the South might have accepted a firm hand at this stage, and Northerners, relieved that the bloodshed was over, might have found the right blend of justice and charity. But the chance was missed and the white South, having accepted the remarkably lenient terms offered by Johnson's program, was bitter and resentful when confronted with much stiffer conditions in 1866 and 1867. The legacy of that bitterness lived on for several generations. Lincoln was sorely missed, and Andrew Johnson had much to answer for.

The problem went far deeper, however, than personal failings or political mistakes. There was an inescapable, and perhaps insoluble, dilemma at the heart of reconstruction: between mercy and conciliation towards a defeated foe, and justice and support for the freed slaves. Because of the obstinacy of the white South, the ambiguities of the victorious North and the racial prejudices of both, any approach to one of these two objectives almost inevitably obstructed achievement of the other.

In 1868 Grant was elected president in succession to Johnson, though not before an extremely violent campaign in the South, which saw 1,000 deaths in Louisiana alone, mostly blacks, and more than 200 in Arkansas, including that of a Republican congressman. The Ku Klux Klan was again very much in evidence, intimidating black and would-be Republican white voters. Still dominated by Confederate veterans, most of them in their late twenties and early thirties, using hit-and-run guerrilla tactics, the Klan was in effect the paramilitary arm of the Southern Democrats. It was especially successful in Georgia, where a 7,000-strong Republican majority in the state elections that April was turned into a 45,000-strong Democratic majority in the autumn presidential election.

Elsewhere in the South the turnout of black voters was drastically reduced. Schoolhouses for blacks were a particular target of the Klansmen and dozens of them were burned. Northern teachers of black children were intimidated too, and many of them took the hint to return home. Blacks who owned land and whites who were considering selling land to blacks also came in for special attention.

Attempts after the election to stamp out the Klan were doomed to failure, since its members worked hand in hand with the local white population, who shielded them and kept them supplied with information on troop movements. Even when caught, few could ever be convicted because of reluctance to testify against them or to serve on juries that would try them. In one instance in northern Mississippi, all five key prosecution witnesses were murdered during the course of a Klan trial. However, in Arkansas the governor, a Union veteran, successfully cleared the state of Klansmen by strong-arm methods, executing those who were caught and convicted. Tennessee was similarly cleared. But when North Carolina's governor tried to emulate such tactics he came to grief and was forced out of office. Congress had to step in and tighten the laws to secure convictions, which it did during 1870 and 1871. This led to a clamp-down on the Klan's activities, when thousands were arrested, though most of those convicted received only light sentences.

In 11 of the 21 Northern states and all five of the border ones, black men still did not have the franchise. Radical Republicans had long been embarrassed by this anomaly, while Democratic campaigners had had a field day reminding voters of such an obvious hypocrisy. As a result in 1869 such Republicans introduced in Congress a constitutional amendment, the Fifteenth, which forbade states to deny citizens the right to vote on the grounds 'of race, colour, or previous condition of servitude'. This was eventually ratified in March 1870. Some Republicans had wanted it to be a simple affirmation that all male citizens aged 21 years or older had the right to vote, in order to prevent some states from bringing in literacy tests and other devices to deny the franchise to blacks — which is what happened in the South within the next two decades. However, it was feared that such a measure was too radical for the times and would never receive the necessary ratification by two-thirds of the states: anti-Chinese sentiment in the far West, along with persistent anti-black prejudice elsewhere, would probably have blocked it.

In 1872, one of the great pieces of unfinished diplomatic business left over from the Civil War was at last settled. The United States had claimed damages from Britain for the depredations caused by Confederate commerce raiders such as the *Alabama, Florida* and *Shenandoah*, which had been built in British shipyards. At some points in the long wrangle over the issue, there were American demands that the damages should include the entire cost of the war after July 4, 1863, on the grounds that only British support had kept the South going after Gettysburg and Vicksburg. Such extravagant claims, like suggestions that the cession of Canada might provide appropriate compensation, poisoned relations between the two countries. Eventually, by the Treaty of Washington in 1871, it was agreed that the question of damages should be submitted to arbitration by a tribunal in Geneva. In September 1872, its award of $15,500,000 cleared the air.

In the same year Grant was returned for a second term. The Republicans once again had a two-thirds majority in Congress and retained control of seven of the 11 former Confederate states. But no sooner was he re-elected than things began to go wrong both for him and the Republican Party. A faltering economy, coupled with rising unemployment and an epidemic of sordid financial scandals involving people close to the presidency, all distracted Northern attention from the South. Northern Republicans had anyway become disenchanted with events there, and accordingly reconstruction began to unravel, particularly as reports mounted of corruption among some of the Republican Southern state governments.

The truth was that the bulk of Northern opinion had never been sufficiently committed to securing the rights of the freed blacks in the South. Great changes had come about, through emancipation, civil equality, black suffrage and black participation in Southern state governments, but the motivation behind them was too often flawed or ambiguous. There were those in the North who were more interested in the punishment of former Rebels than the welfare of former slaves. More pervasive still were the racial attitudes and prejudices of Northerners, and their difficulty in coming to terms with something that few had ever imagined before the Civil War: a re-shaped American society which included several million free black citizens, enjoying (although in practice that was hardly the appropriate word) full civil and political rights. Republican setbacks in the mid-term elections of 1874 accentuated the party's disillusionment with events in the South. The Democrats were now in a majority in the House of Representatives, and the impetus behind the reconstruction programme had almost exhausted itself. The Civil Rights Act passed in 1875, which prohibited racial discrimination in public buildings and on all forms of public transport as well as on juries, was a kind of swan song, but it was rendered ineffective by Supreme Court decisions during the 1880s.

Blatant Democratic intimidation of Republican and black voters in some states led to hundreds of deaths and when, for instance, Mississippi's governor asked for Federal

150. *Rutherford B. Hayes took over from Grant as president in 1877 and ended the process of reconstruction*

troops to help prevent these deaths, Washington turned him down. As a result, at the next elections few Republicans or blacks dared to vote and the Democrats won control of the state. The same pattern was repeated in other parts of the South. Northerners were losing the will, as well as the interest, to persist with further reconstruction there.

The election of 1876 and its extraordinary outcome brought the formal process of reconstruction by the Federal government to an end. The results in three Southern states were disputed and the Republican candidate, Rutherford B. Hayes, needed the votes of all three in the electoral college if he was to succeed — and even then it would be by only one vote. After weeks of crisis, a deal was agreed whereby Hayes became president in return for the withdrawal of the remaining Federal troops from the South. In effect, this meant the end of the few Republican state governments still in business there, and the final return to white Southerners of control over their own domestic affairs. During the next 20 years, a new apparatus of white supremacy was clamped on to the black population of the South. In the 1878 elections, the Democrats captured control of the Senate, and now had majorities in both houses of Congress. Much of their strength lay of course in the South, and many of those Southern members were ex-Confederate officers — no fewer than 18 of them former Rebel generals.

Having regained political control of their section, the Southern white leaders now sought economic control too. This they did, not just by removing, by fair means or foul, many of the Yankee carpetbaggers who had bought up plantations and invested in businesses in the region, but also by developing new industries themselves in the South. Although cotton growers went through a bad time, principally because of stiff competition from India and Egypt in overseas markets, textile production increased. By the end of the century nearly a quarter of the nation's textile mills were located in the South and by the beginning of the Second World War there would be more looms there than in the rest of the country. Also, tobacco output soared in Virginia and North Carolina during the latter decades of the century. Even heavy industry was brought to the South, with the establishment during the 1880s of iron and steel works around Birmingham in Alabama. Further expansion became possible when at long last, in 1886, Southern railroads adopted the Northern gauge which permitted nation-wide networks for the first time. Much of this growth was financed by Northern capital.

Even so, by the end of the century the South's share of the nation's manufacturing capacity was only 10 per cent — the same as it had been on the eve of the Civil War. The disparity in incomes between North and South had actually worsened. By the final decade of the century Southern incomes were on average less than half of those in the North.

The generation that had fought the Civil War was passing away. The Republicans were now a business-oriented party, projecting themselves as the party of prosperity and economic growth. Less swayed by moral scruples than of old, with fewer 'causes' to pursue, they were often the servants of new and powerful interests. Issues like tariffs and trusts concerned congressmen more than the protection of former slaves. The Democrats became more and more the political agency of white supremacy, conservative and backward-looking.

Not until the civil rights movement of the latter decades of this century did Southern blacks again achieve the rights and power they had had in the years immediately after the Civil War. Then, for instance, a black politician had occupied the same senate seat for Mississippi that Jefferson Davis had held a decade before — although there were never more than seven black congressmen at any one time, out of a total of 300, and no black was ever elected a state governor. On the other hand the first black congressman from a Northern state was not to be elected until 1928.

After 1890 a legally enforced system of disfranchisement and segregation of blacks was imposed in all the Southern states. For a brief moment, it seemed that the severe economic depression of the 1890s might unite its black and white victims in common protest. But the conservative white leadership exploited the race issue, and once again black Americans were cast in the role of scapegoat for the South's ills. The apparatus of disfranchisement included literacy tests, poll taxes, ballot-box stuffing and so-called 'grandfather clauses' which restricted the vote to those who could prove that they or their forebears had been able vote before 1867, the year when blacks were first enfranchised in the South. Alas, the North turned a blind eye. Similarly, during the 1890s, segregation in public places and on public transport became the rule in the South and the Supreme Court sanctioned such practices by accepting that the provision of separate but equal facilities for the two races satisfied the terms of the Fourteenth Amendment. In practice there was, of course, no prospect that the separate facilities would ever be equal.

Although the North's victory in the Civil War was conclusive and clear, there is no obvious and irrefutable answer to the question of who won the peace. Certainly white Southerners had staged a remarkable political recovery, but their wounds were still deep and their scars still painful. Equally certainly, black Americans were not among the outright winners of the peace. The abolition of slavery was a massive and irreversible change, though much of the freedom which had been bestowed with one hand had been taken away with the other. The Union had been saved, but at the cost of the lost aspirations of millions of black Americans. Their deliverance would require another civil struggle and another Lincoln-type saviour.

15 Lasting legacy

The Civil War generated a greater outpouring of memoirs, biographies, reminiscences, eye-witness accounts, campaign descriptions, battle narratives, regimental histories, general works, scholarly studies and popular literature than any other war in American history — perhaps more than all of them combined. It coincided with the great surge in literacy and many of its participants kept diaries or journals and most wrote letters home. Commanders were required or encouraged to compile reports, while politicians were forever instituting inquiries. As a result the war is prodigiously well documented. The official records alone run to 154 volumes. For instance, at the United States Army Military History Institute at Carlisle Barracks in Pennsylvania, there are about 20,000 books on the Civil War, approximately 1,300 collections of unpublished letters and diaries, and an estimated 80,000 photographs — and there are literally hundreds of other universities, historical societies and repositories with their own rich collections of books, manuscripts and photographs on the war, not just within the United States but elsewhere in the world. Hardly a year goes by without some new cache of letters or photographs coming to light.

Similarly remarkable is the persistence of interest in the war down to the present day, despite the competition of other, more recent conflicts. Perhaps part of the appeal lies in its romance and excitement. If for some the pain still lingers just below the surface, others have found soothing balm in turning the struggle into a feast of glory and nostalgia, a respite from the real business of American life. Almost every weekend during the summer somewhere in the United States a group of enthusiasts, all impeccably uniformed and equipped, will be re-enacting one of its battles — and their regard for detail would shame any Hollywood designer. Such recreations also take place in Britain and other European countries. Civil War magazines and news-sheets still flourish, while Civil War round-tables meet regularly in most of the major cities of the United States to study some aspect of the conflict or to debate rival interpretations of its numerous controversies. Civil War monuments are a familiar sight in thousands of communities across the American continent, far outnumbering those that recall other notable events in American history, even the War of Independence, while the sites of the major battlefields have been lovingly restored and preserved by the National Park Service.

To the millions of Americans who were involved in the Civil War, it was most probably the central event of their lives. Those who lived through the two world wars this century may well understand their feelings. It was an experience that gave many Americans a new sense of belonging to a nation, for the war stimulated American nationalism in both emotional and practical ways. The victory of the Union dramatically demonstrated the power of the nation in action and the long, hard struggle to achieve that victory helped to create for the majority of Americans a feeling of involvement in their country's affairs which they had never known before. In its turn, that produced a stronger commitment and deeper loyalty to the United States as a whole.

At least one and a half million men served, with varying degrees of enthusiasm, in the Union army, and their families, friends and neighbours shared in their life-and-death struggle on behalf of the nation. The Union army was a powerful agent of American nationalism; apart from anything else, it was by far the largest national organization the United States had yet seen. The soldiers who returned home after the war had recollections of places and people hitherto remote but now fixed in their minds as part of the same American nation to which they belonged; they had witnessed the nation in action as something real and meaningful to themselves. The men who did not return added greatly to that store-house of heroes and honoured memories from which a sense of nationality can draw sustenance. The emotional bonds forged by the war lived on into the peace and became a central part of the national heritage. As time passed, even the Southern experience merged into that heritage and, as we have seen, Robert E. Lee emerged as an American as well as a Southern hero.

Veterans' organizations, most notably the Grand Army of the Republic founded in 1866, were not simply social clubs or welfare agencies but powerful political pressure groups which congressmen and even presidents ignored at their peril. The GAR had over 400,000 members in the mid-1880s and its last 'encampment' was held as late as 1949. Republicans carefully cultivated that close identity between loyalty to the party and loyalty to the Union, which was one of their most valuable assets, and were not above 'waving the bloody shirt' at election time to remind voters which party had led them to victory and, by inference, which party had backed the other side. Similarly, in the South, for many years after the war to have been a Confederate veteran was virtually an indispensable qualification for political office.

For all its scale and drama, however, the war had no perceptible effect on European military thinking, which preferred to ponder the lessons offered on its own doorstep in the Austro-Prussian and Franco-Prussian wars. These seemed to suggest that brief, fast-moving, decisive campaigns were the trend of the future rather than the protracted, ponderous war of attrition waged at such cost by the citizen armies of America. Europe shut its eyes to most of the portents which the war offered. Its general staffs and military academies took little notice of what the Civil War had to teach about logistics and defensive entrenchments, about the deep penetration of enemy territory and the problems of the new armaments.

When British officers turned their minds to the Civil War at the close of the century, they looked to Lee and Jackson rather than Sherman and Grant. It took the blood-bath of World War One to show the value of a study of the campaigns of the latter generals. For the American military, the war obviously had a more direct influence on strategic and tactical thinking, notably in the emphasis on out-producing rather than outfighting the enemy. They also took to heart some of the lessons in organization and management, as well as in technology.

To say that the Civil War accelerated economic growth in the United States, or that it created modern, industrial America, is much too simplistic. Its impact was more

151. *A union wagon-park during the Civil War testifying to the enormous resources poured into that struggle. No one now doubts who out-produced whom*

diverse, although none the less significant. The destruction of slavery, and especially of the obstructive power of the slave-owning planter class, undoubtedly helped to smooth the way for the rise of industrial capitalism. The process of industrialization had begun in America well before 1860 but the Civil War put industry to the test while still in its formative years and, in important respects, gave it a push in the direction on which it was already launched. There was some disruption and deflection of resources to meet wartime priorities but, at the same time, success in coping with those problems increased industry's confidence.

The Civil War encouraged new methods of organization and distribution, as well as new techniques of production. It prompted those engaged in industry and business to think much more in terms of the national market. It helped to redistribute income in favour of manufacturing interests, particularly in the Northeast, and it hastened the movement of labour into industry, particularly heavy industry. It accelerated the replacement of Southern cotton by Western grain as the major American agricultural export and, as a result, during the 1860s American farmers enjoyed a peak of prosperity which would not be matched before the early part of this century.

There was, however, an ironic twist to the story of the economic and social consequences of the Civil War. The Republican Party, which led the North through the struggle, proclaimed a way of life based on individual opportunity and the 'right to rise', where most of the people were small property owners, living on farms or in villages or small towns. Their supporters thought that the war was being fought, and eventually won, in order to preserve that way of life. In fact, what happened, not immediately but over several decades after 1865, was that this America was overshadowed, even overwhelmed, by the new and increasingly complex industrial society of big business, vast factories and great cities.

The Civil War did indeed raise the curtain on modern America. Whatever the economic statistics may say, it remains in the minds of most Americans the great divide in their history. It is the watershed from which, in one direction, the currents run back to the colonial and revolutionary past and to a more innocent, agrarian society, and, in the other direction, forward to the productive capacity and sophisticated technology of the affluent but anguished nation of a century later. The war separates the era of the small workshop and the country store from the age of Standard Oil and United States Steel and of financial moguls like J. Pierpont Morgan.

Southerners date their history from the war, or before the war, and no one asks them which war; they may call it the War between the States or the War for Southern Independence or the War of Northern Aggression or simply 'the late unpleasantness'. Nevertheless, the South emerged from its time of trial and defeat not less distinctively Southern but more so. Its cherished principle of white supremacy survived the military and political onslaughts intact. The war saw merely the transition from the formal to the informal empire of white over black. America remained a white man's country, its government a white man's government. The eventual road to reunion between North and South was paved with the shattered hopes and disregarded rights of black Americans. In ending slavery, the war may even have exacerbated the problem of race. To white Southerners, their black neighbors served as scapegoats for the bitter humiliation they had suffered at the hands of Northern whites; because it was easier, they vented their feelings on the former slaves in their midst rather than the distant Northerners. To others, though, it seemed as if they had a self-torturing obsession with race. Just as the blacks, despite emancipation, were still the odd people out in a white man's world, so were Southerners themselves still set apart, not just on account of their continuing economic and social backwardness, but also their experience, unique in America, of failure and defeat.

As a direct result of the war, white Southerners became defensive, with a feeling of inferiority, a psychological sense of being embattled, which still lingers in some places. They had long considered themselves masters of their own distinct civilization, inheritors of the best of Western tradition, while the Yankees had been dismissed as barbarians, and now they were told that everything they believed in was wrong — their sectionalism was wrong, their peculiar institution of slavery was wrong, their whole social system was wrong. It has taken Southerners many decades to come to terms with this painful experience. There is a prickliness in the Southern mentality which manifests itself in the tendency to take up insults, to feel or imagine slights, and to boast about relatively modest achievements, while perhaps harbouring inner doubts about how the South stands in relation to the rest of the country.

The generation of Southerners who came out of the war was very much a generation of defeat, of people who had experienced defeat on every level. The war had been utterly devastating and traumatizing, evoking bitterness and despair. Their religious faith, predominantly Methodist or Baptist, led many Southerners to see the working out of the will of God in their defeat, although they still found it difficult to accept the notion that God had turned against them; after all they were God's Chosen. Forced to acknowledge the superior weight of Northern armies, they were not prepared to concede any other kind of inferiority. The South had lost only on the battlefield, not in any larger sense. It had retained its honour. It had won the war of spirit and of values — hence the idea of the 'lost cause', which was to grip and fascinate, and some would say hypnotize, the South for a century, and more. The Virginian Edward A. Pollard wrote in 1866: 'The Confederates have gone out of this war, with the proud, secret, deathless, dangerous consciousness that they are THE BETTER MEN, and that there was nothing wanting but a change in a set of circumstances and a firmer resolve to make them the victors.'

The South had been humbled by its defeat but the shared experience of the war years had helped to define it, to give it a new identity in which it soon began to take an intense pride. For whites in the South the Confederacy would be the touchstone of Southern experience, one that became filled with nobility and courage when, as they saw it, their ancestors had fought for principle with determination and with bravery against a more powerful foe. According to William Faulkner, for many white Southerners it would always be the afternoon of 3 July 1863 at Gettysburg and Pickett's charge had not yet begun.

Southerners talk a lot about the burden of their history, meaning the burden of losing the war and of having to get over that defeat. People who lose wars tend to remember them longer than those who win them. But in the bleak hindsight of defeat, Southerners realized that they had been carrying a weight all along, that of coping or failing to cope with their past, of being both a distinctive part of the country which they had helped to found and at the same time a section of a developing society with which they were increasingly out of touch. Southerners were different, alienated in a sense from the basic American dreams of innocence, plenty and success. Because of slavery, and later segregation, they could not consider themselves innocent. Since much of the South was still relatively undeveloped, theirs was not a land overflowing with milk and honey; and within a country which worships success the fact that, at least until Vietnam, theirs was the one section that had known defeat made them once again stand out.

Although the South lost the war on the battlefield, it may well have won the literary one, which lasted many times longer than the military conflict. Southern literature did not come into its own until the 1920s and 1930s, with writers like William Faulkner, Thomas Wolfe and Robert Penn Warren and, more recently, Tennessee Williams and Carson McCullers. Defeat is often more attractive to the writer than victory; tragedy and failure more interesting than success or optimism. The fact that the war took place largely on Southern soil meant that the Southerner had a closer identification with it; Southerners have always been more aware of their past and, many would argue, preoccupied with it.

For at least a century after Appomattox the South faced the agonizing problem of how to catch up with the rest of the United States without being swallowed up in the process. Its lagging and inefficient economy made it both backward and backward-looking. It did not really become industrialized until the 1920s and some would say not until the last thirty or forty years, when, through the notion of the Sun Belt, Southerners began to turn to their advantage some of the region's characteristics, such as its climate, which had hitherto been regarded as a brake on its development.

During that same period the South has also undergone a second reconstruction, mainly as a result of the civil rights crusade. For a while in the 1960s it seemed almost like a replay of the Civil War with 'The Battle Hymn of the Republic' as one of the inspirational songs of the movement, while the Confederate flag and 'Dixie' served as symbols of Southern resistance to it. Our television screens were filled with pictures of over-sized, cigar-chomping Southern white policemen, batons and bulldogs at the ready, blocking the path of peaceful marchers. Southern blacks produced a charismatic leader in Martin Luther

King, Jr, whose intensely moving 'I Have A Dream' speech, delivered in November 1963 in the shadow of the Lincoln Memorial in Washington before the biggest crowd the United States had ever seen, did much to dispel Northern white fears of possible black vindictiveness in the light of such provocation. Even so, it did not discourage rioting and looting by the residents of the black ghettoes in many Northern cities.

But at long last, as a result of the legislation of that decade, the 'Whites Only' signs came down on public buildings throughout the South, while schools and universities there became integrated and blacks no longer had to ride at the back of buses. They were able to vote again and many were successful in standing for public offices long thought the province of whites only — though not before emancipation claimed its second martyr in Martin Luther King, who was assassinated in April 1968. The tragedy helped, however, to close the ranks between blacks and Northern, and many Southern, whites. The United States made great strides within a matter of years towards equalizing the opportunities for blacks and whites, though the task is far from finished. There are still deep-rooted problems of economic inequality and the alienation of so many young blacks, as well as the persistence of white racism.

In many ways, the repercussions of the Civil War are still with us today. Discussing its legacy, the distinguished Southern man of letters, Robert Penn Warren, suggested that what the South gained was 'the Great Alibi', a perennial excuse for all its deficiencies, failures and vices, while the Northern inheritance, he sardonically observed, was 'the Treasury of Virtue', the complacent assumption that might and right had joined hands to bring victory to its cause. Warren's shrewd assessment conveys something of the irony and ambiguity of the war's consequences for both sides, and for America as a whole. The victory of the one was flawed, and in some respects wasted; the defeat of the other was cherished when it could not be reversed.

It should never, however, be forgotten that, as well as preserving the Union, the conflict did liberate four million blacks from the bonds of slavery — and there was surely no other way in which that could have happened in the 1860s. In addition, by way of putting the failure of the first reconstruction after 1865 into its context, thousands of black American males were, for however brief a period, casting their votes and holding political office long before millions of white British workers had the right to do so.

In a wider sense, of enormous concern for the world at large, the war raised a whole series of issues about democracy, nationalism, race, central authority, rights of minorities and the abuse of power.

No one was more aware than Abraham Lincoln of the universal meaning of the United States' ordeal by civil strife. During one of the darker moments of the conflict, he coined perhaps the most eloquent of all his deceptively simple sentences: 'We shall nobly save, or meanly lose, the last, best hope of earth.' After more than a century and a quarter, there is still no final balance sheet of nobility and meanness, and no final verdict on what was saved and what was lost.

Bibliography

There is a huge number of books on the Civil War, and the following list is no more than an introductory sample. It offers a guide to some of the more influential recent works, including those which the authors of this book have found particularly helpful.

Benet, Stephen Vincent, *John Brown's Body* (New York, Doubleday, 1928)

Beringer, Richard E., Hattaway, Herman, Jones, Archer, and Still, William N., *Why the South Lost the Civil War* (Athens GA and London, University of Georgia Press, 1986)

Connelly, Thomas L., *The Marble Man: Robert E. Lee and his Image in American Society* (New York, Knopf, 1977)

Cooper, William J., *Liberty and Slavery: Southern Politics to 1860* (New York, Knopf, 1983)

Cooper, William J. and McPherson, James M., eds., *Writing the Civil War: the Quest to Understand* (Columbia SC, University of South Carolina Press, 1998)

Davis, William C., *Jefferson Davis: the Man and his Hour* (New York, HarperCollins, 1991)

Davis, William C., ed., *The Image of War, 1861-1865,* 6 vols. (New York, Doubleday, 1984)

Donald, David Herbert, *Lincoln* (New York, Simon & Schuster, 1995)

Donald, David Herbert, ed., *Why the North Won the Civil War* (Baton Rouge LA, Louisiana State University Press, 1960)

Escott, Paul, *After Secession: Jefferson Davis and the Failure of Confederate Nationalism* (Baton Rouge LA, Louisiana State University Press, 1978)

Foner, Eric, *Free Soil, Free Labor, Free Men: the Ideology of the Republican Party before the Civil War* (New York, Oxford University Press, 1970)

Foner, Eric, *Reconstruction: America's Unfinished Revolution, 1863-1877,* (New York, Harper & Row, 1988), abridged as *A Short History of Reconstruction,* 1990

Foote, Shelby, *The Civil War: a Narrative,* 3 vols., (New York, Random House, 1958-74)

Foster, Gaines M., *Ghosts of the Confederacy: Defeat, the Lost Cause, and the Emergence of the New South, 1865-1913* (New York, Oxford University Press, 1987)

Frassanito, William A., *Antietam: the Photographic Legacy of America's Bloodiest Day* (New York, Scribner, 1978)

Fredrickson, George M.*The Black Image in the White Mind* (New York, Harper & Row, 1972)

Gallagher, Gary W., *The Confederate War* (Cambridge MA, Harvard University Press, 1997)

Gallman, J. Matthew, *The North Fights the Civil War: the Home Front* (Chicago, Dee, 1994)

Glatthear, Joseph T., *The March to the Sea and Beyond: Sherman's Troops m the Savannah and Carolinas Campaigns* (New York, New York University Press, 1985)

Holden Reid, Brian, *The Origins of the American Civil War,* (London and New York, Longman, 1996

Horwitz, Tony, *Confederates in the Attic: Dispatches from the Unfinished Civil War* (New York, Pantheon, 1998)

Kolchin, Peter, *American Slavery, 1619-1877* (New York, Hill & Wang, 1993; London, Penguin, 1995)

Levine, Bruce, *Half Slave and Half Free: the Roots of Civil War* (New York, Hill & Wang, 1991)

Linderman, Gerald F., *Embattled Courage: the Experience of Combat in the American Civil War* (New York, Free Press, 1987)

McCardell, John, *The Idea of a Southern Nation* (New York, Norton, 1979)

McPherson, James M., *Battle Cry of Freedom: the Civil War Era* (New York, Oxford University Press, 1988)

McPherson, James M., *For Cause and Comrades: Why Men Fought in the Civil War* (New York, Oxford University Press, 1997)

McWhiney, Grady, and Jamieson, Perry D., *Attack and Die: Civil War Military Tactics and the Southern Heritage* (University AL, University of Alabama Press, 1982)

Mitchell, Reid, *Civil War Soldiers: their Expectations and their Experiences* (New York, Viking, 1988)

Morrison, Michael A., *Slavery and the American West: the Eclipse of Manifest Destiny and the Coming of the Civil War* (Chapel Hill NC, University of North Carolina Press, 1997)

Neely, Mark E., *The Last Best Hope of Earth: Abraham Lincoln and the Promise of America* (Cambridge MA, Harvard University Press, 1993)

Paludan, Phillip Shaw, *The Presidency of Abraham Lincoln* (Lawrence KS, University Press of Kansas, 1994)

Parish, Peter J., *The American Civil War* (London, Eyre Methuen; New York, Holmes & Meier, 1975)

Parish, Peter J., *Slavery: History and Historians* (New York, HarperCollins, 1989)

Potter, David M., *The Impending Crisis, 1848-1861* (New York, Harper & Row, 1976)

Ransom, Roger L., *Conflict and Compromise: the Political Economy of Slavery, Emancipation and the American Civil War* (Cambridge & New York, Cambridge University Press, 1989)

Royster, Charles, *The Destructive War: William Tecumseh Sherman, Stonewall Jackson and the Americans* (New York, Knopf, 1991)

Simpson, Brooks D., *America's Civil War* (Wheeling IL, Harlan Davidson, 1996)

Stampp, Kenneth M., *The Imperiled Union* (New York, Oxford University Press, 1980)

Thomas, Emory M.,*The Confederate Nation, 1861-1865* (New York, Harper & Row, 1979)

Thomas, Emory M., *Robert E. Lee: a Biography* (New York, Norton, 1995)

Warren, Robert Penn, The *Legacy of the Civil War* (New York, Random House, 1961)

Woodward, C. Vann, ed., *Mary Chesnut's Civil War* (New Haven CT, Yale University Press, 1981)

Index